GW00504536

ISBN no. 978-1-5272-1878-9

Typeset (information to follow)

Printed and bound in Great Britain by
Book Printing Uk
www.bookprintinguk.com .

# Willies Wheels - Driving the Film Industry

## William Z Fonfe

*Marian*

*With my best wishes*

*Willie*

This book is dedicated to

Ted Morley and Brian Hathaway

# Thank you to:

Helen and Adam Fonfe who first mooted the idea for this book.
Karen Harper and Lainey Mitchell for their encouragement.
Jason Fonfe for his notes and additional material.
Gez Zia for his help recovering pictures from my laptop.
Denise and Gary Skull, Heinz Werner Schneider, Sue and Bryan
Baverstock,Sammy and Sheila Fonfe, and Gary Tuck for
contributing images from their collections.
Keith Hamshere for letting me use some of the still photographs
he shot.
Gary Skull, Colin Morris, Bryan Baverstock, Johnny Morris, Phil
Allchin and all the other old boys who reminded me of events that
I had forgotten to include in my first draft.
Natalie Fonfe for her Photoshop skills.
Phil Buck for his help with reformatting some images.
Grace Taylor for designing the Book cover and Sam Clough for
enhancing it.
John Sargent for persuading his children who now run his old firm
to sponsor me.
Mark Day for being a sympathetic sounding board during my daily
struggle with the publishing world.
Finally, Nicky Davies who for nearly a year typed and retyped,
proof read and edited the manuscript. Her constant
encouragement helped me on many occasions to overcome my
self-doubt and spurred me on to finish what I have started.


Sponsored by : Sargent-Disc Ltd

# Filmography

# Introduction

When President Kennedy visited Cape Canaveral, renamed the Kennedy Space Centre after his death, he was introduced one by one to all its employees. When greeting the man who sweeps the floor he asked him what his job was. "I am helping to put a man on the moon" came the reply.

In a similar way a unit driver, who chauffeurs members of the film crew and the cast to and from the set and occasionally runs errands for the production office, is helping to make the film. He may be a lowly member of the crew but without him the show would not hit the road. The same applies to the transport contractor whose motor homes provide comfort and respite to the actors and whose trucks convey and store the props, costumes, construction equipment etc that make up the film set. His contribution may not be obvious but is nevertheless essential to the smooth running of the show. He may be, as are the caterers, a necessary evil because his input does not appear on the screen yet without him travelling to location or even setting up sets on a stage will be almost impossible.

Having chauffeured and supplied production vehicles on more than two hundred productions I have been fortunate enough to witness many unusual and quirky events. Family, friends and acquaintances have often urged me to write them down and give the wider public an opportunity to read about the life we have led at the bottom of the pile on which show business is built. The most surprising thing to an outsider is the fact that, while filming during the era I have written about, cast and crew members, however famous or however insignificant, formed a close-knit team that shared long hours of hard work and the equally long hours of hard off screen diversions.

I am primarily concerned with the unexpected events that I have witnessed both as a driver in the early days and more recently as the supplier of trucks and facility vehicles. The trucks that come in all shapes and sizes are destined for the props, construction, special effects and camera departments etc, while the facility vehicles consist of make-up trailers, artists' motor homes and mobile toilets etc. I have gone through ups and downs like most of humanity but, fortunately, have managed to forget most of the Downs and have recalled most of the Ups that I am hoping to share with industry insiders and the general public.

# Prologue

The first time my age was mentioned as in "you are getting old" was when I failed to recover from a minor injury sustained whilst playing football. Receiving a knock was a regular occurrence and, what was equally true, was that I recovered sufficiently seven days later to play again. Then, as each week passed, I noticed that I would report to our next game with a niggling pain that remained from the encounter I had experienced the previous Sunday. I thought nothing of it until I started to collect painful bruises that just lingered on and eventually came to the notice of my fellow teammates. Telling them that there was nothing to worry about did not convince them and I was made to miss out on more and more games. "At your age these things take a lot longer to heal" was the general consensus "it may be a good idea if you took up a non contact sport". I remembered not being old enough to do things but being too old came as a bit of a shock. So no more kicking or being kicked!

Hampstead, at the time, was home to what was known as the Bohemian set, consisting of everything that was appealing about London at the time. It was where actors, painters and writers congregated and was only rivalled by Chelsea as the bastion of 'Swinging London' where any number of already famous or hoping to become famous musicians could be found around most corners. Many of them were regulars at the local pubs and the bistros that had sprung up and replaced the tearooms of yesteryear. The Coffee Cup on the High Street served continental breakfast until the late afternoon and beyond and the many pubs played host to all comers for the rest of the day until closing time.

Bring your own food and drink - usually bread, cheese and cheap Algerian wine - parties were nightly venues for the insomniacs. Young female company day and night was largely provided by St. Godric's Secretarial College. After hours of monotonous shorthand and typing practice they deserved some distraction and it was down to us to introduce them to the extra-curriculum pleasures that were on offer. The introduction of the Pill enhanced our lives by allowing us to taste forbidden fruits for the first time in history without the fear of contributing to the population growth.

Once, during one of those parties, whilst I was discussing world events in the kitchen, screams were coming from one of the rooms. I went to investigate, fearing a possible confrontation with a violent intruder, when one of the girls pushed me aside, rushed to the phone and dialled 999. Another stopped me from entering the room from where the scream came yelling "She is having a baby!" The ambulance arrived a few minutes later and helped the mother-to-be down the stairs between contractions and gently out of the house. I knew her. She came from Bochum in Germany and was what one would describe nowadays as weight challenged, always wearing a caftan. I now knew why. A few days later I met her in the Coffee Cup holding a baby wrapped in a pink blanket. She wanted to return home and, as I was at a loose end, I offered to give her a lift in my newly acquired Sunbeam Rapier. I thought it might be fun to travel to Germany as I did enjoy driving long distances especially on the Autobahns that had no speed limits.

I bought this car because my previous car was a Morris Minor van. The local car dealer/garage owner who, for some reason, was known as Boozy although he hardly drank, used to buy vehicles at the car auctions at Alexandra Palace. When he successfully bid for a bunch of ex-Post Office vans, he paid me to shuttle them back to his forecourt in Hampstead. He paid £15.00 each for them and, as I had that sort of money, he let me have one of them at cost. It was late autumn and fairly chilly but I could not get warm air to blow onto my feet. I drove to the garage and asked Boozy to show me how to fix it. "These vans have no heaters, they are an optional extra!" I was not prepared to suffer so I part exchanged the van there and then with the help of a hire purchase agreement for a blue and silver Sunbeam Rapier convertible with an efficient heater as standard equipment.

A few of my elders had lived through turbulent times which they often recalled whether one prompted them or not; fighting in the World Wars and Korea, surviving the Blitz or finding refuge from prosecution. I had had none of it; my past consisted of years living in bedsitter land leading the Bohemian life of an existentialist not worrying about the future, just enjoying every day as it came. I started off by sharing a one bedroom flat with a separate kitchen and bathroom on the top floor (no lift) in a converted five storey building in Gayton Crescent just 200 yards or so from the High Street within sight of the Coffee Cup and the William IV pub that were my regular hang-outs. What I did not realise was that the clientele in the pub consisted largely of men who were in close touch with their feminine sides. At the time homosexual acts committed by consenting adult males were still illegal. The story goes that, when the Criminal Law Amendment Act, which dealt with such matters and applied to both sexes, was put in front of Queen Victoria to sign she refused to acknowledge that women could indulge in such 'perversions' and forced the government to amend the act to target men only. I enjoyed their cutting and outrageous banter borne partly out of their forbidden practices (Galgenhumor as the German expression goes) but eventually moved on to the more heterosexual Flask in Flask Walk.

5

We also took in an au pair who was AWOL from her employers who lived in one of the larger residences in the vicinity. The deal was that she could sleep in our kitchen as long as she kept the place tidy and occasionally cooked a meal. When, however, she was joined by another girl with whom she shared the bed and more intimate yet legal embraces, it all became too crowded and I moved first into a bed sit in Fitzjohn's Avenue, then another in Arkwright Road, always in close proximity to the village centre. When I felt financially more secure, I rented a two-storey studio building with a large north-facing window in Sheriff Road, West Hampstead. The village itself was turning into a destination for the Nouveau Riche who longed to sidle up to the icons of Swinging London and who could afford to pay for it. It was not disloyalty or boredom with the old place, it was just the cost that drove me downhill to the west. On the other hand The Kinks were often seen and heard locally.

I converted the upper floor into a large open plan living room with a kitchen in one corner, a bathroom at the far end with a bedroom on a balcony on the upper reaches of the area and a dining alcove underneath. I sublet the ground floor to a budding photographer in the hope that we would enjoy a steady influx of pretty young things as featured in the film Blow Up. Sadly this was not to be. Soon my tenant returned to the real world of 'cheffing' in a burger joint and later opened up his own fast food outlet in Montpelier in the South of France where I understand he now lives happily ever after.

It was here that Sheila moved in with me, something that at the time was not what well brought up middle class girls from the right side of the track did. Sharing a home without being married may be commonplace today but just a generation ago it was deemed to be 'Living in Sin'.

Finally Sheila inherited a bit of money and with some savings of my own we had enough to leave behind the mice that kept us company in the studio and bought a brand new two bedroom maisonette in Primrose Hill. From now on it was down or uphill all the way depending on one's point of view.

However, before we made the move into middle class respectability, still in my laddish period, my life cycle consisted of getting out of bed at lunch time, often not on my own, and doing odd driving jobs to fund the coming evening's entertainment. Hand to mouth with no responsibilities or stressful ambitions; Jean Paul Sartre, the French philosopher, would have been proud of me. On the other hand, I realised that I was achieving very little with which one day I would be able to impress my grandchildren.

Once during the Three Day Week - when candles were in short supply - my friend Andrew managed to locate a manufacturer with stock somewhere in deepest Belgium. His problem was that he did not have a licence to drive a truck. It so happened that I was qualified to take charge of heavy vehicles and thus the enterprise got on its way. By the time I returned to Dover with my first load the demand for candles turned into a mania and I sold the whole load to the highest bidder at the dockside. I then turned round and repeated the trip with the same result. In the end we made five trips before the factory ran out of stock. Enough money was made to live through the following months in relative comfort.

A similar adventure was on offer when we met with a wholesaler from the East End who was looking for a new supplier of soap as his existing one was going out of business. Again my entrepreneurial friend got on the phone and located a factory in Eastern Germany, then behind the Iron Curtain. We met the Trade

Attaché in his office in Belgrave Square (no socialist modesty there), shook hands and signed our life away on a deal provided we took care of the transport. Moving in and out of the beleaguered part of Germany involved long delays at the border, invasive searches for escapees inside and underneath the vehicle and a mountain of documents. It was worth it in the end. After just four such deliveries, months indulging in small luxuries followed.

One of my more regular jobs was an evening delivery round for a man who peeled potatoes in a cellar under a greengrocer in West End Lane. Once washed and peeled he diced some of them into raw chips ready for the frying pan and others he left whole to be boiled. They were all wrapped in cellophane bags weighing either 14 or 28 pounds and had to be dropped off at eateries all around London. That was my job. I usually managed to complete the task in less than three hours and, apart from getting to know vast swathes of the City (it came in useful later), I had a small income stream with minimal interference to my social life.

I may have been too old for a kickabout but still young enough to have a future. It was just that I was unclear about what my future would be. I had no professional or trade qualifications although I thought I was intelligent enough to use common sense if an opportunity presented itself. My then girlfriend, later to be my wife, shared a bed sitting room with a school friend whose boyfriend worked in the film industry. At one of our frequent foursomes he mentioned that he was setting up a small production company with very little money and he wondered if I knew where he could get hold of a couple of minibuses. This was well before an Internet search would have produced a result. I habitually kept my eyes open during my travels around the capital and I remembered a company in Battersea that hired out minibuses to Australian visitors who wanted to tour Europe. I managed to convince the owner that the film industry would provide an additional income stream. My future had begun.

A popular poster of New York, with the City large in the foreground and the rest of the United States at an ever-decreasing size fading out in the background, made the rounds. It symbolised the fact that it was the city that dominated the known world with all other locations insignificant add-ons. I felt the same about Hampstead with Chelsea just behind and the rest of humanity somewhere else just visible in the far distance.

Within weeks my world expanded well beyond the blinkered view I cherished and, however satisfying my life had been, I was looking forward to a new and different future to be experienced on a much larger canvas. The director and the producer, my new bosses, had homes in Notting Hill. Although it was prior to its elevation as Julia Roberts' favourite part of London, I had no idea that successful people would choose to live there.

In contrast before I visited it with the film crew the town of Aldershot was somewhere beyond the reach of anyone other than square bashing young men with nothing better to do than learn to kill folks on demand. In the following forty years or so the business took me to every corner of Europe, West and East, with hardly a country I did not visit professionally. In fact, the only European Countries in the West I did not work in were Norway and Lichtenstein (not counting San Marino, Andorra, and Gibraltar) while in the East I missed out on Bulgaria, Turkey and one or two of the new countries in the Balkans. Best of all, though, were the men and women that made up the film crews. Their work ethic was infectious; long, dedicated hours of hard work but equally hard and dedicated time to play. In addition, the camaraderie and team spirit appealed to me, dare I say it, more than the superficial friendships I had enjoyed in my previous life.

Away from work my social standing blossomed as I became a source of information about an industry and personalities that enjoyed universal appeal. My children and their friends, as well as fellow partygoers, were always keen to hear my news. It is unfortunate that in the years to come the film industry morphed into a corporate structure where paperwork and mistrust caused by Micro Management dominated. The old structure of one man, the producer, in charge and a director with his crew getting as much on film as time and money allowed, was not to last forever. Michael Winner would turn in his grave if he found out that his idea of teamwork "a lot of people doing exactly what I tell them to do" would fall on deaf ears.

It is fortunate, though, that I lived through the happy years when technicians were hired because of what they knew and not because they could create a paper trail that justified their actions.

# 1 Overlord 1973

## Soldiers in a New Light

In a number of ways this was a first on many levels; first time I went on an 'away' location, first time I worked for a producer who had backed the project with his own money, first time I was introduced to the inner workings of film making and first time I was put in charge of transport.

James Quinn, our producer who owned the Everyman Cinema chain, which specialised in films of artistic merit and was a long-standing member of the British Film Institute, was paying for it all out of his own pocket. His catch phrase became "Is it really necessary?" and was constantly repeated each time an expense was mooted. The Director, Stuart Cooper, a Bafta award winner for best short film and who co-wrote the script, saw this time a chance to produce an epic to rival Ben Hur. He had to be repeatedly restrained by our production manager Michael Guest who had to remind him of the limitations he had to accept.

It was to be a dramatised tribute to an old friend of the producer - hence his funding of the project - who as a young man was conscripted into the army during World War II and consequently took part in the D Day landing, code named Operation Overlord. Transport consisted of three trucks, one each for camera and grip equipment and two more for wardrobe and prop departments. The soundman would bring along his own van. Two minibuses and my car, a Peugeot diesel estate, completed the fleet. The cast included Nicholas Ball who later starred in his own TV show 'Hazell'. As far as I was concerned, most importantly, he was married to one of my favourite comedic actresses, Pamela Stephenson, who later married one of my favourite comedians, Billy Connolly.

We started shooting in a disused barracks in Aldershot which did not need too much 'dressing' as the place had been left untouched since the buildings had been erected at the time our story unfolded. For aerial photography the army lent us a helicopter that we adapted to carry the camera with a special contraption to hold the cameraman safely in place. He was to sit on the ledge of the open door of the fuselage with his legs dangling in mid air.

I drove the production manager, the director and the grip to RAF Yeovil where we checked out the aircraft's suitability for the shots we were planning. While the others busied themselves with tape measures and anchoring points, I chatted to the pilot who explained how his machine worked, i.e. stayed aloft and was extremely easy and safe to fly. I am not a fan of helicopters, having witnessed a couple of accidents that caused them to crash. My concern was heightened when it occurred to me that the pilot's repeated reassurances reminded me of 'the lady doth protest too much'. I returned to Aldershot on my own while the others got a lift, literally, in our flying contraption.

I arrived back at the forest clearing where it had landed just as the cameraman was being strapped into the fuselage and, as planned, was sitting in the open door with his legs dangling outside and the camera held on a frame which he could move up, down and sideways in front of him. The engines - it was a twin-engine model which, we were assured, made it even safer to fly - started up with a splutter and an even louder whistle as the rotors cut through the air. The blades spun round faster and faster until my hands reached up to protect my ears from the overwhelming noise and I had to adopt a forward stance to counter the hurricane that emanated from what could only be described as a wind machine. Eventually, the whole bulk of metal began to lift, a few feet at first, then a bit higher and, just as the pilot tipped down the front of his craft ready to move forward, the whole thing came crashing down, a sheer drop of some 15 ft. It hit the ground with a thud but fortunately the suspension softened the landing enough to prevent a crash that would have seen us picking up pieces of metal or worse, body parts.

Out of the shocked silence emerged an ever-increasing moaning sound from our cameraman who had obviously taken a hard knock on impact. Our unit nurse and an ambulance crew, who were standing by just in case the pilot had overestimated the safety angle of this undertaking, took charge. The cameraman was taken, sirens screaming and blue light flashing, through the woods onto the distant road leading to Frimley Park Hospital. The co-pilot staggered out and limped slightly towards our catering van where a sympathetic production manager met him and sat him down with a cup of tea. My friend the pilot remained in the cockpit glued to his seat staring straight at his instrument panel. He could not be persuaded to leave his position. It was up to me to clamber into the grounded flying machine, balancing a heavily sugared cup of tea, in an attempt to bring him out of his hypnotic state. After some ten minutes it worked. He got up and edging past me our eyes met very briefly. Me, not out loud "You still think it's the safest form of transport?" And he, white with a green tinge, "Sorry, don't know what happened".

When the air accident investigators arrived the next morning it transpired that there was nothing wrong with the aircraft itself but a computer fault had caused the engines to shut down without warning. Brave as they must have been, they got into it and took off, hopefully arriving at their destination unharmed.

The schedule was rearranged, our cameraman released from hospital and we resumed shooting late into the evening in order to make up for lost time. Unfortunately, our caterers could not stay on to feed the crew and I was sent into town to corner the market for fish and chips. The smell in my car persisted well until we arrived at the seaside a few days later for our next locations, Corfe Castle and Swanage beach, where we were going to re-enact the D Day landing.

We were booked into the Haven Hotel in Sandbanks next to the ferry terminal. The craft, unusually, was towed by a chain mechanism across Poole Harbour. It was to carry our cast and crew on the first leg to our sets. In addition to our normal cast, a dozen men from the Special Boat Service (SBS) were recruited from a nearby base to give the landing shots an air of realism. We all assembled on the beach ready to not only defeat the imaginary Germans but also to resist the very real cold and damp weather that was accentuated by a penetrating freezing wind. Building sandcastles and playing ball on this magnificent beach in between takes was not a pastime of choice. What was unquestionably of some comfort was a chance to retreat into the minibuses that stood by on the nearby road with engines running and heaters blowing. The concerns of our production team about the excessive use of fuel were ignored.

At sunset, filming wrapped and the rush to the ferry and the hotel on the far side resembled a flight from a burning building. This was mainly due to the fact that the hotel could not provide enough hot water for everyone to have a bath simultaneously. Being in charge of transport I had to wait until the whole crew had arrived safely and thus I drew the short straw. Still, it was my first film and I was the most junior member of the team. It took about two hours for the water to heat up again so I passed the time with a pre-dinner drink at the bar in the company of other guests who did not seem to mind my rough and unwashed, possibly smelly, appearance. On these occasions I was told about local restaurants that offered a better choice of meals and value for money than the ones in-house. One advantage of having to wait!

Whatever else I did, I always ended up at the hotel bar because it stayed open long enough to enjoy a nightcap. One evening the brave soldiers that we cast as the landing party came over from their barracks and joined us in the bar of the hotel with other guests and local regulars for a drink and an exchange of anecdotes. It was my round and I found myself in the company of half a dozen serving men. They did enjoy working on the film but said they would prefer to see more action. They had already been on two tours of Ireland. They boasted about catching up with members of the IRA (Irish Republican Army) and UDA (Ulster Defence Association) whom they could literally beat up before arresting them. What they most looked forward to was being posted to countries where they had to work behind enemy lines to get their intelligence. In the process, two of them proudly recounted how they had garrotted one of their perceived enemies. I could not believe what I was hearing. The enthusiasm with which they carried out unspeakable deeds not only shocked me but also made me reassess my high regard for the men who are charged with protecting our way of life.

Shooting on the site of Corfe Castle was much less of an ordeal for all but the poor actors who had to clamber up and down the hill on top of which the ruins stood. This they had to repeat time after time to satisfy our director who wanted to capture the action from every angle possible. With only one camera, it meant that each angle required the camera to be moved to a different position that gave the actors a few moments to regain their composure, if not their strength. This set-up was scheduled to be the very last to be shot and, therefore, it no longer mattered if any of the artists were to be incapacitated by injury or exhaustion. A strained foot and a back injury later and principal photography was in the can. Relief all round and a modest end of picture party was organised in the hotel bar where some of the staff and local friends joined in. The hard work we had endured deserved hard play, even if the open bar did not survive for more than an hour. It seemed that nobody objected to carrying on by putting their hands into their own pockets and the drinking, dancing and general merriment continued until the early hours when we retired upstairs into bed, not all of us unaccompanied.

Breakfast was a bleary eyed affair and one by one the cast and crew made the rounds of goodbyes with air kisses and hugs wherever one looked. I drove my car back to London with the minibuses, loaded with the crewmembers who did not bring their own cars down, in tow. The buses were returned to Battersea undamaged and I pulled up in the car outside Stuart's house in Notting Hill with Michael, the production manager. Here the three of us were joined by the producer for a meeting to go over the events of the last eight weeks. I, of course, had no comments to make but found it an educational experience to witness such a debriefing session and the detailed requirements needed for the editing process that was to follow. Later that evening I gave Michael a lift home to Ham and he thanked me for a job well done with the promise that he would bear me in mind for his next project.

I did not have to wait long before he called me about a TV series for HBO, the American cable network, who had commissioned a dramatised documentary with the title The Prize Winners. It was to be a six part mini series featuring a different Nobel Prize winner in each episode. It was to be based in Harefield House in Harefield near Denham Village. With the exception of the leading artist, the cast and crew were going to make their own way to the production base while all the equipment would be delivered and stored there as well. This meant that I was only needed as transport for the leading actor, morning and night. The rest of the day I could run errands and, if time allowed, watch what was happening on-set. In contrast to my first adventure in films, when the actors were newcomers to the screen, this time I was entrusted with well-known faces. They included Sian Phillips, Peter O'Toole's wife, David Warner,

Susannah Fellows and my favourite, Anna Calder-Marshall, all of whom I had watched on TV and the big screens many times before. Maybe not international stars at the time but it would do for the moment.

# 2 Holocaust 2000 1975

## From a Star to a Starlet

In my days in Hampstead and Chelsea I often bumped into celebrities of the day - Ray Davies of the Kinks, Marianne Faithfull, Mick Jagger and his fellow Stones and many others. I met Petula Clark in Majorca where I also first met my wife-to-be, Sheila, and Olivia Newton John of Country Roads fame, who sang at our wedding dinner with just a tape as her backing track. I admired them all but must admit that I reserved my highest respect for successful sportsmen and women whom I would have gladly served unconditionally. Once, however, I met and shook the hand of Peter Medawar, whose sons formed part of my circle of friends. He was the 1960 Nobel Prize winner for his research into how the human immune system works when accepting or rejecting donated organs. He was known as the 'father of transplantation'. His contribution to medical science and civilization is unrivalled and whenever my ego threatens to lift its head over the parapet Sir Peter's discoveries remind me how relatively insignificant my own achievements are.

In my show business world the Hollywood crowd stood apart, mainly because they were so far removed from my daily life. This changed when Michael Guest asked me to join the film crew as a unit driver on The Seven Percent Solution. It's a new twist on the Sherlock Holmes stories where Watson treats his friend's cocaine induced delusions and leads him to meet up with Sigmund Freud. The elaborate sets were designed by Ken Adams who won an Oscar for Kubrick's Barry Lyndon. He is also credited as the production designer on all the early Bond movies which were realized on the sound stages at Pinewood Studios. I began by picking up and dropping off Nicol Williamson to and from his home in Barnes. There his wife often met me on arrival at the front door still in her dressing gown and, when time allowed, brought out

19

a cup of tea while I waited for her husband to appear. He played the lead role but I was more interested in the supporting cast of well-known American actors.

Soon, I was to look after Robert Duval who never stopped recounting the fact that he had turned down the lead in Jaws. Next came Alan Arkin who, when directing a play way back when, gave Dustin Hoffman his first acting job and topped it all by telling me about the time he worked with Audrey Hepburn in Wait Until Dark. He was too modest to brag about the Oscar he won but I found out about it from one of my fellow drivers. Best of all, I enjoyed the company of Joel Grey, father of Jennifer, Dirty Dancing, Grey, and whose part as the Master of Ceremonies in Cabaret won him an Oscar for best supporting role; not only did we strike a cord over our mutual family affairs but he would have me in stitches with his many anecdotes about the bizarre lifestyle choices of his fellow American actors who were chasing recognition and one-upmanship at all cost. It was then that I first heard the saying "the only thing worse than being recognized everywhere you go is not to be recognized."

Holocaust 2000 completed my collection of international stars when I was introduced to Kirk Douglas as his driver. In 1977 you could not get more famous than Kirk although I did wonder why a man of his stature had agreed to appear in what sounded like a B movie; an Anglo-Italian co-production of a horror/disaster movie did not exactly promise good takings at the box office. He must have had his reasons; I was just hoping that his life was not imitating the fictional story told in Sunset Boulevard where an erstwhile diva finds herself descending tragically into anonymity.

A, if not the, cardinal sin a driver can commit is to arrive late for his pickup. I, therefore, always added at least fifteen minutes to the average time that it would take me to pull up outside the home or hotel my charges would be coming out of. When, however, I drove up to Kirk's hotel in Knightsbridge, he was already standing at the entrance waiting for me, ready to go. The next morning I wanted to anticipate his early appearance and made sure I arrived half an hour before we were due to depart. He, obviously, noted my reaction because the following morning there he was standing there greeting me as I came to a halt in front of the doorman. Neither of us remarked on the fact that we were now going to meet the film unit well before we were expected, even though I decided to take the scenic route to minimise the panic that would ensue.

I was not going to be beaten when the following morning I turned up a full hour before his call time. Unbelievably within minutes he appeared, but this time he motioned me to get out of the car and follow him into the dining room where we both sat down for breakfast. It was a silent affair and without a word being spoken we agreed to call it a draw. From then on we returned to the beginning. Me fifteen minutes early and him ready to leave a minute or two later.

While Kirk was on the set I met other members of the cast, one of whom was Simon Ward who made his name when playing Young Winston directed by Richard Attenborough. After some small talk he opened up and started to recount endless stories about his previous films and the stars and directors he had worked with. It would have read like a Who's Who of show business. There was Richard Lester, who directed the Beatles films, Faye Dunaway of Bonnie and Clyde fame, Spike Milligan and Roy Kinnear, the comedic actors, Charlton Heston, the gun toting American superstar, Richard Chamberlain, the cool unflappable Dr. Kildare, Raquel Welch, the overbearing sex symbol and Oliver Reed with his favourite stunts of drinking to excess and dropping his trousers at the slightest provocation.

I worked with Oliver a few years later during The Class of Miss McMichael with Glenda Jackson. On that occasion he invited the director and the producer for dinner to his country estate and, as they were coming up the drive, he took out his shotgun and started firing at them, leaving bullet holes all over the car and a mess caused by fear all over the inside. Needless to say they fled the scene only to be made a misguided laughing stock on the set the following morning. He relished his notoriety, which eventually led to his early demise while on the set of Gladiator.

In the car, Kirk Douglas was extremely personable, always ready for a chat and full of interesting trivia about life with his many friends in Tinsel Town and his exploits on film locations. One should remember that in the days before mobile communications and the internet a passenger was stuck with me for as long as it took to get him or her to location in the morning and back to the hotel in the evening. Apart from the London sets, we filmed in Great Missenden and on the South Downs with both journeys involving at least an hour each way in my company. Once he travelled with his agent back from Brighton to the Berkeley Hotel where he was staying. You could have cut the atmosphere with a blunt knife. Kirk was not happy; in fact, he was furious about the way filming was going, especially about the female lead, the stunning Agostina Belli. She could not speak a word of English and had to deliver her lines parrot fashion. The inference, however, was that the real reason behind his outburst was that she would not welcome his approaches off screen - "How dare she cold shoulder Hollywood Royalty!" I kept my eyes on the road, trying unsuccessfully to ignore the subject of his anger and the repetitive expletives that emphasised his outrage.

Familiarity, as we know, breeds contempt and as soon as we arrived Kirk did not wait for the porter to open the car door for him but pushed himself out of the backseat, slammed the door behind him and poked his head into my side window instantly turning from outrage to sugary sweetness: "You won't say anything about what happened on the way back, will you?" I did not know whether

I should be offended that he thought I would be that unprofessional, or whether he just needed my reassurance. In the event, I said cheekily "Don't worry, sir, I will keep it all back for my book". This did not go down well.

When I got back home, a message awaited me not to pick up Mr. Douglas in the morning and during the following six weeks of the shoot neither of us made eye contact. Many years later I befriended his son Joel (younger brother to Michael) during the making of Jewel of the Nile and, when he got married to our production co-ordinator Patricia, Kirk and his wife sent me an invitation to the wedding. He either did not make the connection, had forgotten the incident or, as I would like to think, he forgave me (unlikely!).

From then on I had to make myself available to the stunning Miss Belli and her entourage, the just as attractive make-up artist and her very pretty personal hairdresser. Too much eye candy for someone who was condemned to keep his eyes on the road. I was made to swap a friendly yet self-important star, who did not share my sense of humour, for a glamorous young Italian starlet, accompanied by two ever-smiling grateful chaperones who could not hide their excitement of visiting England and London in particular. Never mind the language barrier, we got on like a house on fire. Myself, with the remnants of my Latin and schoolboy French, the girls with a few broken words of English. I bought a dictionary which eased communication a little but misunderstandings and mispronunciations aplenty only added to the general amusement that dominated our journeys.

The girls were keen musical theatre fans and I managed to get hold of one of my low life contacts who let me have tickets to Les Miserables at a good price. Not sure who the price was good for - us or, more likely, him. Never mind, they were happy to pay and insisted that I accompany them to the show. My ego was being well massaged by the three muses who accompanied me that evening up to the West End. In the auditorium I initially drew the short straw with a seat that was described as having limited visibility. The upside was that this gave me a perfectly legitimate excuse to lean over into Agostina's space and accidentally make contact. Dirty old man, I admonished myself, but with no regrets especially as she did not seem to mind. On the contrary we exchanged innocent smiles with a shrug of the shoulders every time we touched. All good things come to an end and this one was no exception. Lots of hugs and kisses and they were gone.

Kirk Douglas was being looked after by my fellow driver, Brian Hathaway, who told me how well they got on. When he dropped him at the airport, Kirk had shaken his hand and assured him that if he ever visited LA he would be most welcome to stay at his place. Unlike other departing charges, he failed to reward him financially for the attention he enjoyed and the servitude he took advantage of during his time filming in the UK. Neither did he offer to pay for his flights, something other Hollywood greats have done. Julia Roberts, who paid for her driver to fly on Concorde, springs to mind as do many others who rewarded their drivers with tickets to the States and in one case all the way to Australia in the front of the plane.

Better luck next time!

# 3 The Big Sleep 1977

## If you don't Laugh, you Cry

Like a loveable rogue Michael Winner, now missed by some, could be a man with a sharp and witty tongue and at the same time deride and insult a less articulate and unfortunate human being who, for one reason or another, could or would not fight back. He was an only, I suspect spoilt, son of a well-to-do father who had no qualms about taking out a court order to stop his widowed mother spending what he perceived to be his inheritance while she was still alive. On the other hand, his cutting remarks and somewhat outrageous behaviour were often very amusing as long as one was not on the receiving end. One evening, as the speaker at a charity dinner, he had us all in stitches with his tales and self-deprecating humour.

I was contracted as a unit driver for The Big Sleep and was to report to the production office in Kensal Road first thing in the morning. It was 1977 so no mobile phones, just bleepers – similar to the ones carried by doctors in hospitals – which were then the only method of communication on the move. Driving round the Hammersmith one-way system the bleeper went off. It was then that I had to find a telephone box to ring the office for instructions. Our production manager, Clifton Brandon, who calmed his nerves by constantly sharpening his collection of pencils, emitted a sigh of relief and explained that Mr Winner's driver had crashed his Bentley and that I should make my way as quickly as possible to Michael's house and take him to location somewhere in Chorleywood, Hertfordshire.

Understandably, Winner was in no mood for pleasantries and, from the back, he swung his legs over my passenger seat with his right foot dangerously close to my left cheek. I was not in the mood for pleasantries either; however, he was my paymaster so I let it be for the moment. I turned right into Abbotsbury Road on my way to the A40 when he bellowed that I should have continued straight on into the section of Melbury Road which is a one way street coming the other way. "It's a short cut and I always use it" he added. I ignored him which he accepted with a grunt and some derogatory remark about my professionalism and the lack of comfort my car provided; it was, after all, a diesel powered Peugeot estate, not good enough to accommodate his Rolls Royce of an ego

It did not start well and got worse when, in the pouring rain with deep puddles along the kerb, he kept suggesting I should have used the inside lane for overtaking. Again I chose to ignore his by now rude and personally offensive remarks; not for long though.

When we got to the Target Roundabout I had had enough. I pulled over next to a phone box and asked him as politely as circumstances allowed to get out of the car, ring the production office and ask them to send another driver who would put up with his antics. Reluctantly, he got out and realised that he did not have the necessary change he would need for the phone call. Sheepishly he turned to me, by now soaking wet, to see whether I might have the coins he needed. I did relent when he agreed to get back into my car, keep his feet on the floor and refrain from making any further comments about my car or my driving. Twenty minutes later we arrived at our location where a young man, Crispian Sallis, many years later to become a respected production designer, opened the door and walked two paces behind his boss clutching a cup of coffee in one hand and a script folder in the other. Without turning back both marched into the house that was to feature in the film, and out of my sight.

I returned to town and on to the production office where I made my way to the accountant to settle my float. He did not understand why I should want to do so. I explained what had happened and that I expected that Mr Winner must have called and instructed them to dispense with my services. No such call was received and I carried on with the duties of a unit driver until the end of the filming period. I was even given an extension of contract that covered several weeks of the postproduction schedule. Mr Winner's and my paths crossed daily during the shoot and the only reminder of our confrontation was that, instead of calling me by my Christian name as was his way with the rest of the crew, he always referred to me by my surname just as if I was a naughty schoolboy. I could live with that.

Others, especially the female artists, were often driven to tears by Michael's uncalled for putdowns. I did not hear or see what happened on the set but Joan Collins, before she was famous, and Diana Quick, a respected actress, did shed tears in the back of my car. Consequently they brought along their partners, Ron Cass and Albert Finney respectively, to location for moral support and protection. A couple of years later I worked on The Bitch with Joan when her daughter was hit by a car and would be hospitalised for an indefinite period. Joan and husband Ron were keen to spend time as close to her as possible and I was more than happy to set up one of my trailers in the grounds of the Central Middlesex hospital for their use. (I got a mention in her book about the accident and Katy's slow and full recovery).

Sarah Miles fared better because our lead, Robert Mitchum, took it upon himself to confront Winner and threaten him with a slap if he dared talk to her out of turn. Incidentally, Mr Mitchum was off screen a frustrated stand up comedian especially when he put on an Irish accent to recount his experiences with Burt Lancaster on the Emerald Isle where they shared indiscrete encounters with the opposite sex and which often involved their fellow actresses.

Over the next months our paths crossed several times and I became Willie and Mr Winner became Michael until one day he telephoned my home and, when my wife told him that I was in the USA and could she take a message, he uttered a number of expletives. As she did not realise that this was part of his normal speech pattern she, in disgust, hung up the phone on him. He blamed me for her action and a long period of enmity began. It ended when we 'kissed and made up' during the making of Bulls Eye which he directed and produced and my tender for supplying production vehicles won the day.

At this point I would like to recount one of the many anecdotes of his laddish behaviour. When I supplied a camera truck during the making of The Wicked Lady, Faye Dunaway was asked to appear in the nude for a lovemaking scene. She refused and found refuge in my truck. Michael followed her and explained that he had hired a body double to act out the sequence but would she come on to the set to witness her part for the sake of continuity. She agreed and, when she stood behind the camera to watch the action, Michael directed the double through a megaphone for all to hear "Give it all you can, dear, and don't worry about how much we can see, the audience will think" (and, pointing at Faye) "its all her doings".

A similar, not as crude an incident happened on The Wicker Man when Britt Ekland's character was to expose her posterior. When she refused the director called in a stand-in to act out the scene. The result was that, much to Britt's consternation and protestations, the body double's shape did not resemble her – what she considered to be - much better proportioned butt.

A few weeks into filming my long awaited in-car mobile phone arrived. It was operated by the then General Post Office (GPO). It was a one way at a time communication device. It meant that one could only hear the other side until, when pushing a button to cut off the speaker, one could then talk to the other party. It was of the type used by ship to shore radio and mini cab companies to direct their drivers. I had to wait for two years and pay the equivalent amount of a month's takings to acquire it. The way it worked was that by pressing a button you would alert the operator who would then put you through to the number you wanted to call. Because there were only a limited number of channels available she would cut you off after just two minutes and charge a small fortune for the privilege. Impractical today but the height of communication technology then.

Mr Winner heard about my new acquisition while filming a scene in the middle of Kensington Gardens, a quarter of a mile away from the nearest point where I could park. He had to have the use of it. I was made an offer I could not refuse and the chippies (carpenters) had to build a crate that could hold two car batteries while the sparks removed the phone from my car and mounted it on a console next to the battery pack. A lot of swearing later it worked and Michael had a new toy. He proudly called one of his friends who on several occasions boasted that with his mobile telephone his car is now his office. Michael was about to demonstrate that he was not going to be left behind in the one upmanship stakes. He pressed the call bottom and asked the operator to put him through to his friend's chauffeured limousine. Then to everyone's amusement (loudspeakers were the only option), the put down came: "Just a minute, Michael, I am on the other line".

Towards the end of the schedule we shot a scene in Margate that involved a car driving off the pier into the sea with onlookers bearing witness to it. At that time the extras, who formed the crowd, were being paid in cash at the end of the day. The assistant production accountant with the cash in the boot of his car arrived at the location later than Michael expected and was immediately summoned to explain what had kept him. In the rush he had left his car unattended. It was no secret that the money to pay everyone was left in the vehicle while the accountant was being admonished for his failure to turn up on time. When he returned the boot was open and, surprise, surprise, the attaché case with the money was gone.

It was three forty five on a Friday afternoon. Banks had closed fifteen minutes earlier and, whatever swearwords were spouted out, no cash could be made available, especially in far away Margate. I was having my afternoon break in the London office when our production manager, eyes more blood shot that usual, asked me to drop everything and go to the ATV offices in Cumberland Place where Lew (later Lord) Grade would hand me a load of cash that I should as quickly as possible take down to the location by the seaside. With the help of one of his assistants, Greg Smith, later to become a prolific producer and client, I rummaged around in a number of safes that were spread all over the building. I ended up with bags full of bank notes, enough apparently to cover the cost of the day's filming.

Off I went over Vauxhall Bridge and into Camberwell on my way to the A2. I was getting slightly apprehensive sitting in rush hour traffic. (Why is it called rush hour, it should be the slow hour as my young son Adam once remarked). Most cab drivers, concerned for their safety, would often refuse to accept a fare south of the river, which at the time was notorious for the criminal activities that took place there. A different kind of apprehension came over me when a policeman on a motorbike pulled up alongside and signalled for me to open the window. I froze at the realisation that I was in a traffic jam south of the River with bags full of cash under the passenger seat about to be questioned by the Law. Fortunately, I had misunderstood his interest in me. He was, in fact, there to escort me, blue lights flashing, out of town. Being able to overtake all and sundry and jump red lights with a police outrider to clear the way reminded me of the lyrics in the musical Sweet Charity "If my friends could only see me now".

It was Michael's good standing with the police force that enabled him to call on their help to usher me with my urgent delivery through town and on to the M2 which then took me to Margate where the crowd was being entertained until I arrived with the fresh supply of funds. When it came to the actual payout everyone was accounted for, which meant that whoever was responsible for the theft of the original money did not forego his legitimate pay out.

I worked with Michael on several of his other projects, famously on his insurance advertisement that was shot in Reigate and where he coined the phrase "Calm down, dear, it's only a commercial".

When it came to lunch Michael insisted that he would only eat off a white starched tablecloth which was placed amidst the unit vehicles in the car park of Holland Park. It is just a stone's throw away from his home and had bemused passers-by believing it to be part of the film set. The rest of the crew ate in the dining bus and, when one of my drivers could not resist a sarcastic yet apt comment and I refused to sack him, our relationship soured again.

It recovered briefly when his production manager, my old friend Ron Purdie, asked me to tender for one of his projects. I spent a bit of time in Michael's Kensington mansion, which doubled up as his office. There the central hallway with its sweeping staircase was dominated by a larger than life portrait of his lordship (to his great sorrow he did not even make it to a knighthood). When my wife and I were celebrating one of our many anniversaries and I had difficulties getting a table at a suitable venue, he used his influence and booked us into Chez Nico in Park Lane, one of the top eateries with over the top attention to service in London. With what seemed half a dozen waiters to each table who pounced every time one dropped a napkin on to the floor and who provided an escort when one would visit the washroom, it was not a restaurant we would normally visit. Nevertheless we enjoyed the experience of witnessing how the other half lives.

Sadly another incident involving one of my drivers and my misguided reaction to Michael's complaint again cut short our friendship which I was unable to rekindle before he passed away.

# 4 The Legacy 1978

## Going into Business

I had just finished working on The Big Sleep with its offices at Kensal Road Studios, a converted dog biscuit factory, when the next production for a film titled The Legacy was moving in. I was carrying books, files and furniture down the stairs while on the return up the stairs I was carrying new books, empty files and new furniture into the vacated offices. I was already doing voluntary work for my upcoming employer. It would have been churlish of him not to offer me a job and I was not going to be disappointed.

Later in the day I went to meet my new production manager. I knocked at the door and entered the familiar but now newly furnished production office. Ted Lloyd rose from behind the desk to greet me. He rose and rose until I had to pull back my head and look up to meet this giant's gaze and, when he took my hand, it disappeared from view well beyond my wrist. His hand shake was not as crushing as I had feared and, having welcomed me to the fold, he sat me down and told me what, at this early stage of pre-production, he understood this project would involve and what I would be expected to contribute.

Richard Marquand would be directing. Unlike my counterpart I knew him and had worked with him on a TV series titled The Prize Winners. We also shared a close friend, Michael Guest, who in turn gave me my start in the industry. I impressed myself that, after only a few years in the business, I had actually met someone whom the man with an armful of credits - starting in the 1950's including such classics as Fiddler on the Roof, Rollerball and Wuthering Heights - did not know much about.   My first medal!

It was going to be Richard's first big movie with an international cast and, in order to assist him but more likely to control and guide him, an established Hollywood producer would be coming on board. All we knew about David Foster was that he had produced such major box office successes as The Getaway which was directed by the legendary Sam Peckinpah with the even more legendary Steve McQueen and the well connected Ali MacGraw, who at the time was married to Robert, The Godfather, Evans. She was later to become Steve's wife. They were all personal friends of his. His business partner was Lawrence Turman who had produced The Graduate which was Dustin Hoffman's big break and Katherine Ross' first step to stardom. She later appeared opposite Paul Newman and Robert Redford in Butch Cassidy and the Sundance Kid. (Katherine on the frame of a bicycle ridden by Paul Newman to the sound of the theme tune is one of my favourite movie scenes of all time). It was for these reasons that to describe David Foster as a Tinsel Town heavyweight would be an understatement.

The Legacy is an American/British Horror film about two architects from the United States who get trapped in an English mansion and witness a series of mysterious murders. The cast includes John Standing (now Sir in real life) as the baddie and Roger Daltry of the Who as one of the houseguests. Though it only received lukewarm critical acclaim it returned a respectable profit for this type of low budget movie.

We did not know what to expect. All we knew was that he, David, was going to arrive in a few days time with wife and three teenage sons in tow. I would be meeting and greeting them at the airport and reporting back to the office my first impressions.

When meeting people at the airport I often play a game with other drivers who hold up boards displaying the name of their expected passenger. It is called 'Where do they come from?' and involves guessing the nationality of the individuals emerging from the Customs Hall. There were no prizes for identifying the Fosters as California meets London. David, just south of fifty with baseball cap, designer facial hair and trainers, Mrs. Foster two steps behind, immaculate short haired brunette, (should have been blonde) colour co-ordinated outfit with a large stone on her finger. There followed three baseball-capped teenagers in trainers and jeans, pushing a trolley each with the suitcases, coats and plastic bags balanced precariously on top of one other. We made contact, I introduced them to a fellow driver we had hired for the trip because my car was clearly not going to be big enough to accommodate five passengers with their luggage. I ended up with dad and the two older boys, Greg and Gary, who, many years later, became a top executive at IMax and the producer of Sleepless in Seattle respectively.

All of them were very excited to be in London and marveled at anything that was more than a hundred years old, which is quite a lot. In love with the ancient, they rented a house in Cleveland Row next to St. James's Palace. It was going to be their home for the next six months but, as it dated back to the 17th century, the Fosters soon discovered that it was not quite the home from their LA home they had expected.

They were prepared to slum it without a swimming pool, garden or a basketball stand. However, draughts, noisy plumbing, low ceilings and doorways (the men folk were over 6 foot tall), tiny rooms with furniture that belonged in a museum, not to mention the white goods (fridge washing machine etc) that belonged in a dolls house were, as was pointed out daily, just impossible to live with. It was a constant reminder that there is a price to pay for the romantic notion of an extended stay in historic London. I am not sure how many of these shortcomings could or would be rectified, as I had to chaperone dad who had more pressing things on his mind.

To start with he was unhappy with the script and this meant meetings with the writer and the director. When I say meetings, I mean all night sessions with me in charge of provisions - pizzas from the nearby Chicago Pizza Factory were favourites and burgers and fish and chips with gallons of diet coke served up occasionally when a change was called for. I spent a lot of time (all bookable for overtime payments, of course) in the house and befriended the boys and their mother who showed a lot of interest in what the city had to offer. Occasionally, I was invited to attend the script meetings and found that heads turned to me for approval of some of the changes that were suggested. It was fairly embarrassing as I felt it was not my place to comment.

Back in the office David buried his head in the shooting schedule and budget, neither of which involved me. This gave me time to help out with the minutiae of pre-production. The special effects supervisor needed to rent a van for the duration and I drove him up to Swans car hire yard in Finchley. When we got there and we asked to keep the vehicle for 14 weeks the manager insisted that we pay for the whole period in advance. I could have bought such a van for that amount of money. Ted was outraged by the rental company's demand and, when I told him about what I could do, he agreed to let me, rather than them, have the advance payment. I had regularly on my way to and from home passed a small forecourt displaying vans for sale in Chiswick High Road. I spotted one that was just right for the job with an affordable price tag on the windscreen. That was it. I stopped and bought it without haggling over the cost on condition that the dealer guaranteed it for the 14 weeks I needed to put it out on hire. It turned out to be a fortuitous arrangement as the van broke down a couple of weeks later and the dealer exchanged it for another one without the blinking of an eye. A few days later another van for the prop department made the wish list and we managed a repeat performance.

It also transpired that my Peugeot estate car was not quite what our man from Hollywood was expecting. He never complained; we just had a feeling that a less utilitarian car would please him more. I put a driver on to my station wagon to work to the office's instructions and, with a decent bank loan, bought a Mercedes for me to chauffeur our leader in.

Ten days before principal photography was about to begin, a truck to carry costumes was delivered to our base. The wardrobe master, Don Mothersill also known as Mother, climbed into the back and immediately slipped on a puddle of oil that covered the floor. Then, when he grabbed the rails along the wall, his hands picked up dirt that should have been wiped away weeks ago. He, unsurprisingly, lost his temper and rushed up to the production office to demand a wardrobe truck from anyone but the supplier of the one he had just inspected. No one else's was available and in his outrage he suggested he build his own. That is where I came in. We found a suitable van, which we set about equipping with everything that would make it the best wardrobe truck in the business. It had rails with locking straps to secure the costumes whilst on the move, large tanks to hold enough water to run a washing machine, a tumble dryer and plenty of power points to plug in a heater, an iron and, most importantly, a fridge for the wine and, when the occasion warranted, for champagne. It was all funded, as before, by a generous advance payment, a small bank overdraft and a loan from Mother, which I repaid out of my earnings at the end of the shoot. By the time we moved to our new base at Bray Studios near Windsor I was the proud operator of two vans, a truck and two cars. Onwards and upwards!

The most exciting aspect of this production was the fact that one of my favourite actresses was cast in the lead. I had first encountered Katherine Ross when she appeared in The Graduate and later practically fell in love with her when I saw her in Butch Cassidy and the Sundance Kid. I was, unusually, so taken by her presence that it took me weeks before I plucked up courage to talk to her. I even overlooked the fact that she was chest challenged when I normally preferred a healthily curved figure. It was her facial expression with her smile, which she delivered with a vulnerable light tilt of the head that would catch me unawares almost forgetting that I was, after all, a happily married man with a young family to cherish.

In reality I was the producer's driver and far enough removed from her not to speak out of turn. There was, however, an incident that brought us together for a day or two. She was at the time engaged to be married to an assistant director in LA who decided to come over and pay her a surprise visit. This is never a good idea, in particular in her case because she enjoyed the company of her co-star, Sam Elliot, not just on but also off screen. So when the boy from California showed up at the Carlton Tower Hotel I was approached by the producers and asked to intercept him and, as gently as possible, persuade him to go home without causing a scene. I took it upon myself to consult Katherine who suggested she would prefer to handle the confrontation herself with Sam by her side and me in the background ready to intervene if things got out of hand.

I did feel for him when he got into my car teary eyed on his way to Heathrow to catch a flight back home. Katherine and Sam in the meantime embarked on a more permanent relationship and, as far as I know, after some forty years are still living together happily ever after.

On the eve of our first shooting day the production co-ordinator noticed that we had not secured enough unit cars to transfer all the artists from their homes to our location at Loseley Park near Guildford. A friend of mine, Morris Newsome, had often wondered if he could one day join our motley crew of unit drivers. That day was going to be tomorrow. I rang him and asked him to pick up Charles Grey from his flat off Exhibition Road, bring him out to us and then stand by until the evening to take him home again. As Charles was going to be with us on most days Morris would have a good chance to stay on the payroll for weeks on end.

In the morning a black London cab appeared with Morris and Charles stepping out of it. What had happened was that Morris' car had been serviced the previous day and was due to be delivered to his home early in the morning ready for his first assignment. Well, the mechanic did not turn up and there was nothing for it but to blow the expense and bring our artist in by taxi. As time went by Morris managed to pursue a very successful career as a unit driver and later, as a sought after transport co-coordinator, even though he did not escape a regular ribbing about the unconventional way his film career began.

Another problem arose when the artists' caravans that were allocated to our American cast did not meet the standards they had expected or indeed were entitled to. Nothing suitable was available or, for all we knew, existed in the UK. Katherine and Sam accepted their fate with good humour but our producer was not at all happy about it and often mentioned it on our journeys to and from location. He even asked his secretary in the States to send over pictures of the type of motor homes that were part and parcel of any self respecting outfit back home. They were obviously in a totally different class from what we could offer. In his eyes we were just a second rate country to work in and "he wished he had known it before he agreed to produce this film." I made a mental note of his idea of location facilities and left it at that for the moment. During the wrap party I was given a pair of expensive looking slippers as a thank you present and an invitation to stay at his home in Beverley Hills if I ever found myself in the U.S of A.

His remarks about us being a third world country when it involved film production stayed with me and little did he realise that, less than a year later, I would visit the States to purchase my first American motor home. I would then turn up on his doorstep to enjoy the hospitality he had promised. Contrary to the perceived wisdom that one should not take up such invitations, I was not to be disappointed. He was the most generous host inviting me, at his expense, to dine in the Universal Studio Commissary, the Beverley Hills Hotel and other celebrity venues. He even lent me his classic Mercedes convertible to drive around in while he had to attend to matters in the office. The only curious incident happened when I wanted to telephone my recently widowed mother and, because of the time difference, I found myself in his office at an opportune moment. I asked him for permission to use the phone, which he was happy to grant but, as we went past his receptionist on the way out, he turned to her and inquired how much that phone call had cost. It came to just a few dollars which I obviously handed over hiding my surprise that, having spent hundreds to entertain me and put me up in his fabulous home, he had no qualms about collecting this trivial amount of money for what he regarded as a business transaction.

# 5 The Thief of Baghdad 1979

## Naming the Enterprise

Peter Diamond impressed me when, during the filming of The Legacy, he jumped off the top of the stage that was 30' high, through a glass ceiling into a tank 25' below which was dressed as a swimming pool. That is what stunt men do and thus earn the reputation of being slightly unhinged. Between takes we often met by the catering truck and exchanged anecdotes mainly about family and friends. During one of these sessions towards the end of the filming schedule he confided in me that he had lined up his next picture The Thief Of Baghdad (yes! another version) and, if I contacted Chris Sutton, the production manager, I would have a good chance to get in on the act.

When I met Chris at Shepperton Studios he explained that this production was mainly studio based with only a few days towards the end of the schedule on a local location. He was, therefore, at this stage not looking to order any trucks but only unit cars for his director and the cast. We shook hands on a deal for my Peugeot with a driver for the Thief, Kabir Bedi, and me in my Mercedes for the director, Clive Donner. The rest of the cast included Roddy MacDowell, Peter Ustinov - later Sir Peter - and Terence Stamp. My other vehicles would not be required until the production moved out of the studio on to location. Therefore, if I received a request from another company, I would be free to accept it.

This is how my camera truck, which I had bought from another facility company whose owner had retired, ended up on Yanks and my costume truck on Quadrophenia where my driver broke several overtime records. On Yanks, however, my man felt he was unfairly treated and I fell out with the production manager over a broken promise; in fact, he turned out to be the first of several enemies I had to contend with during the 35 odd years that followed.

In the car Clive Donner sat in the back with papers spread all around preparing himself for the day's work. He made notes and sketches that he would, on arrival, hand over to his first assistant. He, in turn, would pass on the instructions to the relevant technicians who would set up the staging. At the same time the players were given ample notice before they had to deliver their appropriate lines and rehearse their movements. He was a man who did his homework and consequently he and his crew were always well prepared with no time lost to indecision or second thoughts.

On the way home he was more relaxed and we often engaged in conversation. I particularly remember his aversion to the British pre-occupation of owning property with the emphasis on ownership. For his part he would always prefer to rent and invest his money in more pleasing objects such as paintings and similar artefacts, the ownership of which would give him pleasure with little responsibility other than a decent insurance cover. When I mentioned rising values and the security that bricks and mortar provided he countered it by listing the increase in values of his art collection. I did not argue but indicated that I was in no position to differentiate between worthy and worthless pieces of art. I, therefore, had to stick to the advice that had been handed down by my elders and the building society, which would grant me a mortgage but laugh me out of the building if I proposed to borrow the money for a painting. Never mind that I would have to deal with defective boilers, rising damp, faulty electrics and innumerable other urgent (everything is urgent to an impatient wife) repairs, I would be basking in the knowledge that I owned (or would do when the mortgage was paid off) my home and it would provide shelter for me and my family for evermore. In hindsight, though, there is a lot of truth in what he said. On many occasions I wished I could just ring a landlord who would have to listen to my complaints and worry about rectifying them.

During the day, while my charge was busy directing on the stage and I was not asked to run errands, Roddy McDowell and Peter

Ustinov often joined us drivers outside the building for a chat. Roddy was full of infectious fun and had us rolling in the proverbial aisles for hours on end. It came as a relief when he was called away to the set and we could resume normal conversation.

Kabir Bedi, who was being chauffeured in my Peugeot, felt he deserved better because everyone else was allocated a more prestigious car. Lots of whingeing; first to the driver and then up through the hierarchy via the assistant directors to the production manager. Finally to the producer, Aida Young, whose no nonsense manner and judgement elevated her to become one of the first female producers in the industry. We could only imagine what was said because, following that meeting, Kabir accepted his fate.

I knew Terence Stamp, one of my sixties icons, was in the cast but somehow I never saw him. He must have slipped in and out of the studio avoiding contact with all but the most essential crew.

Peter Ustinov was carved out of a very different stone. He was a true renaissance man with credits as a writer, a director of opera, film and theatre, not to mention his winning two Academy awards for best supporting actor in Spartacus and Topkapi with a further two nominations for Quo Vadis and for best screenplay for Hot Millions jointly with Eli Wallach. He also enjoyed recognition with a BAFTA win, countless other nominations and wins in Berlin, at the EMMYs, GRAMMYs and many other ceremonies. In academia he was awarded honorary degrees in no less than ten universities.

What brought us closer together was our mutual interest in cars; new, classic and vintage. He was also a keen motorist and dispensed with a driver for his way to and from the studio. Instead he was given a product placement car from Rover to assess and comment on it. It was a brand new Rover SD1, the successor to the much-maligned P 6. It was less angular and promised better reliability; the build quality and finish, sadly, did not show much improvement. Peter described it as a Volvo built by Citroen. He let me have a go in it and I could not have summed up my impression any better. It was not only this car that we both found equally disappointing, we also agreed on which car would be our favourite one. There was, of course, a vast number to choose from and we discussed over many days the merits and shortcomings of dozens of the ones on our shortlist. In the end we came to the conclusion that the Maserati Quattroporte was the car that, money no object, we would most like to own. The only difference was that, to me, it represented wishful thinking while Mr Ustinov actually owned one that he kept in the garage of his house in Switzerland. Still, he did promise that if I ever turned up on his doorstep he would let me take it out for a spin. Unfortunately, I never made it and the dream remained a dream because only a few months later someone broke into his property, made away with it and, to my knowledge, it was never found.

Another topic of our frequent conversations was my ambitious plans to build up a location facility business with the most up to date equipment on offer. By then I had started to run a few trucks and cars and was in the process of forming a limited liability company to front the enterprise. It was for this reason that I began to play around with possible names that would both reflect the nature of the business and the fact that I would want to be a 'hands-on' operator. Peter had recently been working in Wales where he noticed that his driver was referred to as 'the Wheel'. It did not take long to decide, at his suggestion, to christen me 'Willie the Wheel' and my new company 'Willies Wheels'. I cringed a little because I tend to shy away from putting my name so blatantly forward but soon realised how much it reflected my idea of associating myself with the 'wheels' which symbolises what I do, namely drive. So Willies Wheels Ltd it was going to be.

Soon after wrap Chris Sutton, our production manager, started to prepare another project, The Class of Miss McMichael, to be shot entirely on location in the deep East End of London. It was described as a comedy drama played out in a school for incorrigible children where Glenda Jackson was the teacher with Oliver Reed in charge as a nasty headmaster. The base and sets were all housed in an old disused school and the facility vehicles were parked on the concrete playing yard adjacent to the building. One driver would be required to look after the circus and both my cars, supported by a third one, would shuttle artists, director and producers to and from the set. All very contained and straightforward except that our main lead was a well-known troublemaker and unpredictable. In reality he was very predictable, regularly making his driver, Sid Checkter, stop at a pub on his way home. There he would attract the attention of the crowd by drinking to excess, dropping his trousers or starting a brawl, often all three. He just could not help himself; exhibitionism to him was just like a drug. However, it did not matter what state he was in when Sid dragged him into his car and got him home, Oliver would be sober in the morning, would never be late and always delivered a faultless performance with perfectly articulated lines.

I was put in charge of Glenda, which was a piece of cake. She was always ready on time and the journey from Blackheath through the Blackwall Tunnel was only rarely, unlike nowadays, subject to major hold ups. The conversation was restricted to a "good morning" with "how are you" and further polite nothings. Some months later when Glenda appeared in a film about the Russian dissident writer, Sakarov, she played the grandmother to a baby that happened to be my daughter Natalie. The signed photograph, dedicated to her, still hangs on our wall albeit demoted from the hall to the downstairs cloakroom.

# 6 Quadrophenia 1979

## The 25 hour day and 8 day week

This production took me back to my own time as a Rocker sympathiser and a detractor of the Mod culture that I regarded as narcissistic and overly concerned with appearance. Their clothes bought from Carnaby Street and their garishly decorated motor scooters (Vespas and Lambrettas) reminded me of a peacock's effort to impress the opposite sex. I preferred the more manly pursuit of a leather clad warrior whose vehicles of choice were proper oil spluttering motorbikes with their innards on display, fuel tanks wedged between their thighs and, above all, a loud and healthy roar that announced one's arrival and left heads shaking in disbelief on departure.

I am a grown-up now, less opinionated and even less impressed by the use of violence to prove one's manhood. Therefore, I looked forward to contributing to a film showcasing the Mods and starring the likes of Sting, Ray Winstone and the then relative newcomers Phil Daniels, Toyah Willcox and Leslie Ash before her unfortunate facelift.

Quadrophenia has since become a cult movie recalling the way the baby boomer generation, with their newly found freedom from conventions and financial dependence, rebelled against society's conformity. It celebrated the 'Mod' culture, with their smart dress code, as opposed to the ' Rockers ' with their provocative metal and leather attire. Inevitably the two trailblazers clashed and fought running battles wherever they met. Calls for the (Gun) Fight at the OK Coral went out at weekends and bank holidays at seaside resorts such as Clacton, Southend and, most famously, Brighton, which was the main location for this show. As it dealt with events that took place in the sixties, when the style of dress was very different from the time the film was shot, it was to be what we called a period piece with clothes of the time that had to be made to order or collected from specialist outlets from all over the country.

Joyce Stoneman, the wardrobe supervisor of The Thirty Nine Steps fame and whom we had met on The Class of Miss MacMichael, wanted to use my wardrobe truck to help her manage the movement of costumes between the various locations and the studio in Wembley. She also felt that my driver, Phil Knight, would be best suited for the task ahead and I, naturally, complied with her wishes. Unlike many other drivers Phil was more than someone who waited around to receive instructions. He was always ready and keen to help out the wardrobe department with any menial task that needed doing; sweeping up the floors, loading and emptying the washing machines, polishing shoes and running errands often to the bookmakers. He thus kept himself busy and popular with his co-workers.

The main location shoot took place in Brighton and the wardrobe department was split between a hotel basement along the seafront and its main base at Wembley's Lee International Studios, a stone's throw away from the twin towers, since then replaced with an arch. For some four weeks Phil had to shuttle costumes forwards and backwards between these two centres sometimes covering the 120 mile round trip two or three times a day from northwest London to the south coast. During daytime hours it would take him anything from three to five hours, depending on traffic, to reach his destination while at night he could manage it in less than three hours. He did, in fact, travel at all hours of the day and night to ensure the costumes ended up where they would be needed either to be worn by the actors or returned to Wembley for alterations, repairs or cleaning. It was not for us to question the efficiency of such an arrangement, suffice to say that Joyce seemed very happy with the way it all panned out.

In order to get paid Phil, like everybody else, had to fill in a time sheet. This was not as straightforward as it would normally have been. The unorthodox hours he spent driving, the tasks he performed while standing by to embark on his journeys and the loading and unloading times needed a sophisticated understanding of his entitlements. Fortunately we had a rulebook to refer to whose relevant passages went as follows:
(I paraphrase)

The basic working week covered five days Monday to Friday from 8.00 am to 5.00 pm with one hour for lunch unpaid i.e. eight hour working day. Any hours worked in excess were chargeable at time and a half.
Saturday' s first eight hours also at time and a half, overtime at two and a quarter times (1 1/2 x 1 ½ = 2 ¼). Sundays would be booked at double time with overtime at treble time. If one got no lunch break or had to take it on the 'hoof,' which meant unable to sit down, it entitled one to charge it at the relevant rate of time and a half, according to the day to which it applied. After 8pm one should be provided with a supper break and after 11pm a ' late supper break'. Failure to provide any of these should be booked at time and a half. One can also expect a 10-hour break between shifts and any hour short of such a break, known as 'hours off the clock', should be booked at the prevailing overtime rate. If on any given day one missed breakfast, lunch or supper a meal allowance must be paid out in cash.

In Phil's case he worked through Sunday into the following week, which meant that his basic pay started at time and a half the following week with the overtime rate increasing in proportion. He then worked through the subsequent Sunday into a third week his basic pay increased to double his original rate i.e. double time for the basic hours, treble time for overtime and four times basic for the third Sunday. This went on for four weeks. Once his time sheet for the fourth week arrived in the office I could not resist framing it and hanging it up in reception. When visitors noticed and inquired about the meaning of it I pointed out that, though it was legitimate, it was also 'A Work Of Art'.

Unfortunately these rules, designed to protect trade union members from exploitation by unscrupulous employers, led to wage claims that could only be described as bizarre. It was not only the film industry that exploited these arrangements. One of my neighbours was employed on the nightshift by one of the Sunday newspapers. He used to attend the printing works only once every two weeks where he would clock in himself and another absent colleague who, in turn, would have clocked him in the previous weekend. Thus either of them would only have to go to work every other week yet be paid as full-time employees. To rub salt into such practises his official job as a print setter lost its relevance to an automated process controlled by computers. This meant that, because he could not be made redundant, he turned up for duty, clocked in and returned at the end of the shift to clock out without having done any work at all. It was alleged that they even had beds brought in to allow the likes of him to enjoy a good night's sleep.

Unlike the newspaper industry, whose products had to be realised locally, filmmakers were and are free to set up productions wherever they were deemed to be most convenient and economical. With the increasing wage demands and belligerent union rules, the following year only one picture, Britannia Hospital, was produced here. New projects were set up abroad and it was left to the infamous Margaret Thatcher to rein in the more extreme trade union practices especially the closed shop policy. It thus opened the film industry to all comers, many of whom were willing to work at more reasonable and often reduced rates. In addition companies were offered tax incentives to film in the UK and the industry began to recover.

# 7 Dick Turpin 1980

## Lost Colleague Remains a Friend

On the film set it is the first assistant director who is charged with getting all the technicians ready before the director issues his last instructions to the actors and signals his approval for the camera to roll. He is the one who has consulted all the heads of departments, the director and producers before preparing the shooting schedule. Consequently, it is his responsibility to lead his team and complete the shots the director is looking for in the time that has been allocated during the pre- production meetings. From his point of view he has to check that everything from the set to the lighting, from the camera to the soundmen and, most importantly, the actors are on their marks ready to go. His voice should be heard above the general din of moving props, construction tools and lights, urging the crew to meet his shooting target.

Once he is happy with the state of the set he notifies the director who will give him the nod to carry out a final check with the camera operator and the soundmen who confirm their readiness to roll. This will follow with a loud "Action" to begin and a little later "Cut" to end the filming of the scene. It is the mark of a good AD that he can command the respect of his crew and is able to motivate them to bring in the show without falling behind schedule. His main problem is that, with a constant barrage from instruction-seeking technicians and his need to inspect every aspect of the set, he does not get a chance to sit down. Thus he spends his working hours on his feet; an extremely tiring and painful occupation. Jake Wright was just that man on The Class of Miss MacMichael and unsurprisingly was looking forward to a desk job for his next project.

The production manager's brief is closely related to the one the first assistant director carries out. He too has an input when the shooting schedule is being discussed because it is up to him to hire a competent crew and contract suppliers at a cost commensurate with the budget. He then has to ensure that, during the shooting period, the budget is adhered to which means constantly liaising with the first assistant regarding changes that may have to be made to the original schedule. The two jobs are so closely related that they are interchangeable, with first AD's often taking on the job of a production manager and vice versa.

Paul Knight and Sidney Cole offered Jake Wright the position of production manager on their forthcoming project, the television series of Dick Turpin. Because Jake was looking forward to resting his feet and giving his voice a chance to recover from the strain of making himself heard on the floor, he accepted this new challenge. Once his current commitment terminated he moved into the production base, a manor house near Maidenhead, where the first series of the Dick Turpin saga was to be filmed.

When we met up he explained that the initial series would run for thirteen episodes with each one scheduled for a two-week shoot. In addition another 26 episodes were planned over the next two years. A quick and optimistic calculation and I made it potentially 78 weeks' work over the next three years. Wow!

I went for it and Jake awarded me the contract. I was three vehicles short and even shorter on funds when Collingdale Motors, the VW agents, came to the rescue. They were advertising brand new VW transporters for sale, financed without a deposit on a three-year deal. After a quick phone call I showed up at the showrooms and things got even better. Not only was I offered a no deposit finance deal but I was also entitled to a 12% discount if I committed to the three minibus versions of the vans they had in stock. The three on offer were just what I needed, one as a minibus for the crew, one for the props and another for the costumes department, all of which needed to be shuttled from the manor house we used as a base to the various sets strewn around the fields and copses in the grounds. In addition, the salesman was willing to put the full sale price on finance and hand over the discount to me separately. "You have to be lucky sometimes" I thought as I walked away, not just with the vehicles but also a wad of cash in my pocket.

We were based in White Waltham near Maidenhead and never moved more than a few hundred yards. On the other hand we had to be extremely careful not to churn up the beautifully tendered lawns or to damage the outbuildings or walls that surrounded this listed property. Unfortunately we did not always succeed and, on one or two occasions, I had to arrange for repairs to be carried out. No one would admit responsibility and, as usual in such cases, my drivers had to take the blame and I had to pay the price. By now business was expanding with vehicles on hire not just on this show but several others such as Quadrophenia and Yanks, with other projects on the horizon.

I, therefore, was able to give up driving myself and employed drivers to take my place. It left me free to pursue more productions and design and build bespoke vehicles that I felt would improve the conditions under which the cast and crew had to work. Dick Turpin was so well managed with both producers, Paul Knight and Sydney Cole, always on hand to oversee matters that I was hardly ever called upon to deal with unforeseen problems. In fact, I only visited the set as a matter of courtesy, to present my invoices and to listen to my drivers' demands for better pay and conditions which I tactfully rejected. Occasionally, as a consolation, I would join them and the crew for a visit to the local pub where I stood my round.

It was there that I re-established my friendship with Greg Dark, the 1st AD, whom I had met when he worked in the cutting rooms for Michael Winner's The Big Sleep and I was the unit driver. The drinking, however, had to come to an end when one evening Greg, driving the wrong way up the M4 motorway, was pulled up by the police who threw the book at him. Both the producers and I appeared in court to provide character references and plead for leniency but to no avail. Apart from a hefty fine he received a two-year driving ban. Inexplicably Greg reasoned that he could continue drinking to even greater excess, as he was no longer driving. Unfortunately, he soon had to join Alcoholics Anonymous to control what had become a serious addiction.

A few years later he moved to southern Spain where I had a holiday home and where we often met for a chat about the happy times we had shared in the industry. Occasionally, however, we shed a tear or two when we bemoaned the fact that times were a-changing. I must admit, though, that my times were changing for the better and the tears I shed were in sympathy for the lack of fortune he had to cope with. At one point Greg wanted to show me the site on which the set for Eldorado was taking shape. We met at the temporary production office just off the road that led from the sea to the mountain village of Mijas and beyond.

As we edged out of the driveway on to the main road I was taken aback when he turned right uphill instead of left down towards the sea. I had just assumed that a soap opera about life in southern Spain would be shot in and around one of the many marinas and surrounding housing developments in sight of the sea with the beach playing a central role. Not so! The road took us past Mijas further up the mountain into the deep interior towards Coin with scraggy fields on either side as far as the eye could see. Eventually, half an hour later a wooded hillside appeared to our left. Greg pointed to a wide gap running up through the trees from top to bottom of the mountainside. "Its just to the left of this firewall" (the gap in the wood was there to stop wildfires spreading). We left the main carriageway and hit an unmade dirt track that led us through the forest to the site that was going to be Eldorado. An artificial lake, village square and church in the midst an assortment of houses, shops and restaurants were nearing completion.

I was surprised to notice that all the buildings were constructed for real and not, as would be common in the film industry, as facades supported by scaffolding. After all, why go to the trouble and expense of erecting three-dimensional sets when only the fronts would be visible on screen? As far as interior scenes are concerned it would be a lot easier to shoot them if the walls could be moved out of the way of the camera instead of being restricted to close ups because one would be working in an enclosed area. John Dark, the producer of the show, and Dan, Greg's brother and the prospective site (studio) manager, were so excited by their designs and the upcoming programme that I did not air my doubts for fear of dampening their enthusiasm. I visited the set on several occasions and was always made to feel welcome. Even though I had no professional contribution to make to this ill-fated project I was sorry to witness its premature demise - very sad!

Dick Turpin the Highwayman starred Richard O'Sullivan who had established himself as a comedy actor in the Doctor in the House franchise and such programmes as Robins Nest, Man about the House and many others. This was to be a dramatic, as opposed to a comedic, role which he carried off with aplomb; so much so that the two following series were supplemented with a full-length feature film co-starring Mary Crosby, the old crooner's daughter. I often chatted to her about all sorts but she always avoided talking about her father and changed the subject when she was pressed. I later found out that she did not have a particularly happy childhood. What a shame!

After the first series the production moved to Stockers Farm near Rickmansworth where the Black Beauty series had been shot. Because this time the offices were in what seemed to be an old farm worker's home, the vehicles would be parked alongside some old barns and disused stables and, therefore, less care was needed when moving them about. Any damage we caused could only improve the place!

A new production manager, Ron Fry, was appointed who in time became a loyal client and a friend. Once Sydney Cole had passed away Paul Knight carried on producing other TV shows such as London's Burning where I continued to have an involvement. Sadly, Richard O'Sullivan, married to Tessa Wyatt at the time, began to have some marital problems which meant he had to be handled tactfully especially after joining the crew in the pub. It needed more than just the lady driver, whom I had employed to look after him, to keep him under control. We, therefore, found an excuse to have somebody ride shotgun with her in the unit car. I never had another opportunity to work with him again but I did meet him occasionally when he came up to our respective sons' school to watch them playing football and where I was one of the other parents on the sidelines cheering them on. I must admit his son was the second best player on the field!

# 8 The Sphinx 1981

## A Call away from Solvency

Just three years since Willies Wheels came into being and the company had expanded ruthlessly, operating twelve trucks and four minibuses. I remembered my friend David Foster and his condescending remarks about the inferior quality of the location facility vehicles on offer to the industry in this country. I decided, with the help of a generous overdraft from my bank, to go to town or, more precisely, to the USA. There I purchased three large American artists trailers and a motor home ready to welcome to the UK the next batch of Hollywood stars who, thanks to my new acquisitions, would appreciate finding a home from home on our shores.

Well, they took their time. The dream of conquering the film industry by offering the most up to date and luxurious facilities, good enough for the rich and famous that were being spoilt by our American cousins, was turning into a financial nightmare. I sat in my office in the newly opened Cricklewood Studios and contemplated the errors of my ways when Ariel Levy, the line producer, who had just had a fall-out with one of my competitors, rang me to find out about the availability of my equipment. I did not know him other than he had directed the second unit of The Spy who Loved Me and worked as an assistant director on The Greek Tycoon. I guessed that his producer, Stanley O'Toole, whom I had worked with some six years earlier on The Seven Percent Solution as a unit driver, had put my name forward as a possible alternative to the company that had fallen out of favour.

He was looking for artists' facility vehicles for his forthcoming production, The Sphinx, to be shot entirely on location in Egypt. The artists he had to accommodate included Lesley Anne Down of Upstairs Downstairs fame, Frank Langella, who later played

Richard Nixon in the Frost/Nixon confrontation, John Gielgud, who needs no introduction, and several other lesser known actors all of whom required comfortable and air-conditioned dressing rooms in the hot climate they were going to encounter on and around the sets. In addition an air-conditioned vehicle was needed to provide a refuge for the director/producer, Franklin Schaffner, who had previously directed The Planet of the Apes and was later going to make an impact with Platoon. Naturally my two mentors, Stanley and Ariel, deserved and were entitled to similar treatment. In the event and totally by chance the trailers and the motor home I had earlier in the year imported from the USA turned out to be just the ones that would fit the bill. Solvency beckoned!

The motor home was to tow an artist's trailer while two pick-up trucks were going to be hitched up to a trailer each, thus forming three road trains. Two drivers in the pick-ups and me in the motor home left the yard on Boxing Day on our first stage to Munich, a journey that took us eighteen hours to complete. The following day, due to heavy snowfall, we could only make it past Innsbruck, a mere 120 miles away. On the plus side we managed to overnight in an Austrian Gasthaus where a gaggle of young female guests were holding a pre New Years Eve party. The least we could do was to provide them with some male company. We must have had a great time as none of us remembered exactly how the evening ended. Suffice to say we emerged from our rooms well into the following afternoon.

Naturally we were now running late. We crossed the Austrian/Italian border over the Brenner Pass. From then on it was downhill on a proper motorway all the way to Venice where we boarded a roll-on roll-off cargo vessel that was to take us to Alexandria. Although my road train was loaded on to the ship I did not join it but left the two drivers to undertake the voyage while I had to make my way to Cyprus. There I met with a senior officer of the British forces stationed there who escorted me to the NAAFI (the store serving members of the British armed forces and their families abroad). There I made arrangements to purchase, on behalf of the production company, a container load of bottled water to be shipped to Alexandria and onwards to Luxor where it would be handed over to our caterers who in turn would distribute the water to the cast and crew.

I then flew to Cairo and on by road to Alexandria where I waited to help disembark our vehicles and load them on to a truck carrying train on the two-day journey to Luxor. In the meantime the cast and crew took a charter plane that also carried equipment such as cameras, costumes, props and make-up on a direct flight from London.

It was the first day that, as part of the Middle East Peace Process, the border between Israel and Egypt had been opened to each other's citizens. Ariel, who had dual UK and Israeli nationality, thus became the first person to enter Egypt by producing an Israeli passport. He felt he made history and never tired of recounting the tale.

Strangely enough, on arrival in Luxor I noticed in a field a few hundred yards away from our hotel a number of American luxury trailers of similar specifications to mine. I was curious to find out why Ariel had not rented them instead of bringing mine all the way from the UK (I obviously did not mind). He explained that the owner was trying to hold the company to ransom by demanding so much for their use that it was just as cost efficient to pay me to rent my vehicles even though they were subject to hefty transport costs. I don't know what the Egyptian owner of the trailers' reaction was when he saw my equipment arrive but had it been me, I would have been as sick as the proverbial parrot. Years later my son Jason visited Luxor and noticed the very same trailers still parked up where they stood all that time ago. Now with broken windows, flat tyres and covered in dirt they made a truly sad sight.

Once we all assembled and settled down in our hotels everyone was invited to an eve of production party. Drinks with our Cyprus water, food consumed and endless anecdotes listened to, we retired to our rooms and made ready for an early start.

Unlike a first normal shooting day with everyone ready and eager to go, half the crew were laid up in bed with varying degrees of stomach aches. The symptoms pointed to contaminated drinks but they were initially dismissed as only bottled water had been available. When questioning the various patients to find out a possible common cause of the problem it transpired that all the affected technicians and artists used ice cubes to cool down their drinks. Yes, you guessed it; the ice was made from local water!! A day or two later all was well and, as there were no more moves planned and Richard and Roy, my drivers, managed to recruit an army of local boys to help them keep everything clean and supplied with the necessary, I left to return home to a bank balance that had come out of intensive care.

Towards the end of the shoot I returned to Egypt to help with the preparation for the return trip and, whilst there, I got to know our little helpers. There were five of them, all from one extended family. Whatever they were paid it was more than they had ever hoped to get yet a pittance to us. Coca Cola seemed to be their favourite drink and the drivers from time to time rewarded them by letting them take a crate of cans home to share with their friends and family. On the last day of filming their father arrived and insisted that we join him at his shack, that's all it was, for coffee and a snack.

We couldn't refuse for fear of offending him and so, stuffed with indigestion pills and a dose of another medication, which I suspected, contained an illegal substance, we set off to join our host. Food and drink i.e. coffee and goats milk Egyptian style, which is definitely an acquired taste, was on the menu and we bravely played the game. What surprised and humbled us most was that the shelves around the wall were filled with the Coca Cola cans, like prized possessions, which they had kept back for special occasions. In the early morning we bade a tearful goodbye with a further couple of crates of coke to soften the blow and loaded our vehicles on to the Alexandria bound train. My drivers accompanied the vehicles on the journey while I stayed behind, flew back home on the plane chartered by the production company and joined them again in Venice for the last leg back home.

However, prior to leaving Luxor when I was back in the hotel I witnessed a forceful argument between our producers and the local fixer. Apparently we had greased the palms of an imposter while the deserving official had gone unrewarded. In reality what should have happened was that both the so-called imposter and the fixer's contact should have been paid but our bosses were not prepared to pay twice. The argument came to a head when the fixer walked away in a huff threatening to get even. He did. The rushes of the last day's shoot mysteriously disappeared.

Ariel Levy moved to the United States but returned a few years later with Rene Dupont, another one of my previous clients, as unit production manager and producer respectively to set up The Man in the Iron Mask in France, of which more later.

I don't know whether our fixer succeeded in blackmailing the producers, who were forced to pay up, or whether the rushes were lost forever and somehow the movie was put together without them. Unfortunately, whatever happened, the film was not well received and did not live up to its commercial promise – c'est la vie.
For my part, a few weeks after we returned with nothing on the horizon, another of those unexpected phone calls led to me servicing Better Late Than Never in the South of France. A year that had started in despair ended in jubilation.

# 9 Better Late Than Never 1981

## A Working Holiday for the Whole Family

1981 was a very quiet year. In fact, I believe only three feature films with a British crew went into production and these were The Sphinx, on location in Egypt from January to April, and Britannia Hospital of which I know only that it was directed by the legendary Lindsey Anderson with John Comfort in charge of production. John had for many years been loyal to one of my competitors and only became a client of mine several years later when my friend Richard Marquand directed The Eye of the Needle. The third British project was this one! It turned out to be the most outstandingly pleasant production I took part in, not withstanding the fact that my family - wife, children and nanny - were asked to participate.

The story involved a couple of crinklies; David Niven and Art Carney. Both claimed to be the grandfather of a 10-year-old orphaned heiress chaperoned by the awesome Maggie Smith and living in the South of France. Locations were, as the script demanded, scattered along the Côte d' Azur and included the marina of Monaco, the bay of Villefranche, an estate in Antibes and a number of those beaches that are hoovered daily and where the cost of sun loungers rivals the price of a room in an upmarket hotel.

Kimberley Partridge, who was cast as the young heiress, was only available during the summer holidays. So it was that the filming had to be scheduled to fit into the 8 weeks which coincided not only with her but also with my children's time off school. Such an opportunity for my family to join me on a working holiday was not to be missed.

As the business grew I stopped driving myself, leaving it to my motley crew of drivers and mechanics to get on with it while I attended to sales and administration. However, an eight week project being shot exclusively in one of the most glamorous locations in Europe proved irresistible. Back at the wheel of one of my motor homes with wife, three children and a nanny (surely one cannot function without one) in the rear we set off in a convoy of production vehicles. It consisted of two American motor homes, one each for David Niven and Art Carney respectively, American trailers for Maggie Smith and our director, Brian Forbes, a European type motor home for young Kimberley, a make-up trailer and costume truck with a couple of service/tow vehicles. We overnighted in a service area somewhere near Aix and arrived the next afternoon at our base at the Victorine Studios in Nice.

The deal was that each driver (including me) received a living allowance to cover the cost of accommodation and 'per diems' to save us from starvation and dirty underwear. The money was good enough to rent a brand new three-bedroom apartment in Saint Laurent du Var overlooking the marina and the tennis club and just a ten-minute drive from the studio.

Our first location was the harbour of Monaco where the production took over one of the largest boats in the port which belonged to Bernard Matthews, the (bootiful) turkey breeder from Norfolk. He also insisted that he was cast as the skipper in the film which, after all, he was in real life. This was before the Russians arrived and when Mr Green was still paddling his wares in and around Great Portland Street. I was looking forward to boarding her and finding out what it must be like to be envied by all who came to get a good look at what they thought to be an extremely wealthy person. It then occurred to me that the passers-by were gawping at me in a way I would be doing at an animal on display in a zoo. Making an exhibition of myself by posing as a curiosity to be stared at by all and sundry was something better left to the people who have the need to demonstrate that they are considerably richer than their fellow men. Even if I was able to afford such ostentatious luxuries I would have loathed flaunting it and I, therefore, abandoned ship and made my way back to the quayside.

Renowned French caterers served lunch and, unusual for the British contingent, it was a sit down affair of four courses with wine, cheese and coffee served in a swish marquee on the quayside. One could only imagine how much the bill would have come to for such a meal and in these surroundings had I been a mere tourist. On the contrary, not only did it not cost us anything but we got paid to enjoy such privileged treatment.

During an after meal chat on one of the neighbouring boats a little girl, the owner's daughter I believe, fell and hit her head on the edge of the table on deck. She started to bleed profusely and, without hesitation, I offered to take her to hospital in my pick-up truck that was parked at the end of the pier. Even rich people can lose their composure when blood is involved and so mother picked up her daughter with a towel pressed against her forehead and followed me barefoot to the truck screaming and gesticulating at a policeman who was standing by the entrance gate to the marina. She was convinced - or so it seemed - that her child was about to bleed to death. He kept his cool, mounted his bike and motioned to me to follow him. Racing a pick-up truck, headlights flashing, with a police escort up Monte Carlo's hairpin bends with screeching tyres is something only stunt drivers experience. Where was the camera when I needed one? An hour or so later, the girl was back on board her parents' yacht with the tiniest plaster stuck to her forehead.

As a member of the film crew, we enjoyed access to all areas, including the famous casino where I managed with no difficulty at all to lose a modest amount of money in an even more modest time span. I understand that some of my predecessors had lost a fortune big enough to make them end it all by jumping off the cliff at the edge of the gardens into the sea below.

Finally, I could not leave town without working out where and which streets doubled up as the track for the Monaco Grand Prix.

Jean Pierre, who worked as a maintenance engineer for the Harbour Authorities, volunteered to take us round the track and, once we had memorised it and were left to our own devices, the race was on. It was a time trial that meant each one of the many crew members that wished to compete was to take a turn in my pick-up truck and race against the clock with the one returning the fastest circuit declared the winner. Entrance fee would be £50.00 per head and the total amount in the pot would be the prize money awarded to the fastest driver. We drew lots for the starting order and I was to hit the road in third place.

It seemed that our bunch of would-be racers and dare-devils were not the first ones to run the circuit, cutting up and harassing the locals who were going about their daily business. Just as my turn came to show my friends and colleagues what I could do, the Gendarmerie appeared and put a stop to my endeavours. An hour or so later - and just for the fun of it - I secretly completed the circuit in a time so slow I am too ashamed to disclose it.

Next stop, Cap D'Antibes. The location, a magnificent villa (later featured in Dirty Rotten Scoundrels), overlooking the sea with our boat anchored some 100 yards off shore. We spent a week there walking the gardens and chatting to the actors; David Niven in particular showed off his raconteuring talents and we were most impressed by the fact that he knew everyone by name. I also fondly remember the hairdresser, Ramon Gow, who entertained us all with outrageous anecdotes of irreverent and light-hearted confrontations with the stars, especially Maggie Smith and Lionel Jeffries. Sadly he was an early victim of HIV and is greatly missed.

Next was the beach. The beaches in Juan Les Pins to the west of Cap d'Antibes are the most manicured I know. Each morning a bronzed army raked the sand in even patterns and put up sun loungers and umbrellas in neat rows like soldiers on parade. Under normal circumstances, at a price, they would then attend to all your needs from serving food and drinks to realigning your sun bed from east to west to ensure one does not have to contort one's body to achieve an even tan. Most importantly, however, they paraded their perfect physiques like models on a catwalk to give all comers an opportunity to admire their six packs and lunch boxes. I never understood the point of such exhibitionism, especially as there were no mirrors about for these Adonises to be turned on by their own images. When the film crew arrived, these perfect specimens failed miserably to draw attention from whomever they wanted to impress. In fact, our director felt that featuring in his film should be left to professional actors with obedient extras in the background.

The whole section of this seafront had been secured and paid for by the film company and, in order to ensure continuity, the production hired its own crowd to populate the sand with each background artist being paid for his trouble. This was just a job my family could do; wife, nanny and three children had to spend every day for three weeks on the beach pretending to be holiday makers (not much pretending needed), occasionally listening to instructions from the assistant director to be quiet or to readjust their positions.

I was told that Adam my then youngest did not always respond to the commands but it made no difference; they all got paid daily. Mind you, it was I who collected their wage packet every evening. After all, as a member of the film crew, I could jump the queue that the crowd had to form for their pay off. Thus I got my kin home with no delay, ready for a shower and the evening meal in one of the many restaurants on the promenade in front of the boats in the marina across the road from our apartment.

Next came Villefranche for a night shoot and we travelled there in convoy. As we entered Nice on the Promenade des Anglais, I noticed that Raymond, who drove the costume truck a couple of vehicles behind me, had pulled over. I followed suit but within minutes he was on his way again. As we were coming out of Nice by the old port he pulled over again and I noticed immediately that he was being shouted at by a youngish, heavily made-up woman and that two unsavoury characters were attacking him (it was a right hand drive vehicle with the driver on the pavement side). The other drivers and I stopped and rushed to see what had caused this uproar.

In his naivety, the woman he thought he was giving a lift to was not a grateful hitch hiker but a prostitute and what he thought was his lucky day was in fact a sexual service she performed. Naturally she wanted paying and her FRIENDS were making sure that she got what she was entitled to. Confrontation was not called for and we clubbed together to save him from a bleeding nose or worse. Whatever it cost it did not seem outrageous compared to the beach fees and I believe that, out of my sight, the boys later took advantage of this service on several occasions.

The night shoot on the waterfront in Villefranche began with the obligatory multi course meal overlooking the bay with our boat moored just offshore. The warm night air made our skin tingle and again I could not work out how much I or any one of my drivers would have had to earn to afford such luxury. I spent every spare minute - and there were many - just gazing alternately at the star filled sky, the twinkling lights of the properties on the opposite shore and our brightly lit boat in mid harbour. Unfortunately dawn was nigh and it all became just a memory to last a lifetime.

What remained a memory with my family was the whole experience of enjoying a holiday that lasted eight weeks. It became a rod for my own back and from then on long summer holidays were a must. Fortunately, business improved and therefore money became less of an issue. We – or more precisely my family – repeated the experience for two years running in Mallorca followed by an annual vacation in the South of Spain where I eventually bought a holiday home. For my own part, I managed to run the business during the week and commuted to and from Malaga at the weekends to refresh the funds and, with a bit of luck, top up my sun tan. Spending summers in this manner has become a family tradition to this day - long may it last.

They say that happy people make lousy movies. In this case I am afraid it is true. The film was panned by the critics and sadly was not a commercial success.

# 10 The French Lieutenant's Woman 1981

## A Lucky Escape

This takes me back to the very early days of Willies Wheels when I met, for the first time, Chris Burt, the production manager later to produce such classic television dramas as Inspector Morse, Lewis and the neither so classic nor successful Revolution. The other future success story belongs to David Barron, then a location manager, who since has taken charge of several projects that I was able to get involved with; The Princess Bride stands out in my memory. Unfortunately, once he advanced to the top job of producer with a credit for most of the Harry Potter film franchise, our relationship had descended to a friendly smile at arm's-length. However, recently I bumped into him when he produced the latest Tarzan movie and the way he greeted me betrayed a willingness to welcome me back into his fold. Hope springs....

First things first though. Our leading lady was crossing the Atlantic on the Queen Elizabeth II accompanied by husband and children. Incidentally, Jeremy Irons, who was to play opposite her, was also on board with his next of kin. Apart from the leisurely progress and luxurious environment such a voyage offers, the passengers were able to carry on an unlimited amount of personal belongings without a surcharge for excess baggage which they would have incurred, even in first class, when travelling by air. Mind you, travelling expenses were not a serious concern to any of these superstars especially because they were being recharged to the production company.

The luggage, which included the proverbial kitchen sink, had to be transferred from the boat to Meryl Streep's London apartment adjacent to the Athenaeum Hotel off Piccadilly from where she later moved on to lower Hampstead. The producers wished that a luggage vehicle should closely follow the car that carried Her (Show Business) Majesty's family in order that both would arrive at her new home at the same time and that our star would be reunited with her belongings without delay. In addition, the producers were anxious that the whole operation would be carried out without any fuss, with utmost discretion and without exposing either Meryl or her family to harassment by the media or members of the public.

For some reason the answer to their paranoia was to ask me to join Brian Hathaway, one of the most experienced unit drivers in the industry, to meet and greet the family as they disembarked at Southampton Docks. Brian would be there for the passengers and I, with my station wagon, for the luggage.

We drove down the M3 in tandem and arrived at the vast terminal building into which the passengers would be directed as they came off the gangplank. There they would be able to point out to the porters the suitcases and other possessions that they wished to be reunited with. The Queen Elizabeth II was slowly moving alongside and, with every inch it came nearer to the quay, the expectant families and friends as well as numerous lackeys, of which we were two, began to nervously move closer to the railings that prevented the entry gates from being stormed. For our part we played it cool. After all we knew that our charges were not going to leave without us. Both of us had been introduced to Meryl during her last visit to the UK and were confident that we would recognise each other in good time.

A quick look around and we spotted a bunch of photographers looking to corner any celebrities that may be arriving and whose pictures would be of interest to the media. What we did not know was whether or not Meryl or Jeremy wanted to be featured in the morning papers. Consequently, Brian wriggled his way to the front of the crowd where he addressed one of the burly porters and offered him a couple of large banknotes in return for letting him through the barrier. There he managed to swim against the tide of the disembarking crowd, intercept our charges and ask the question. Apparently they did not mind as long as the paparazzi kept a respectful distance.

In the event we had nothing to worry about although I am not sure what our celebrities thought of it when, as they came into the terminus surrounded by well-stacked luggage trolleys and families, the men from the media did not spot them and hunted down some other faces that we did not recognise. We thus made our way to the cars parked across the road unhindered. Husband and most of the suitcases in with me, Meryl with the children and a couple of bags which contained, I suspect, her most treasured possessions, in with Brian. A quick goodbye and air kisses to Jeremy whose driver ushered him towards his car a few paces behind ours and off we went again in tandem up the M3 and on to Down Street to the side entrance of the Athenaeum. There we discharged our passengers and allowed the hotel porter, who expected to be handsomely rewarded, to carry up the luggage into the flat that was going to be Miss Streep's home from home until she could find a more suitable and more family friendly residence. After all she would be based in London for several months. For us a firm handshake from husband, a less than firm handshake with a simultaneous thank you and a gentle smile from her, and ignored by the offspring signalled a job well done.

While in London Meryl Streep was entitled to a permanent driver exclusively at her beck and call. Neither Brian, who had other duties than just driving to perform, nor I who was only there to help out on that one occasion but was responsible for the supply of all transport needs, were available for such a task. A new driver had to be appointed and Colin Morris was interviewed and found to fit the bill. I am not exaggerating when I say that he subsequently became one of her life-long friends. Every time she visited the UK from then on, she insisted on him being hired to drive her. I believe she even attended his wedding.

The main locations for the shoot were in Lyme Regis and its environs some of which were, due to the English summer, often covered knee deep in mud. It called for 4x4 vehicles to be employed, one of which was going to be a Jeep Wrangler that appeared in my yard. It was up to me to deliver it to the set before Monday morning's 'Unit Call' (film speak for reporting to work). Coincidently at the very same time I had booked a gourmet weekend with Sheila, my wife, and Jason, my 8 year old first born, at the Imperial Hotel in Torquay, not a million miles away from where the Jeep was expected.

The plan wrote itself; Sheila in her car and I in the Wrangler would travel to the hotel on Friday evening. We would do our eating and drinking Saturday and, on Sunday after breakfast, make a day of it delivering the Jeep and Sheila, having followed us, would then give us a lift back to the hotel for another evening with the master chef. Then, after a last breakfast and intending to embark on a strict diet, return home. Before that, however, on Saturday morning at breakfast we, I mean Jason, noticed the then famous, later infamous, Jimmy Savile sitting a few tables away from us. I later found out that he was there on a freebie that would give the guests a chance to 'celebrity spot' and publicise the venue. His pictures would hopefully adorn the local and national press with the Grand Hotel Torquay added to the by-line. Such a practice is still commonplace and a major publicity stunt popular with many eateries around the country that tip off the media when a celebrity visits their premises. On television at the time he was hosting Jim'll Fix It, a show during which he would in turn invite a member of the public to express a wish that he would then arrange to fulfil.

Here was a chance for Jason to ask the great man to fix his action man figure that he had broken in the car on the way down. We nodded permission and off he went to appeal for help. We watched them in conversation for a few minutes and Sheila, always respectful of fellow guests' right to privacy, got up and rescued Mr Savile from the attention he was receiving from her son. Knowing what I know now, I realise it was more a case of rescuing Jason from the attention he was receiving from Mr. Savile. The action man figure remained broken until recently when we discovered what super glue could do.

Mud, rain and more rain not withstanding, filming proceeded without too many problems although the famous shot with Meryl at the end of the pier defying the stormy weather took a while longer to satisfy the powers that be (I believe it was either a stand-in or one of the assistants who was volunteered to face the raging storm). My input as a driver and supplier of facility vehicles won no special award though it enhanced my reputation and helped me expand my business to become, at one point, a leading player in the industry.

# 11 Enigma 1982

## A Morning Surprise

The producer in charge of this project was a man who could easily be mistaken for an old fashioned father figure of a family doctor who sympathetically listens to all your woes. A squint in his eyes, however, which rarely manifested itself, betrayed the fact that Ben Arbeid's velvet glove concealed a fist of iron. This film was going to be shot entirely in France starting in Strasbourg, moving on to Lille and ending up in Paris. The cast, headed by Martin Sheen, one of the most prolific actors fresh from Apocalypse Now and Eagle's Wing, included a string of British theatricals namely Sam Neill, Derek Jacobi, Frank Finley and Warren Clark, all before they became famous and entitled to extravagant pampering. As all the filming took place in and around city centres, dressing rooms, make-up and wardrobe facilities were set up in hotel rooms while the trucks were all hired locally. No good to me!

I was, however, a personal friend of the now first time production manager and, when he married his long-term girl friend, I was naturally invited to the reception at Pinewood Studios. It was held on the evening before he, with his cast and crew, left for France where his new wife and his daughter from his previous marriage were to join him a couple of days later. For my part I offered to be the production's London contact but did not expect to be called upon. Monday lunchtime's call changed all that.

Each day, once the exposed film had been developed, the director, cameraman, designer and all other interested parties assemble to watch and evaluate the previous day's results. Usually a local cinema would be made available for this purpose. In Strasbourg, the first filming venue, the projector in the cinema turned out to be incompatible with the type of film used on this production. The solution was to hire another projector and set it up in the hotel in time to watch the rushes in the morning. No such projector was available to rent in France. Airfreight was not an option as the paperwork alone would take a couple of days to process. Trucking was equally unsuitable as it would take at least 48 hours to get to Strasbourg, especially in those pre EU membership days with unpredictable delays at Customs.

Me in my car it had to be! I reported to the rental company, Samuelsons in Cricklewood, to load all the boxes that contained the bits and pieces that made up the projector. My poor car! Boxes on the front passenger well and seat, on the back seat - in both cases up to the roof lining - and, of course, the boot which was so tightly packed that I could only just about pull down the lid far enough to lock it. With only the driver's wing mirror useable I set off. Dover then Calais and bypassing Paris on to my destination with very few motorway miles to help me along.

I arrived in the morning ready for a good day's lie down. However, before I could relax, I had to call our production manager to announce my arrival and hand over my cargo. I rang his room and was taken aback when one of our female crew answered the phone. It was not the wrong number. I explained where I had left the car for them to unload and make sense of the many boxes I had brought with me which, once assembled, would make up the longed for projector. I then retreated in wonderment into my room. He had only been married for one day but who was I to judge? The saying "What happens on location does not count" did, in this case, not ring true or appropriate.

I woke up after lunch to a phone call from my friend who asked me if I could pick up his wife and daughter from the airport later that afternoon. I was happy to do so; after all I knew his wife who had worked at the studio for many years and there was no way she would suspect any unfaithfulness because I was convinced that discretion would save her from finding out the worst. Unfortunately, it was newly found 'true love' and, irrespective of the consequences, it had to be declared openly. Therefore, this time a fling on location was made to count and yesterday's wife had to make way to a love sparked off just a few hours earlier. Ex-wife-to-be with stepdaughter in tearful embrace left in the morning. Luckily it was not I who had to give them a lift back to the airport. In the event, divorce followed soon afterwards and a new family, with what now was his third wife, came into being.

A few years and a son later on another location, this time in Germany, I witnessed a repeat performance though this time no one, including the mother of his child, was taken by surprise. A buxom lady working on the show took his fancy and again he could not contain his need to advertise his conquest. Again according to my friend, this was going to be a life changer and would last until 'death do us part'. At the last count, two children followed but it was not death that parted them. This time I did not witness the relevant events but found out from mutual friends that a new relationship which, on this occasion began in Wales, was going to survive the test of time. Though we have since lost touch with each other I wish him well in his new life. Long may it last (this time.)

I took a couple of days off before I made my way back home and particularly enjoyed the food in the restaurants that were frequented by the producer and his lead artists. I was there as his guest because he felt he owed me thanks for going beyond the call of duty when I had travelled overnight to save the day. I was introduced to the local Alsace specialities of choucroute, sauerkraut with a selection of salted meats, sausages and charcuteries which are now some of my preferred dishes when visiting France and the Alsace in particular.

Five hundred miles to the east and many years later I was introduced to another local speciality. My friend (sort of) and potential client, Angus More Gordon, was on a reconnaissance mission for a Spielberg project in Wroclaw, Southern Poland. I had to attend to some business in Dresden, Germany, just a three hour drive away, and used that opportunity to contact him and meet up for a late lunch. I was hoping to fnd out more about the impending production but it was too early to discuss my possible involvement.

What was on the agenda, though, was Angus's eagerness to introduce me to the local delicacy of Pierogi. The last time someone in Eastern Europe enthused about a local delicacy was on one of my visits to Russia. Blini consisted of a thin type of pancake made from buckwheat and served filled with caviar. I should have known better than to expect a similar treat in the university canteen into which I was led. Suffice to say that here caviar was not on the menu. I was too polite to remark that stuffing a dumpling with minced pork meat (I think) did not bring back memories of my trip to the Soviet Union. On the other hand the meal cost only a few Zlotys which cheered up Angus no end. After all, getting value for money is in his DNA.

I left the projector in the producer's care only to return and pick it up when a suitable cinema on the next location in Lille became available. I took a leisurely drive back, stopping over in Paris to call on an old friend who happened to have been my best man and was now making a living as an art dealer. Very posh!

I got back home and, apart from picking up the projector, I only had to undertake return trips with various props and replacement lenses. Prices in France, at the time, were quite reasonable and crew and cast could not stop shopping for anything from clothes to electrical gadgets to cameras. When they found out that I was travelling backwards and forwards by road, any spare room in my car would be taken up by their new acquisitions which thus would not be chargeable as excess luggage on their flight back. When arriving in Dover, Customs were initially happy to let me through when I declared that I was carrying personal effects belonging to friends of mine. As I could not be sure of what they contained I always drove into the bay marked Something to Declare and invited the officers to inspect my load.

 Inevitably on my last trip they discovered an expensive camera and an electronic gadget (I never found out what it was) which they advised me were subject to import duties. I did not have enough money on me (credit cards were not yet available) which meant I had to leave them behind and return home without them. They belonged to one of the American members of the crew who, as it happened, would take the goods back to the States with him i.e. export them, and would therefore be exempt from paying import duty. In the event he was booked on a flight back the following morning. I was, as drivers always are, blamed for the debacle. I had to return to Dover and persuade the Customs officer that the offending pieces belonged to a US citizen who was about to leave the country the following day. To cut a long story short, and because of the lack of time available, I had to pay the duty in the hope that the production would refund it. I got back in good time to reunite the American with his camera and gadget. I cannot remember if he thanked me but the production duly reimbursed me.

# 12 The Wall 1982

## The Lone Honey Wagon and Organised Sex

Not to be confused with the 1982 Alan Parker Film featuring Pink Floyd or the 2017 thriller directed by Doug Liman. In the days of the Cold War with the Iron Curtain that descended from Stettin in the Baltics to Trieste in the Adriatic (Winston Churchill) very few productions ventured out into the Eastern Bloc countries. At the time I recall that the only locations used by international filmmakers were in the old Yugoslavia that now, after a bloody civil war, has split into several independent states and Czechoslovakia that, after a peaceful understanding, split into the Czech Republic and Slovakia. In fact, even then, both countries had already begun to rebel against the socialist doctrine imposed on them by their big brother, the Soviet Union. Three years earlier Force Ten From Navarone was successfully shot in the Yugoslavian Federal State of Montenegro and Bosnia Herzegovina, which, after a bloody civil war, gained its own independence. The film featured the young Harrison Ford and Robert Shaw and the even younger Barbara Bach. It was followed by the made for television All's Quiet on the Western Front with Ernest Borgnine and Donald Pleasance shot entirely on location in Czechoslovakia.

Ron Carr, having supervised the production, was asked to take charge of The Wall to be shot on location in Southern Poland. There he would be presented with similar problems to the ones he had encountered and overcame during his time in its neighbouring country with which it shared a political system and a socialist doctrine. Katowice, an industrial city and transport hub in Upper Silesia with the only western style hotel for miles around, which was managed by a French company, was chosen as the production base. A large part of the city, with its early twentieth century buildings that had not seen a coat of paint in decades, was due for demolition and, therefore, it suited both our special effects department and the town planners if we blew up the buildings for real; after all, the script told the story of the 1943 Jewish Warsaw Ghetto Uprising when the Germans flattened the area before they transported the survivors to their near-certain deaths in the nearby death camps of Auschwitz and others.

Shockingly the Authorities were eager to please the producers and keen to collect their fees prematurely. They gave permission to set off the explosions before the residents had a chance to remove all their possessions and place them at a safe distance from the imploding buildings. The poor souls would hardly have had time to move into their new homes in the grey prefabricated high-rise dwellings that could not possibly improve their life style but, more likely, drive them to drink and despair. Our crew, to their credit, refused to push the button and held back, forcing a costly delay, until the inhabitants could be evacuated in an orderly manner.

The budget did not allow for the rental of location facility vehicles to be shipped from the UK. However, at the time the Polish film industry did not have the wherewithal to treat its cast and crew to anything but extremely basic provisions when filming on location. Fortunately everyone on set agreed, for the sake of the picture, to slum it. In addition our cast headed by Tom Conti, the prolific theatrical actor later to star in Shirley Valentine, and Lisa Eichhorn, whom I met during the making of Yanks and who later worked with Matt Damon on The Talented Mr. Ripley, did agree, like the old troopers they were, to endure the discomfort they were exposed to. However, there was a limit to how much suffering for 'Art' would be tolerated and the toilet facilities on location were definitely it.

The management was forced to operate a minibus to shuttle those in need back and forth to the hotel and thus an unacceptable amount of time was lost on the set, especially when the cast were caught short. A few frantic phone calls followed and a deal was struck to send one of my mobile toilets, tow truck and driver across the Iron Curtain to provide relief to the desperate. Because there was some urgency to deliver the trailer to the set, I volunteered in order to save time to act as a second driver. We hit our first hurdle when we were about to enter what was then known as the German Democratic Republic. I remembered my time as a truck driver in these parts and, therefore, did not unduly fret about the four hours it took to reach the front of the queue of vehicles waiting to enter the country. We were granted a transit visa to the Polish border with the proviso that we overnight in Babelsberg Studios near Potsdam. Once there, the East German Film Authority would arrange for hotel accommodation and issue us with an exit visa to allow us to leave the country at the allocated border crossing - hard to believe now since German unification and the falling of the Berlin Wall with Poland a member of the EU allowing free movement of goods and labour.

Just after lunch the following day we hit the German-Polish border where the Customs officers and heavily armoured guards proceeded to inspect first our documents then our truck and finally our honey wagon trailer. Once I opened the door to the mobile toilet the two guards (they did not do things unaccompanied) started to egg each other on as to which one of them should take a closer look at the toilet bowls. They managed to call over another officer who displayed fewer stripes on his shoulders to undertake an inspection of the sewage tanks under the floor. At pain of severe punishment he refused (who could blame him?) and a standoff ensued. Eventually an English-speaking officer arrived and, having explained ourselves, he pronounced that "These mad Englishmen don't trust the Polish standard of hygiene and are dragging their own facility with them." A rare outburst of German laughter followed and we managed to clear another hurdle. I later found out that, in the same way we like to belittle the German sense of humour, the Germans belittle the Polish sense of hygiene.

A few hours later we arrived in Katowice and were directed by the location manager to a large compound where we were to park overnight before travelling to the film location the following morning. To our surprise the pound was full of UK and Irish freezer trucks transferring beef carcasses on to Russian lorries that were due to deliver them to the Olympic village in Moscow. So much for Thatcher's boycott of the Games!

We checked into the hotel in mid evening and, as soon as I signed in, our UK electrician, an old friend who inquired about my room that happened to be on the ground floor, welcomed me. "I need you to put your per diems into the pot" he said and, when I looked perplexed, he added "don't lock your window tonight". Whatever!

A shower and change of clothes later I went to reception where a number of the crew, surrounded by a bevy of young ladies, were ready to go out. They beckoned me to join them which I did. Poland at the time was a Communist state in the midst of the Cold War. The American and British boycott of the Olympic games, which were held in their friendly neighbour's country, did not exactly make us flavour of the month.

Living conditions from what we saw were unbelievably rough with streets lined with drunks and factories emitting smoke reminiscent of paintings of the Industrial Revolution with their chimneys in full flow. Russian (old fashioned) trucks with black clouds in their wake huffed and puffed along the unlit roads and the few cars were reminders of the mid fifties when air pollution was not yet heard of. In other words, outside this French run hotel the scene was pretty grim, not helped by drizzling perma-rain that would, it seemed, never stop. On the other hand my fellow crewmembers with their entourage seemed cheerful and, when we arrived and entered what was a nightclub, all was revealed. In an instant we were spiralled into a scene from Cabaret with flashy women, champagne, music and a floorshow introduced by a Joel Grey look-alike and of which

Raymond's Revue Bar would have been proud. Deutsch Marks and Dollars were king with the local Zloty a definite no-no. Both my companion of the last three days and I could not keep up and we returned to the hotel well before midnight; after all we had an early morning to look forward to. I did remember not to lock my window and dropped off into a deep sleep.

I am not sure what time it was when I noticed a woman climbing in through the window and letting herself out through the door of my room into the hotel corridor. I started to believe I was dreaming when another woman followed with another in tow, then another one and another. I slipped under the bed sheet covering my face on the basis that if I didn't see them they didn't see me. My alarm went before dawn and, as I was shaving, the earlier procession of now somewhat dishevelled women crossed my room from the door to the open window and disappeared into the morning mist. Explanation, if this is necessary: the women were sex workers who were not allowed room visits but, at a price, paid for partly by the per diems I handed over on arrival, they would bypass reception and provide their services where required. This was a daily event and quite a few members of the crew took turns to receive these visits. Needless to say several doctors' appointments were required on their return home.

For these women this was a regular, if only temporary, income stream and they dished out entertainment beyond the call of duty. A rumour spread that some of the ladies of the night were encouraged by the more sinister branch of the government to monitor our activities and report back to their masters any misdeed or remark by any one of our crew that may subvert their authority. Knowing our interest in politics and the like we had nothing to fear because all we wanted was to complete the shoot, collect our wages and return home as soon as possible.

Although eggs were aplenty and to our taste, the bread in the hotel was always stale and inedible. The girls took turns to volunteer every morning to go out to a local baker and bribe him to supply the crew with fresh bread. They did the same with the local butcher who was persuaded to cut the bacon into rashers the way we were used to. They also ensured we retained access to the dens of iniquity that provided distraction from the miserable location and the even more miserable storyline of the film.

Having set up the mobile toilet, I left my fellow traveller to it and got one of the unit cars to drive me to Warsaw to catch a flight home. This trip was uneventful other than the unbelievably bad state of the road, a motorway built during the 2nd World War by the Germans but which had not seen any maintenance since then. The driver had no sympathy for either his suspension or my discomfort and we spent over two hours with him staring straight ahead obviously resenting the fact that he had to work for his living (just a miserable so and so?) and me being tossed up and down over the countless cracks and potholes in the road.

Many years later when we worked on Schindlers List I drove through Katowice on my way to Kraków. It was unrecognisable with its newly tarmac'd roads and freshly painted houses. Even the chimneys, now carrying large filters, no longer emitted their poisonous exhaust. I was in a hurry so did not stop to see what had happened to the hotel and the locations we used. Maybe next time.

# 13 Slayground 1983

## The Fastest Unit Car in the Business

Times were good and a bit of an indulgence was called for. In the event it was a petrol blue Porsche 928S. Unlike the usual sports cars built by Porsche with their engines in the back, this one had its engine in the front with the gearbox in the rear. This arrangement gave the car perfect weight distribution and, therefore, handled like a grown up go-cart. The price put it beyond the reach of boy racers and thus made it an ideal carriage to ease my oncoming mid life crisis. It helped that Sheila did not threaten me with a divorce but insisted that I promised to be very careful driving it, something she would have said even if I turned up in a Land Rover. It was a wholly inappropriate grand tourer for a father of four though, in my defence, I could fit in three of my children aged eight, five and three on the occasional seats in the rear and the baby, just a few months old, crossways in a carrycot in the glass covered luggage compartment. No room for nappies and all the other paraphernalia but we had the use of a people carrier with a sticker proclaiming 'My other car is a Porsche' for longer journeys.

Not that many years ago I would have belittled a middle aged (anyone out of their twenties) man with greying sideburns and a comb-over, driving an expensive Super Car, as a sad case. Cruising up and down the Kings Road on Saturday mornings and showing up outside the Playboy Club at any other time was not for me. I was only, if you can believe it, attracted by the engineering prowess of this machine and my ability to handle such a beast at high speed, both in traffic and on the open road. Never mind the fact that in reality city streets were too congested to travel at anything faster than a mini van and that exceeding the speed limit on the open road risked being caught for breaking the law.

Slayground is the fictitious story of a girl who, as a result of a botched robbery, is accidentally killed. Subsequently the members of the gang find their comeuppance when one by one they go to heaven - or more likely to hell - in mysterious circumstances that were borrowed straight out of a Hammer Horror movie. The last remaining gangster found himself being followed into a fairground where the chase across the various rides ended up in a blood bath. For Terry Bedford it was his first step on his directorial journey out of commercials into the world of feature films. However, what interested me more than his plans for the shoot was the fact that he had a collection of Citroen Traction Avants that were produced in various guises from 1930 until they were replaced in 1955 by the equally revolutionary DL and DS ranges. These front wheel drive low slung limousines with large wings over the front wheels - that supported a flimsy bracket holding oversized headlights - usually came in black. They gained fame as the archetypical French getaway car. At the same time, they were used by the police and made famous by Jean Gabin and more recently by Michael Gambon in the Inspector Maigret TV series.

I could go on about this most advanced design and good looks but suffice to mention that a friend of a friend of someone I met in my hitchhiking days let me take the wheel of one of these monsters. Without power steering and with front wheel drive it was only possible to steer it on the move and the faster one drove the easier it was to turn the steering wheel. However young and strong I was, parking was only possible if one threw caution to the wind and sort of raced backwards into the desired gap. It was then, I believe, that the French lost interest in keeping their bumpers dent-free, a habit they have adopted and cherish to this day.

Two producers were in attendance. Gower Frost, relatively inexperienced but an old friend and business partner of Terry was to provide moral support and protection from the other producer, the very experienced John Dark who would inevitably interfere with and frustrate the ambitions of our artistic leader.

As much as I enjoyed John's company his manner and appearance were often a source of embarrassment especially in the presence of members of the general public not familiar with the antics of one of the most prolific filmmakers in the industry. He made up for his below average height by overcompensating with an ostentatious dress sense; brightly coloured trousers with an even brighter coloured jacket accessorised with an even brighter, if that was possible, shirt and tie. A pantomime dame would have had a hard time outshining him. He had by this time spent a lifetime in the business and hardly ever stopped recounting tales of his encounters with the stars, crews, studio executives and directors. The punch line of these anecdotes reflected without fail his superiority over his hapless opponents.

I too was subject to one of his assertions about the need to provide shelter from wind and rain and a sit down facility at mealtime. "No dining bus" he pronounced. The production manager supported my argument to provide one yet it was beyond John's remit to admit to the error of his ways. Technicians and artists had to retreat into local eateries for a roof over their heads and a table and chairs to sit down at when food was served. It did not matter to him that paying to rent such a space and purchase meals at restaurant prices, rather than utilising the services of a caterer, ate much deeper into the budget than necessary. What mattered above all was that the producer did not lose face by admitting that a mere driver won an argument, whatever the cost to the production.

I knew my place and had learned my lesson not to contribute any further notions as to how to employ resources more efficiently. After all, my producer, as they say about any customer, is always right especially as he was a veteran of countless productions and was soon to head the ill-fated television soap, Eldorado, in Spain.

Ron Fry, a production manager whose credits included The New Avengers and Dick Turpin, where I first met him, came on board. With my new wheels waiting for an opportunity to hit a fast road I offered Ron a lift to Southport, our first location, 225 miles away on a motorway nearly all the way. When John found out that I was going to travel with Ron he insisted that he should join us. My and Ron's protestations that my car was a two seater with only tiny casual seats - as becomes a sports car - in the back drew no response. John used his seniority to direct the 55-year-old grandee of the industry into the back and remain there in the foetal position for the three hours that it took to get to our destination. Poor Ron took days to recover from the ordeal!

Next was the question of hiring a local car suitable for our producer to be chauffeured around in. He expected, as was his right, to be conveyed in a limousine where there was enough space in the back to hold meetings and do some paperwork. The location manager, whose task it was to contract such a vehicle, explained that there was only one such car in town which was owned by a company of undertakers whose manager was not authorised to hire it out. John summoned me and we drove to meet the undertakers where the conversation went thus: "If the Queen comes, would you let her have the limo?" "Of course" said the hapless man. "Well" retorted John "I have got news for you, she is not coming. Therefore, can I have the car then?" A phone call to his head office later, a chauffeur appeared and ushered John into the black limo which remained with us for the period. Needless to say daily bon mots about funerals and dead bodies abounded.

One of the duties of a unit driver is to transfer the daily rushes to the labs for development where they get checked for any imperfections. For this purpose the labs work throughout the night so they can report back in the morning. However, to be able to do so the rushes have to be delivered before midnight and would have to leave Southport by 8 o'clock to allow for traffic or other hold-ups. When John discovered that I intended to return to London in the evening he roped me in to do the first rushes run.

On the M6 I cruised at about 90 mph, a bit over the speed limit, but very comfortable in my new GT. North of Birmingham I noticed a Ford Capri on my tail too close for comfort. I put my foot down and soon lost him far in the distance and carried on, now at 100mph + on a deserted motorway. Driving past Newport Pagnell Services I caught from the corner of my eye a marked police car about to join me on the motorway. I immediately slowed down to the national speed limit that, after cruising at 100mph, seemed like standing still. In no time the police car pulled up next to me and beckoned me to move over on to the hard shoulder. Well I did as I had been told and no sooner did I get out of the car than my old friend, the Capri from Birmingham, turned up. He was an unmarked patrol car and I was duly cautioned for exceeding the speed limit by at least 20 mph; the summons and the resulting points on my licence an inevitability.

I delivered the rushes in good time and in my mind tried to work out the defence I would put forward in court. One of the best options I thought would be to sell the car and plead that, having disposed of it, this would demonstrate my resolve not to exceed the speed limits again. So I did, much to the relief of my wife and much pain to me. I kept on rehearsing my mitigating circumstances over and over again. Someone must have heard my pleas because the summons never came and I never found out why, not that I wanted to know. What a pity I so prematurely got rid of what was and still is my favourite car.

I returned to Southport and later Blackpool on several occasions and helped out with the rushes in a sedate Toyota Landcruiser which was a more appropriate mode of transport. In fact over the years I bought and drove seven of these extremely versatile and dependable vehicles.

The film, like many others I worked on, came and went without returning a profit. As a rule of thumb only one in ten pictures made could look forward to breaking even and only one in possibly dozens would be a box office hit and would make somebody richer than they were before they handed over the funds to realise the project.

# 14 The Curse of the Pink Panther 1983

## I met him when still alive

While working on The Thief of Baghdad, Peter Sellers was also working on the Prisoner of Zenda on one of the other stages at Shepperton Studios. I can't remember the circumstances but I befriended his dresser and was surprised when he came up to me to tell me that Peter Sellers' driver had been taken ill and asked if I would be able to drive 'a friend' of Peter's back to town in his Roller. I got permission from our production manager to help out and went over to meet Sellers in his dressing room.

I was introduced to his 'friend' and all three of us walked in the drizzling rain out to his car where I was handed the keys with instructions of what was what and told to take good care of my passenger who wanted to be dropped off at the Royal Garden Hotel in Kensington.

In her large sunglasses, a scarf over her head tied under her chin and wrapped in a coat that could only be described as frumpy, this five foot nothing lady was hardly the tall blonde sex kitten I would have expected his 'friend' to be. I had to do a double take when I realised it was Princess Margaret. I tensed up which is not like me; after all I have met and befriended quite a few celebrities. Almost immediately she put me at ease by starting a casual conversation about nothing in particular. I did ask about her bodyguard and she explained that she had released him the previous evening and was meeting him with her car outside the hotel from where she would drive round the corner to her apartment in Kensington Palace.

I returned the car to Shepperton where Peter questioned me informally about the journey gave me a generous tip and asked me to reassure him that I would be discreet. It's only the thirty-year rule – and that they are no longer with us - that allows me to tell this story with a clear conscience.

Alas, The Curse of the Pink Panther had to be shot without Peter as he had passed away some months earlier. The story establishes that Inspector Clouseau, usually played by Sellers, had gone missing and another detective took his place. It was to be shot in the South of France and I had been contracted to only supply a camera truck and a car trailer for one of the action vehicles. Still, I towed the action vehicle, a Citroen 2 CV, to Nice where I met for the first time David Bickers who was going to convert the car in such a way that it could slide on its roof down a mountain road. The comedy moments occurred when it was heading straight at a hairpin bend and should have gone over the edge but would, at the last minute, turn and follow the road round and continue down the hill.

To achieve this effect Dave inserted a platform inside the roof of the car with wheels protruding on to the road. These were so small as to be invisible on film. In order to avoid the cliff's edge the front wheels were steerable from inside the car where Dave would lie on the platform, that was attached to the inside of the arched roof, in such a way that he was hidden from view. In other words, he used the roof as a kind of skateboard with the rest of the car as a backpack. Rather him than me, but then he was a world champion sidecar racer - twice!

Blake Edwards, who had originated the series back in the early sixties, would direct and produce the film. To help him with his creative juices we had to attend to some of his more eccentric demands. His room in the then five star (four stars today) Meridian Hotel was not furnished nor decorated to his liking. Consequently he flew in all the way from Hollywood his favourite interior designer to breathe new life into his suite. The management, however, did not share his tastes and, once he had checked out, we had to repaint the walls and refurnish it to restore it to its original splendour. His other preoccupation was that he wanted to spend as much time as possible with his family who spent the summer months at their home in Switzerland (he was married to Julie Andrews of Sound of Music fame). To this end he would order his private jet to come and pick him up from Nice every Friday afternoon and return with him on Monday morning to resume filming. The Victorine Studios are located half way up a hill that overlooks the airport. As he felt that every moment was precious, one of his assistants had to stand on the studio's back lot and look out for the arrival of his plane. Then, as it approached the runway, he would have to advise Blake of its impending landing. At once our director would drop everything and leave the rest of the day's work to his assistant to complete.

When in the studio, between takes, he needed to relax and prepare for the next scene to be shot by playing on a pinball machine in his trailer. Unfortunately the entrance to his trailer was too narrow for the machine to fit through. Nobody volunteered to tell him that he would have to retreat to another room if he insisted on unwinding with this toy. We, therefore, had to dismantle the doorframe to his trailer, cut into the wooden support of the walls and bend back the outer skin of the vehicle far enough for the pinball table to fit in through the gap. Once in, we rebuilt the doorframe, reattached the wooden support and peeled the outer and inner walls back into their original position. The same in reverse order had to be carried out once the show wrapped and the machine had to be shipped to its next destination, the cutting rooms where the film would be edited.

It also reminded me of a problem we encountered when we had to accommodate Prince during the making of Under the Cherry Moon, again in Nice and again involving his hotel suite, this time in the five star Hyatt Regency. He had no objection to the décor of his suite; however, he explained that he was unable to function without his piano, which coincidently was awaiting collection from his private jet at the airport. The first part of this undertaking was straight forward enough. A few telephone calls by one of our local assistants and we secured the services of a removal company that specialised in transporting pianos. The next challenge would not be as easily met. The door to the room was not large enough to allow a grand (grand in more than one way) piano through. "What about a crane to lift it up and through the French window?" one of the singer's entourage suggested. The suite was on the fifth floor so we would need a very large crane which, with money no obvious restraint, was ordered. When the crane arrived the operator explained that, in order to carry out the task in hand, he would have to place the outer support legs of the crane on the adjacent road which, in turn, would need to be approved and supervised by the police.

More phone calls and haggling over the fees demanded by the gendarmerie and the piano was ready to take to the air. When it reached the height of the fifth floor, the crane had to swing the piano towards the men waiting to receive it on the balcony of the target room. Suddenly a gust of wind caught the sail-like grand and it began to swing from side to side threatening to smash into the building with disastrous consequences. The operator quickly decided to bring his load down to earth and abandon the attempt to lift it up again unless the wind dropped. According to a hastily acquired weather forecast, this was not going to happen for at least another day or two. Unfortunately Prince would be unable to wait that long so we had to return to the drawing board. I remembered Blake Edwards and suggested that we enlarge the aperture of the entrance to the room in question. Unlike our previous experience, which we managed to handle 'in house', this would require specialist construction workers and decorators to go to work. The hotel manager needed a promise of enough money for a holiday in the Bahamas before he agreed to let the builders in. Ironically, Prince hardly ever played it because, as he said, he spent the day on location and did not want to disturb his fellow guests in the middle of the night.

Another tale involving eccentric demands unfolded when I was asked to supply motor homes for Omar Sharif and Ryan O'Neal on Green Ice that was to be shot at Elstree Studios. Omar, as a fanatical bridge player (I think he was a champion of some sort), wanted a full size card table with four chairs to accommodate a card school in his trailer. This was at a time before such vehicles featured a slide out facility which meant that the built-in sofa and part of the galley had to be removed to make room for his furniture. Compared to Ryan's fixation about the bad luck the colours green and purple represented, this was relatively easy to comply with. The soft standard furnishings, the curtains and carpets in Ryan's appointed vehicle, all contained traces of the offending colours. This meant that, at great expense and chargeable to the producers, all of them had to be replaced. An army of buyers had to locate suitable materials and an even larger contingent of seamstresses had to be employed to bring in new décor in time for his first call. To describe this effort as stressful would be an understatement. Shame that, in spite of meeting his demands, this production did not bring Ryan the luck he needed for this show to go into profit and relaunch his career.

Blake would not leave his pinball machine alone, even if it meant that he had to delegate directing some key scenes to his first assistant. I often wondered how he managed to communicate with his lead actors, David Niven, Robert Wagner, Herbert Lom and the young Joanna Lumley, from afar.

# We call this work!

photograph Keith Hamshere

Glenda Jackson, Jason Robards , my Natalie and others

Operation Overlord on Swanage Beach

Swanage Beach Today

Volga river with boat and explosions
Crossing the Volga at Stalingrad   (Enemy at the Gate)

Volga location; the abandoned water filled open mine.

# The South of France

On the way to work

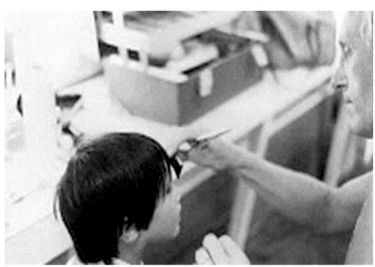

My Sammy with Raymond Gow (Better Late Than Never)

# La Victorine Studios

Just a Memory

Before my Time

# Bryan Baverstock (Schindler's List)

With the wrong chair

With Steven Spielberg

With Liam Neeson

With Ben Kingsley

With Anthony Hopkins

With loads of money

# Willies Wheels

Motorised Honeywagon

The Original Gully Sucker

Motorised 3 Position Artist's Truck
and Interior

merican 3 Position Artist's Trailer

# More Wheels

Double Decker Dining Bus    Dining Bus Interior

Make up Bus

torhome

rowler

Star Trailer

No more Star Trailer

# Just two of the six million

Grandmother with her Pooch

Grandfather with his first grandchild( (Tammi)

## 4 Generations on

Oscar, Alfie, Isaac, Bertie, Elijah and Harry

# Budapest

Madonna (Evita)

The Rocky Horror Show with my Sammy about to start.

# 15 Hart to Hart 1984

## The Oracle and Rhodes Island

The rumour goes that, by 1983, Coca Cola was amassing a great deal of money in Greece and, with exchange controls in place, could not easily get it out of the country. They, therefore, got together with Columbia Pictures and formed a joint company which they imaginatively called Colgems. The idea was to fund television productions in general and in Greece in particular, all paid for from the funds that Coca Cola made available. Once the resulting programs were sold in the USA and other territories they would receive that income in the rest of the world thus circumnavigating the financial restrictions imposed by the Greek government. This was, of course, just alleged but reinforced by similar methods employed in South Africa and other countries with exchange control legislation

The next step was to find projects that could be shot there and scriptwriters were commissioned to produce suitable material. The team at the production offices of Hart To Hart developed two storylines that would fit the bill and a largely British crew was employed to realise them.

The first episode was to be shot in and around Delphi, famous for its Oracle and its significance some two and a half thousand years ago. That's a very long time since its heyday. The town, if one could call it that, was perched on a god-forsaken mountainside. A fair amount of ruins stood randomly about the place with a three star hotel by the roadside being the only hint that tourists would visit it from time to time. The parking lot to the front of the building was no bigger than my front garden which, at best, could accommodate six cars. Even our experienced production manager, Malcolm Christopher, was unable to find enough space for our motorcade and had to send us miles away to find a secure overnight holding area. Yet, as difficult as it was to settle into a workable unit base, it faded into insignificance when compared to my journey from the UK.

I volunteered to drive the honey wagon with one of the artist's trailers in tow. I did so because what I feared most of all was crossing borders, especially into Italy, which more often than not would invite a bureaucratic nightmare. Before I had to face it, my truck broke down just short of Koblenz on the German autobahn. The back axle had seized and there was nothing for it but to lift it off the autobahn and into town to the Fiat garage for repairs. The mechanics felt they would need at least a couple of hours to find out what needed repairing or replacing before I could resume the journey. I chose to use the interval to take a trip down memory lane.

I remembered the town fairly well because for several years my father, a lawyer, maintained a practice there. With time on my hands I decided to look up some of my old haunts. The larger than life statue of Kaiser Wilhelm I, grandfather of the infamous Wilhelm II, on horseback mounted on a 30 ft high plinth was still there on the corner that marks the convergence of the iconic rivers of the Rhine and the Mosel. The sweet white Mosel wine and the not so sweet one of the Rhine spring to mind, best drunk mixed with sparkling water as a spritzer, a sure way to offend the local growers.

The old town centre with its row after row of small shops selling local produce interspersed with ironmongers, barbers, hairdressers, watchmakers, dressmakers and countless other specialist outlets, each with its colourful crest on display, had all but disappeared. What was left behind were a couple of pubs (Gasthaeuser) advertising their brand of beer and large multi-storey department stores with anonymous wares on display. I ventured into a coffee shop with more varieties of cream cakes than I thought was possible to produce, stacked up neatly on three glass 15 foot long vitrines. Just looking at them was enough to put on a stone in weight. I bravely avoided eye contact with the buxom lady behind the counter and made for a corner table laid out with white starched cloth intricately crocheted around the edges, a dainty porcelain cup and plate with silver cutlery ready to receive one of those 'cream with a bit of pastry' dishes from the showcase by the front door. I asked for a coffee only which, from the daggers drawn look of the waitress whom I had obviously insulted by my meagre order, indicated I was lucky not to be directed to the door there and then. Coffee arrived in a silver jug accompanied by a glass of water that I did not really want. I later found out that this is how coffee should be served but why it should be so remains a mystery to me because, if I had wanted water, I would have asked for it.

I can speak and read German and therefore spent the next hour engrossed in a newspaper that was freely available and at the same time protected me from the penetrating gaze of the staff who were wondering why I would reject the offering which was this establishment's pride and joy. Maybe they thought that I could not afford to pay for it, which in turn would mean that I had no business being there in the first place. They never found out because I was too polite to tell them that just looking at the cakes and the sight of their clientele who were gorging themselves on them put me off their shop forever. Back at home I could have had a full English breakfast for the price of the weak but drinkable coffee I consumed.

It was now time to return to the garage for its verdict on the cost and time it would take to get me going again. "Come back in four days" I was told unceremoniously with no ifs or buts and, when I mentioned costs again, the answer came back "cannot tell, but international transfer will do". Credit card? What credit card? Its 1983! I left the garage to it and rejoined my drivers who were getting a bit of a rest on the road opposite the premises. I was, therefore, able to act as a second driver who could, at various points during the journey, relieve anyone who was in need of a rest;

thus we were able to make up for the time lost due to the breakdown.

An eight hour uneventful stint on the autobahn with only a couple of stops for fuel for the motor homes and German sausages with fresh bread rolls and sweet mustard for the drivers, of whom I was one, and we hit the Austrian border. Here there were no official formalities to endure. As the forthcoming motorway is a toll road, money, at pain of a heavy fine, must be handed over. That done, it was getting late and an overnight stop was on the cards. We followed a bright green neon sign to a hotel a few hundred yards off the main drag and, having checked in, I showered and after a change of clothes went down to the bar where I was meeting my drivers for dinner. It was a warm spring evening that hailed one of the many local bank holidays. The other guests were joined by a local bevy of youngsters who were going to celebrate their day off work. I remembered a similar experience when travelling to Egypt (for the making of The Sphinx), albeit in mid winter. Whether we wanted it or not, we were sucked into the festivities. I must admit that I impressed myself, and possibly others, with my rock'n'roll moves helped along by my very rare indulgence in the local beer. My drivers did not comment on the evening which I took to mean that I embarrassed them like a middle-aged uncle would have done at a wedding reception.

The morning saw us at the Italian border and an unexpectedly easy crossing. It was downhill all the way, literally, to Ancona. Here the drivers with the motor homes would board the ferry for the 24-hour sailing to Patras in Greece and on to Delphi for our first location. I, in the meantime, would catch the night train back to Koblenz where my honey wagon with its new back axle would be waiting for me.
Then off on my own through the rest of Germany into Austria and to the Italian border. As soon as the Italian Customs officer realised what searching for contraband inside a mobile toilet entailed he just waved me through. In Ancona I drove on to the boat and made for

my cabin for the night crossing. As a commercial vehicle my fare included me as the driver and up to two passengers free of charge. Two German girls knew about this concession and asked me to give them a lift onto the boat. I, being all heart and happy to have some company during the trip, agreed to take them on. They were fortunate that I did not realise prior to departure how irritating their constant giggling and teasing about the vehicle I was driving would be. To the rescue came a party of Danes on a camping holiday who entertained me and fellow passengers with risqué anecdotes supported by alcoholic drinks that were too cheap not to be taken advantage of. It all went on late into the night - or was it early morning?

Off the ferry in Patras and into Greek traffic. Surely not everybody is late for work or on his way to a maternity hospital with a baby about to pop out? But that is how they drive. No giving way, winning the race between traffic lights at all cost and most of all not allowing themselves to be held up by a long slow travelling road train like mine. I didn't mind being overtaken but witnessing such manoeuvres on blind bends crossing the white central line reminded me how squeamish I was at the sight of blood which is surely what I was about to encounter. In the event, after a short river crossing and innumerable hairpin bends up the Delphi mountains, no blood was spilled but I did espy from the corner of my eye a car that had rolled down into the valley some 300' below and another jammed against the upside wall bordering the road with excited onlookers crowding around it. I was sure this one had overtaken me earlier on. At the end of the climb I tried in vain to turn into the hotel car park so I left the truck parked outside until I got directed to our secure pound a mile or two further along the road.

Most of the filming took place on the roads in and out of the area and involved a lot of road closures to allow for the stunts to be carried out. Greek drivers do not tolerate hold-ups lightly. A lot of arm waving and shouting had to be endured by my drivers, who were seconded to traffic control. All was well, though, as soon as the proverbial brown envelopes (that's how we received additional pay) arrived. Then another few shots at the temple of Apollo and on to Athens where the rest of the episode was to be filmed. While in Delphi both Robert Wagner and Stephanie Powers each rented a palatial mansion straight out of Hollywood. On the weekend some of us in the company of Jackie Chan and John Standing, who made guest appearances in the show, visited – by invitation of course - Stephanie's abode where a barbecue was on offer. During a brief conversation with our hostess it transpired that, far beyond her talent as an actress, she was extremely well informed, had an extensive knowledge about a great variety of subjects and was fluent in several languages. Respect!

Before we left we were enlightened about the significance of the sheer 150 high rock face that towered over the unit base. Apparently in the good old days, when one needed to find out whether or not an accused was innocent, he would be led up to the top and pushed down over the side. If he turned out to be not guilty he would survive but, if guilty, he would be smashed to smithereens. Surprise, surprise not many, if any, innocent people were ever tried!

A car rally played a key part in the story and Athens streets, not forgetting the ancient monuments, formed the backdrop to the drive-bys of the rally cars. Pretty tame compared to some of the stunts I have witnessed on other productions but who am I to offer an opinion?

The next episode featured the Aegean Sea with a base on the island of Rhodes. As a lot of sailing was involved and my vehicles did not float, we boarded a ferry and set up a unit base by the quayside where we were going to settle down for the period. No need for me to stay, so back home for two weeks until the shoot was due to wrap.

On my return I was met by Malcolm, who had stayed behind to wind up outstanding matters and help to manage our next production in Greece which was due to begin in a few days. In the meantime he was at a loose end and we decided to do a bit of sightseeing. He was still in possession of the rally cars we used as action vehicles on Hart to Hart and we were able to pick out an Audi Quattro for the trip. This car was extremely powerful and uniquely boasted permanent four-wheel drive. In real life it won every rally it entered and turned heads wherever it appeared. We took turns competing with the indigenous boy racers and obviously left them all behind to lick their injured manhood. We drove to the Isthmus and back in Clarksonesque style and, as he would say years later, it was "the best car in the Woooorld".

# 16 The First Olympics 1984

## Competing with the Present

To celebrate the Summer Olympics that were due to be held in Los Angeles, this two part mini series about the first modern Olympics had been commissioned and was going to be shot in part at St. Hubert's near Gerrards Cross but mainly on location in Athens and its environs. With some of my vehicles already in Greece, left behind from the filming of Hart to Hart, my ongoing association with its producer, William Hill, and both production supervisors, Dimitri Dimitriadis and Ray Frift, I was an obvious choice for supplying the necessary facilities. This was to be a much larger project than the previous one and many more vehicles had to be employed to meet its full requirements. (I satisfied the requirements for the UK shoot from my stock that was left behind.)

After inspecting what was available locally it became clear that eight more vehicles, four trailers each towed by a costume truck and generator truck, were needed with two motor homes making up the numbers. We had ten days to get ready which gave us enough time to fly me and the other drivers from Hart to Hart back home to collect the additional road trains and deliver them by the same route we used five weeks ago to Athens; this time, hopefully, without having to deal with a breakdown. I did not join my crew but flew out to Athens to acquaint myself with the proposed locations and unit bases where my vehicles would be parked up. Normally I would not get involved with these details but, from experience, I knew not to rely on information supplied by our beloved Greek location manager whose job included setting up a workable base from which we could service the shooting crew and cast.

This meant ensuring drainage facilities for the grey and black (sink and toilet respectively) water tanks either directly into the sewers or locating a specially equipped tanker truck (gully sucker) that could pump out the dirty water and move it off-site to a waste treatment plant. At the same time we would need a fresh water supply to refill the clean tanks feeding the costume truck with its washing machines and the make-up trailer where it would be needed for the hair wash and the washing up bowl. Most of the water, however, had to be made available to the mobile toilets where it would be required to flush away the waste and also be piped up to the hand wash basins. As far as the artists' trailers and motor homes were concerned they would be continuously monitored as their demand for tap water depended largely on how often the bathrooms and/or the showers were being used. Again I would have to determine whether we could access the mains or whether we would have to secure the services of a tanker and, depending on its capacity, how often we would want him to call on us.

Next I would have to ensure that there was an adequate power supply available to satisfy the demands of all the electrical equipment on board; everything from lights to air conditioning units, washing machines and heaters for when the temperature drops (unlikely but must not be taken for granted especially for the night shoots) to battery chargers and fridges. If, however, no such power source could be secured we would have to (as we actually did) bring over our own generator. Finally I was looking to pace out the site so that we could park up the trailers far enough apart in order to leave sufficient space between them to allow for the steps in and out of the cabins. These had to be positioned in such a way that one could easily use them without having to squeeze past the adjoining trailer. It was also important that the fridges and other white goods in the trucks were operated in an upright position and, therefore, every vehicle should be made to stand on level ground. If that were not possible I would have to organise for chocks (wooden ramps) to be placed under the wheels and jacks front and back to achieve a perfect horizontal stance.

I was shown a number of sites that were cheap to rent but unsuitable for our purposes and finally decided on setting up the circus in a car park right in front of the original Olympic stadium. With its hard standing surface and its proximity to the main set it could hardly be more ideal. Why I was not offered it in the first place remains a mystery, though I suspect that using this one would not benefit our location manager, as it was not owned by one of his cousins, allegedly.

My drivers with the additional vehicles arrived a couple of days later and we spent the following day setting up the unit base ready for the onslaught of the crew that flew in on a charter that afternoon. We were all booked into the five-starred Intercontinental Hotel. Here we, that is every one from producer down to the drivers and the most junior runners, were to be treated equally well in equally best available rooms. The drivers found the five star atmosphere not only inappropriate and over the top for their liking but, more specifically, they did not appreciate the cost of the drinks which would exhaust their weekly meal allowance in a matter of hours. It did not take them long to negotiate an exit from the hotel and use the money the production saved, and subsequently refunded, to find their own digs and bars, not to mention houses of ill repute, which financially were now well within their reach.

If that was not enough, they discovered that no provisions were made to hire night watchmen to keep unwanted visitors away from the set and the unit base. The prospect of even more money made them offer themselves up as security guards at a reduced rate as long as they could use the artists' trailers to sleep in between shifts and without impinging on the trailers' availability to the actors. No more rent to pay, however little the digs were costing. Production thus saving money and the drivers pocketing even more cash. A Win, Win arrangement. The next unit move was scheduled for three weeks into the shoot and, with an experienced and well off crew looking after the vehicles, I returned home and resumed my family holiday in Spain.

On my return I found myself surplus to requirements as the boys had everything under control and felt it would be better that what I didn't know should remain so. The producers and the other 'powers that be' seemed happy with the arrangements so I was left to do the touristy things and a bit of networking with Dimitri, our Greek counterpart. All of it involved food and drink, some of it better than others. I particularly enjoyed lunches and dinners in the port of Piraeus where fresh fish abounded and olive oil was used sparingly. Other eateries seemed to drown their wares in olive oil and it reminded me of the slogan 'chips with everything' except here it was olive oil with everything. On my last night of this week long stay John Sergeant, our financial controller, his assistant Val and I made for the roof top restaurant in the Hilton a few hundred yards from our Intercontinental. There we enjoyed, for a change, a Japanese meal.

On our way back, with John one side and me on the other flanking his assistant, I suddenly found myself walking next to John with no girl in between us. We looked at each other momentarily when we heard a meek "Help" coming from below. Our poor friend had stepped into a manhole and fallen into it with just her head and shoulders visible and her arms reaching out for our ankles. We managed to pull her out of the hole and fortunately, other than the shock and a bruise or two, she was unhurt. It was difficult to know what to do about it. The hotel receptionist and the night manager consulted in Greek and I suspected that they thought a drink too many was the cause of this incident. They suggested the best option would be to wait until the morning and invited us to free drinks on the house at the bar. We skipped the drinks and made our way upstairs.

In the morning I went out to inspect the scene of the incident and the manhole cover was still missing. Back to the hotel with the day manager who promised that he would report it. "Thank you" I said and made my way to the airport knowing full well that he would forget to do anything about it. Three weeks later the cover was still missing but at least the pavement was cordoned off.

On this visit I rented a car and was promptly stopped by a policeman who, with the help of an English speaking bystander, explained that, in order to cut down on air pollution, cars were only allowed into the city on that day if their number plate ended with an odd number and, as my plate displayed an even number, I could only enter the next day. When I mentioned this to our Greek contact he explained that we had twice as many unit cars than we needed with half displaying even and the other half displaying odd numbers and that is how we maintained an uninterrupted service for the cast and crew.

For my part I left town to visit Marathon to see how this legendary city had fared over the years. It was the most disappointing experience I ever had as a tourist. Marathon, for the record, consisted of nothing more than a bunch of low slung nondescript houses dotted about randomly between scraggy olive trees and unkempt fields. Can you believe it? I was not impressed. Even if Athens had not won the Battle of Marathon the famous soldier had good reason to run away.

The production was due to wrap on December 18th giving the drivers plenty of time to return to the UK in time for Christmas but, as luck would have it, a ferry strike threatened to delay their home coming. After much huffing and puffing it was agreed that they could fly back with the crew and return after the holidays to bring the vehicles back. However, I still had to go back to Athens to liaise with our Greek production manager about secure parking and, more promisingly, the possibility of further films to be shot there.

The cast and crew were due to fly back on a plane chartered from Monarch Airlines then based in Luton and, as I wanted to go back to Athens, I managed to get a lift on the empty leg. It was a surreal experience to sit in the departure lounge and be called to board a flight on which our travel agent and I were the only passengers. The plane was a brand new 757 that had just returned from its maiden flight - how cool was that! Champagne breakfast in an aircraft with 190 odd seats, 7 airhostesses with nothing else to do but keep us entertained. To top it all, I was invited onto the flight deck to witness the landing into Athens airport. I did notice that after touchdown we took the wrong taxiway to raised voices from the control tower. The captain laughed it off and we soon disembarked to live another day.

In the New Year nine drivers flew out to bring back our vehicles and, to avoid causing congestion, they travelled in threes. One of a group of three stopped at a service area in Italy and checked into a motel for the night. A shower and change of clothes later they went into the restaurant for an evening meal. While waiting for the food to arrive they looked out of the window and noticed that one of our trucks had begun to move. They rushed outside just in time to catch a couple of guys trying to steal the motor. My drivers, none of whom a sane person would challenge to a fight, dragged the two culprits out of the cab and, by all accounts, gave them and a third accomplice a good thrashing, good enough for two of them to need hospitalisation. Unfortunately, instead of enjoying a large steak they ended up in a police cell due to the fact that, as a translator put it, they had used disproportionate force. The English Consul had to bail them out in the morning and we all felt it was worth it, even if it only meant that we could tell our grandchildren what we had been up to.

This concluded our Greek adventure until years later we returned to service Captain Corelli's Mandolin on the island of Kefalonia.

# 17 Jewel of the Nile 1985

## Driving a Jet Fighter

I am a Jew by birth if not by conviction. Nevertheless, I often take offence when a non-Jew makes a derogatory remark. Conversely when someone stands up and defends my fellow semites I am filled with respect, especially when they risk retribution.

Two instances among many others that took place during the Second World War are imprinted on my memory. When the Germans occupied Denmark they pronounced that all Jews had to publicly display a yellow Star of David on their lapels. Within hours the Danish Royal family stepped out on to their palace balcony, each with a Star of David sewn on to their clothes. Unfortunately this act of defiance was short lived and many Danish Jews were rounded up and sent to the gas chambers.

Once the Germans moved into France and installed the infamous Vichy Government, Hitler sent a message to the then Sultan, later King, of Morocco, Mohammed V, to single out the Jews in his Sultanate and ship them across to France from where they were going to be sent on to one of the many concentration camps in the Third Reich. "I have no Jews in my country" he responded "only subjects". To my knowledge no Moroccan Jew was ever deported.

I had never visited Morocco and would have welcomed any opportunity to visit or, even better, work there. Derek Kavenagh, whom I met briefly when I ran a few errands for the Pink Panther franchise back in Shepperton, called me from Nice and explained that he had since relocated to LA and had now returned to Europe to supervise this project. He vaguely remembered me (not sure if he was just being polite) and, as I had been put forward by one of his old friends, Bryan Coates the location manager, he wanted me to confirm that I would be in a position to cope with the demands of this production with its mega stars, Michael Douglas, Kathleen Turner and Danny DeVito, in the line-up. The call came as I was spending a few days with my family in Javea on the Costa Blanca and was planning to return to London via Barcelona for a meeting about a forthcoming TV series, then on to Paris for a quick reunion with an old friend before I would board the evening flight home.

Suddenly Nice became a priority and I broke my own record of catching the most flights in one day. Very early morning from Valencia to Madrid, on to Barcelona, back to Madrid, on to Nice for a late lunch, then Paris followed by the last leg to London. That's six flights in one day, something even a pilot with Ryan Air would find difficult to match.

I arrived at the Victorine Studio, which is set on a hill overlooking the western part of Nice and the airport, just as Derek and his party were starting to tuck into the main course of what was going to be a prolonged working lunch. The dining area extended on to the terrace of the restaurant that doubled up as the studio canteen. It was enveloped by climbing plants (I think they were vines) and, with a light breeze fanning the air, the mood around the table could not have been more relaxed and, to me, welcoming. Derek introduced me to his companions, Joel Douglas, Michael's younger brother who was to be one of the producers and Richard Dawkin, the production designer with overall responsibility for the sets of the movie. Bryan, an old friend from the UK, Patricia Reed, the co-ordinator, later to become Joel's wife, and Bernard Mazauric whom I had met before on Better Late then Never made up the rest of the party

This turned out to be more of a social gathering than a negotiating session. I had to assure them that I had enough equipment and experienced drivers to deliver a faultless service. It did not take much convincing because Bryan had already recommended me for the job and both Bernard and Patricia had witnessed the efficiency with which we worked on a previous show. I was confident that I would not be beaten on price and, on this basis, a deal was struck in time for me to hurry back down the hill (in a unit car) to catch my connection to Paris. Morocco here we come!

Breakfast on the terrace of our Marrakesh hotel should have been a laid-back happy affair overlooking the enormous pool with loungers all laid out ready for a spot of sunbathing. Not so because, whatever we talked about, the conversation kept on turning back to the terrible accident that had befallen us a couple of weeks earlier. Bryan Coates, our location manager, and Richard Dawking, our production designer, had hired a light aircraft to go on a scouting mission into the desert and, on their return, hit a sandstorm that damaged the engine and they crashed into the mountainside. They and the pilot lost their lives. Ironically, another aircraft had followed them with other crewmembers on board. Both aircraft landed at the chosen location but, after a while, Bryan and Richard felt that they had seen what they wanted to see, left the others to carry on discussing items with which they were not concerned, and took off. The sand storm subsided shortly afterwards and the rest of the party returned, unaware of the disaster they had so narrowly missed. If and when you watch the film and stay on long enough to read the credits you will notice that the film is dedicated to their memory.

Compared to this, the next problem confronting the producers seemed trivial but still important enough to warrant concern. One of the main scenes was to feature a Starfighter jet making its way through a busy street market. It had been loaded, with its wings detached, on to an articulated truck and was due to leave Marrakech earlier that morning. However, it seemed that the driver was missing and no replacement could be found. There were also problems with the right type of driving licence and insurance. Panic was the order of the moment. It was already getting late and, for reasons that I am unable to explain, I volunteered to drive it. I had the relevant licence and my company was covered by an international fleet insurance policy that allowed me to take charge of any vehicle anywhere in Europe and North Africa.

I cancelled my flight home and was ushered two blocks away to a gated pound. There it was. The A15 Jet minus wings loaded on to a semi trailer at an angle that made its nose extend forward over the cab by some 3 meters. Looking upwards through the windscreen I could see at least a meter of it sticking out. I familiarised myself with the controls of the 10 year old Berliet tractor unit and motioned to the two police outriders that I was ready to go.

I have been driving large and long trucks for over 40 years but nothing then or since would prepare me for what followed. The road to Ouarzazate wound itself up over the outer reaches of the Atlas Mountains wide enough for two cars to just pass each other but, with my load and the suspiciously loose verges, I had to take the centre line. My police outriders were kept busy throughout directing cars out of the way; however, when meeting another truck heading towards me it was a question of 'chicken' ending with one of us having to reverse into a wider section of the road. This manoeuvre on these barely made-up roads would take in the region of half an hour each. In addition, on the many hairpin bends all traffic had to be halted as I needed the whole width of the road to swing my truck round it, often with the front of the plane protruding into the sheer rock face on one side and overhanging the drop into the valley on the other.

Darkness in Morocco arrives suddenly and it was not deemed safe to carry on. I now had to endure a night on the floor of a roadside cafe. It was not too bad as I was dead tired and Moroccan cushions made up a decent enough resting place. Breakfast was nothing like the one I got used to in Marrakech so, for fear of upsetting my stomach, I made do with a coffee and plain pita bread dunked in olive oil for a bit of flavour.

Eventually, what seemed like hours later, we got to Ouarzazate where the street market was set up in a newly built Atlas studio complex and where a crane was waiting to lift off my load. I did not wait to find out what happened next. I waved goodbye to my police escort who were waiting to be paid off and managed to get a lift to the airport where the twice-a-day flight to Casablanca was ready to board. Incidentally, the aircraft is still standing where I dropped it all those years ago (1983). I assume nobody is fool enough to make the journey back across the mountains.

At Casablanca Airport I was met unexpectedly by an enthusiastic young man who introduced himself as Mohammad and insisted I stay the night in his father's hotel. The hotel I was booked into by our travel agent was, according to M, full of prostitutes and gangsters and he had come to save me from the debauchery that would await me there. I did not have the heart to tell him that I was a big boy now and a bit of debauchery would not do me any harm. I became apprehensive when we got into a chauffeured limousine for the journey to his dad's place. I later found out that the hotel and the car belonged to a cousin. Nevertheless, it was a five star establishment with a 6'6" tall doorman dressed in a colourful uniform of, I believe, Arab design to escort me into the grandiose marbled foyer. He then ordered one of the dozen or so bellboys to take me straight up to my room. I was obviously expected with no need to sign in at the reception desk. M enjoyed my surprised look at the hospitality he showered me with and then added that I would be expected for dinner in the restaurant in an hour, "If that is OK" he added.

To turn down an Arab's invitation is tantamount to treason or worse if there is such a thing. A shower and change of clothes later I made my way down to the foyer to discover that the hotel had three different restaurants. This meant I had to take a peek into each one in turn to find my host. It had been a while since I last suffered the indignity of being stood up but that was exactly how I felt when there was no sign of my date. I only knew him as Mohammad but, even though it must be the commonest name in town, I approached the reception desk and meekly asked if they knew where I could find him. I was met with a blank expression that did not change when I added that he was the owner's son. After a minute or so a suited gentleman appeared from behind the screen that formed the backdrop to the reception area. He then revealed that my Mohammad was a distant cousin and had booked a table but would not be able to keep me company and, by the way, my meal would be on the house. It all sounded very odd to me and the nearest I got to an explanation was that his family was indeed very wealthy and did own Atlas Studios in Ouarzazate but, most importantly, they were closely related to the King and, therefore, free to roam around the city and play host to whomever took their fancy. I felt uneasy about eating on my own and went to the bar, had a beer and returned to my room for a surfing session with the TV. Years later, while working on Spy Games, I mentioned my adventure to the owner of the car hire company we used who explained that Mohammad was slightly unbalanced (not a surprise) but that for years his antics were tolerated. Recently, however, he was admitted to a mental institution in France where, it is said, he is living happily ever after. I knew there was something odd about the boy.

Principal photography began in France aboard a magnificent sailing yacht in the bay of Villefranche. I could only watch proceedings from the quayside where my facility vehicles formed the unit base. We were scheduled to stay there for a few days before we had to pack up and make our way to Marseille from where a roll-on roll-off service shipped our trucks, motor homes and trailers across the Mediterranean to Tangiers. The drivers in turn flew there via Madrid the following day and embarked on the two-day overland journey to Ouarzazate. All went to plan and nothing worthwhile had been reported en route.

My location facility vehicles, which I met on arrival, were then parked up on the studio lot before being escorted into the desert where they were scheduled to spend the next eight weeks, miles away from what my motley crew understood to be civilisation (a pub at least.) With just some alcohol and very little casual sex they had to survive on a diet of healthy food as provided by our caterers (no fast food joints anywhere) and endless video games. The constant heat did offer slight diversity when they had to carry out running repairs to the air conditioning units and the generators that powered the circus. Cleaning the equipment was subcontracted to a bunch of local youngsters who were happy to do the necessary in return for a small and very affordable reward. They also survived a minor fire on set with the damage being taken care of by the production company.

Following the end of principal photography another movie was being set up a few miles away; Ishtar with Dustin Hoffman and Warren Beatty. It would require my type of facility vehicles. Unfortunately the production supervisor, who was well known to be careful with money, had a personal issue with me that made him forget his raison d'etre and decided to order identical vehicles all the way from the UK, thus landing his production with the substantial transport costs this involved.

A few weeks later in the cutting rooms at Twickenham Studios I bumped into Michael Douglas and, in passing, he was curious to know how I had got on with Warren Beatty and friends on Ishtar. I told him that I had not been asked to tender for it, something that seemed to surprise him. I later found out that when Warren Beatty's assistant approached the production manager (the one who let me down on Yanks) about my availability he was told that I was too busy with other projects. Professionalism for some is set aside to satisfy petty squabbles.

# 18 Widows II 1986

## Birth of the Three Position

The first thing a production manager has to learn is to say convincingly: "Whatever you were told or think, this is a low budget production", with the emphasis on the low. It does not matter that it is common knowledge that this may be the biggest project undertaken by this particular outfit with the biggest names signed up to star in it. Neither does it matter that monumental sets are being constructed on the stages and on the back lot and that some of it will be shot on exotic locations all over the world, where cast and crew are going to enjoy staying in five star (drivers are catered in four star) hotels.

The opening gambit remains unashamedly "We cannot afford to do business with you unless you drastically reduce your prices." With that experience in mind my opening rates make allowance for a reasonable discount. Then, before we shake hands, he would be taking in a deep long breath of air emitting a faint whistling sound through his clenched teeth accompanied by a grimace similar to the one a dentist would pull at the very moment he is about to inflict pain. The deal done, he would utter a hint of an apology for forcing me to ostensibly admit defeat: "I would have accepted your quote but it's the budget you know. It was not my doing, just been made to work with it". No one could recite these lines better than my erstwhile friend, Ron Purdie. He had graduated from the School of Albert Fennel of The New Avengers and Johnnie Goodman of Minders fame.

They were pioneers of independently produced television programs allowing broadcasters to purchase ready-made shows at fixed prices without committing to the long term and open-ended expenses they would incur by employing in-house labour. The broadcasters were bound by the rules that made it almost impossible to dispense with the services of their workers and thus they had to be retained on a full time basis whether or not they were needed. In addition the trade union enforced a closed shop policy that meant that only its own members could be engaged. In order to ensure that the management respects its employees' need for a social life, heavy surcharges for anything but an eight-hour working day Monday to Friday had to be paid for. Producing dramas, especially ones that required travelling to away locations and long hours, would be prohibitively expensive and, most importantly, almost impossible to budget for in advance.

Mark One Productions and Euston Films, Albert's and Johnnie's respective companies could, as independent entities, negotiate their own terms with the relevant unions and thus create a framework that allowed for a much more efficient and financially viable agreement with cast and crew. Suppliers, too, who within the old system would have had to wait for months for their bills to be settled and, therefore, increased their rates to allow for such late payments, were now, because they were being paid weekly, willing to substantially reduce their rates. (Historically, the BBC would wait three months before they even looked at invoices and took at least another sixty days to make a payment). Soon other independents followed and they accounted for such classic television series as The Sweeney, Minders, The Saint, The Professionals and many others.

The Professionals reminded me of the day I had to deliver cans of film to the editing suites at Delane Lea in Dean Street, Soho. As I was about to enter the building Gordon Jackson was coming out, we made eye contact, acknowledged each other and started to discuss the weather, the traffic and a few other issues that resulted in a ten minute long conversation. He then hailed a passing cab, told me to take care and departed. As I reflected on this casual encounter I began to wonder whether I really knew or had ever met this man in person. Did he just look familiar because I must have seen him on the box? A few years later when I visited the set of The Professionals one of the assistant directors was about to introduce me to him. After a moment's hesitation he responded in his broad Scottish voice that he remembered me from our conversation all this time ago and that he, too, wondered whether he had met me before or whether he was talking to a complete stranger. I must admit that I have had similar experiences since. Do I ignore and risk appearing to be rude or do I acknowledge a familiar face and risk embarrassment all round?

Widows II was another of the many projects of Euston Films and of which the said Ron Purdie, a stalwart production supervisor, took charge. To make his transport budget balance a fresh approach was needed. The problem was that he had four leading actresses of equal standing to look after. Historically this would have meant four caravans each to be towed by a truck with four drivers on the payroll. To complicate the matter the show was to be shot at various London locations with up to three unit moves a day (in those days there was no such thing as a unit base, all vehicles were parked up in the streets with parking dispensations to be paid for). Finding enough spaces for the traditional number of vehicles would be a nightmare if not impossible.

Thinking outside the box was needed. Firstly we had to establish the minimum requirements that would keep our girls happy. These were a private space big enough for two (the actor and a dresser) to swing the proverbial cat in, a sofa, a full length mirror and a chest of drawers on which one could stand a TV/video player, in other words a room 6' x 7'6" would suffice. It dawned on me that a 19' truck box body could accommodate three such cabins and that, if hooked up to a 24' trailer, this could offer the fourth such cabin with room to spare to fit in two make-up positions and allow access from the rear to two toilets. I had purchased a left hand drive (a coincidence) 7.5 ton truck that was previously used as a mobile showroom for some sophisticated radar equipment and which already featured a side entrance with steps. We then set about cutting two additional doors into the side and erected two partitions to make up three little compartments that we wired up for electric lights. Once we furnished them with a sofa and TV stand they became cosy little retreats for three of our four leading actresses.

I travelled up to Telford where I met with a trailer manufacturer who took on the job of building a 24' long box trailer with three doors on the sidewall and two doors at the rear. It was to contain three dressing rooms that, with a width of 6' each and allowing another foot for the partitions, took up 19' of the length of the trailer. The remaining 5' was to be halved and access would be through two rear doors. One half would be the men's and the other the ladies' toilet. For the purpose of this show we would remove one of the partitions to create a double room for the make-up artist and the hairdresser. The first multi-position vehicle was born and later became the template for the popular three and two position trailers that we employ nowadays.

That was it! One driver instead of five, (4 caravans and a makeup trailer). The overall length short of 60 feet would be less than half the one required for a conventional set-up. Unfortunately, none of the savings which benefitted the production were passed on to me; however, to Ron's credit he did appreciate the skill and commitment of the driver, Chris Streeter, who found his reward in a brown envelope, a long lost method of handing over untraceable cash.

The truck part of this road train was soon afterwards sent to a location in Morocco to service a commercial for an Italian company. They found the vehicle to be so useful that they made me an offer to buy it at a price I could not refuse. It coincided with one of my trips to the USA where I intended to buy some more trailers. When I showed the American manufacturer pictures of the 3 position trailer I purchased up in Telford, they offered to build similar ones with much more luxurious fittings at a fraction of the price that would include the shipping costs from the States. Thus the American 3 position made its first appearance, soon to become standard issue on nearly every production since. Over the years improvements and upgrades were incorporated. Firstly, individual bathrooms were added to each section, then showers and, most recently, they feature a wall that can slide outwards when stationary and thus substantially increase the size of each room. These additional features have come at a price. The latest trailers are now longer and heavier and can only be towed by tractor units with Large Vehicle Licence holders at the wheel.

# 19 Lady Jane 1986

## Actors - with the Accent on the TORS

If there ever was one true highbrow costume drama with Shakespearian actors vying for stardom, directed by a leading light of British theatre, Trevor Nunn, then this was it. This heavyweight cast was to support the leading lady (more girl), the twenty-year-old Helena Bonham Carter fresh from her success in A Room with a View. She played the part of Lady Jane, the unfortunate young Royal who, as a pawn in some unsavoury aristocrats' conspiracy, was crowned Queen of England only to be deposed and sent to the Tower of London where she met her gruesome end by decapitation. Filming was scheduled to spread over a dozen locations that would make up a catalogue of English country houses and castles.

Although I had imported my first American artists' trailers I did not have enough of them to be able to supply all that was needed, neither had the production enough money in the budget to allow each of the artists the luxury of an individual trailer. Only Helena, as the fragile lead, was granted the comfort of an American motor home.

The first location was Hever Castle near the village of Edenbridge in Kent, Ann Boleyn's family home. It had been recently converted to an upmarket bed and breakfast hotel. It was surrounded by a double moat and featured award-winning gardens. It was declared out of bounds for our vehicles, however carefully we intended to traverse the lawns. The drivers were directed to a field at the edge of the estate. There we had to lay down metal tracks to drive and park on to avoid sinking into the soft soil if and when it rained. The cast and crew had to make their way to the set on foot with only an umbrella and an overcoat as protection from the downpours and the cold that dominated our stay there.

A few days later it was the turn of Haddon Hall, a fortified medieval manor house in Derbyshire, dating back to the 12$^{th}$ century. The Duke and Duchess of Rutland who made it habitable had restored it in the 1920's. We met the 10$^{th}$ Duke who graciously took us on a conducted tour of the house and very proudly walked us through the immaculate gardens. Fortunately some parts of the estate along the front of the building were less cared for and it was there that we could site our unit base, as long as it did not include heavy vehicles that could, in wet weather, sink into the soft grass and leave a trail of mud in their wake. We set up seven artists' caravans, Helena's motor home, two honey wagons (mobile toilets), and the make-up coach on this patch of grass and powered them up with more than ten silent petrol generators. The stand-by trucks, two for the prop department, one for the construction crew, one for the camera boys and the costume truck had to be left across the road in the visitors' car park. Five small 4x4 pick-up trucks carefully shuttled equipment to and from the heavy goods vehicles to the set. In addition my drivers had the use of a couple of small vans and my Landcruiser as a tow vehicle to enable them to collect supplies needed for the facility vehicles and fuel to keep the generators topped up. Malcolm Christopher brought along his VW camper that he used as his production office from where he managed proceedings. Ted Lloyd, our supervisor, had to make do with one of the caravans if and when one became available and, when not, he had to find himself a corner in the manor house where he could sit down and scrutinise the paper work.

To keep the generators topped up we filled army issue jerry cans and stored them on the back of a pick-up truck. On one of the rare cloudless days the cans were inadvertently exposed to the sunlight with the petrol inside building up pressure from the heat. When the driver was about to refill one of the generators and attempted to open the lid the content shot out and covered him from head to toe with petrol. Even though health and safety still had years to establish themselves the potential disaster was plain to see. These petrol driven generators had to go. I managed to locate a company in Birmingham that hired out large 40 KVA diesel-driven ones that on their own could power up the whole circus. We did have to rewire them first to provide the single-phase 16 and 32 amp outlets to feed our equipment rather than the standard three phase ones mainly used on building sites and industrial plants. Having witnessed the benefit such a power source offered I bought two of them, mounted them on trucks that could double up as tow vehicles and introduced them into the industry where they quickly became irreplaceable. Another first: The Facility Generator!

The cast and crew were booked into a number of hotels in nearby Bakewell, of tart fame. I, too, stayed in one of them for the first two nights while everybody settled down and got acquainted with each other. Unfortunately, but not surprisingly, one of my drivers enjoyed himself too much when, after more than a few drinks and egged on by his fellow men, he invaded a wedding party, proceeded to take off his clothes and, without a stitch on, dragged the mother of the bride on to the dance floor. He then lost his balance and as he fell to the floor took the startled woman down with him. The guests, in shock, then witnessed a simulated sex act with the drunkard on top of his hapless victim. A moment later the men folk took over, lifted our man off the floor and, before his mates could intervene (I suspect they did not want to, preferring to stand there and laugh their heads off), threw him head first out through an open window. It was hard to clarify what followed. The bride was screaming hysterically, someone was helping her mother back on to her feet and a bevy of male guests strode towards the door to the bar where our crew quickly and successfully barricaded themselves. The unit nurse who sat at my table got up and pulled me out on to the street were a crowd had gathered around our evicted ex-friend. He was wrapped in a blanket and when asked how he felt he could only respond with an incoherent whimper. Someone said he was a doctor and pushed us all aside. "He has broken his collarbone and may have sustained internal injuries" he pronounced "do not move him until the ambulance arrives". I felt surplus to requirements and walked back into the hotel wondering what the consequences would be.

First things first, I would have to apologise for my driver's laddish behaviour and hope that I would find a sympathetic ear, then beg forgiveness from the hotel management and possibly the bride and groom. Whilst I contemplated my future Ted walked into the bar, sought me out and led me into the corridor for a 'quiet word', as he put it. He had witnessed such outrageous exhibitionism from film crews before. Nevertheless, he could not tolerate such behaviour on this show and, therefore, I should round up the drivers who were involved and replace them in the morning. Also the hotel management had threatened to ask every member of the film crew to leave unless he, with me in tow, promised to keep our people under control, especially when drinks were involved.

I had no choice but to agree, and sent two drivers home while two new recruits joined us the following evening. I also banned my drivers from the hotel bars, not only in this place but also on any other locations that were coming up while working on this shoot. "If you must have a drink, then find a pub as far away and out of sight from where the crew is staying". Our stripper had indeed broken his collarbone, cracked a couple of ribs and needed some stitches on his forehead but also had to look for another job. Tragically, alcohol became an obsession from which he never recovered and led to his early demise.

A few miles to the north on the far side of Bakewell from Haddon Hall is Chatsworth House, our next location. We did not have to change hotels though by now my drivers busied themselves on night security duties and taking turns sleeping in the artists' caravans. Thus not only did they receive additional pay for their trouble but also pocketed the hotel money the production no longer had to find. Another bonus they benefited from was that they took turns to run the daily rushes to London, which gave whoever did it the chance for a short family visit. The rushes run was usually a job for a unit driver but, because we were based so far away from home, they demanded, according to our production manager, more money than he was prepared to commit to and thus the job with the lower pay-out came my drivers' way. For the first time drivers were earning more money than they could spend and returned home with newly opened savings accounts.

It was then time to head south to our next location at Broughton Castle near Banbury in Oxfordshire. It's a medieval castle and is the home of the Fiennes family, who are the Barons Saye and Sele. It sits amid parklands that include formal gardens and is surrounded by a moat. As the property was not open to the public we could use the tarmac covered visitors' car park. It was also just an hour's drive from home and it only involved a day trip for me to check on the state of my vehicles and drivers.

Dorney Court at Dorney near Eton was even closer to my yard. If pushed I could walk there from my home in Datchet. I had befriended the owner, Peregrine Palmer, some years ago when we used it on The Legacy. At that time his father was still alive and his brother kept wolves that he took, tethered to chains, for walks in the back garden in full view of - and uncomfortably close to - the cast and crew. For the record, the Palmer family has lived in this Tudor manor house for over 400 years and the estate would not be the same without an eccentric son to liven up the place. I was saddened to hear that Peregrine, who was my age, just a few years later passed away leaving a young family behind.

Winchester's Great Hall, where we featured what was supposed to be the famous round table where the Knights of Olde held their meetings, was next on the agenda. For some reason I remembered that an old flame was living nearby and we arranged a reunion to which she appeared with her mother as chaperone. No recalling of our intimate experiences then. "I don't know what you mean" remarked my friend when she read this paragraph. Memory loss may be a good thing.

The production supervisor was our gentle giant, Ted Lloyd, assisted by Malcolm Christopher, the production manager. I had worked with both of them before, Ted on The Legacy and Malcolm on a number of shows going back to The Return of the Saint and several Michael Winner productions. It took people of their calibre and experience to appreciate the logistical problems we, that is I, faced in moving as often as we did setting up a unit base on the treasured and manicured lawns of the iconic properties we used, thus keeping the production running to the satisfaction of so many cast and crew members. I must credit them for, without them, we would have had great difficulties keeping the show on the road. Particularly helpful was their willingness to allocate additional funds to the transport budget so that the extraordinary effort of the drivers could be rewarded (brown envelopes). On to Dover Castle, which was dressed to mimic the Tower of London, the art department excelled themselves by crowning the towers with onion shaped roofs identical to the ones in London. They also cleared the lower courtyard to accommodate the scaffold with the block that supported the victim's head before it was chopped off.

It transpired, though, that our caravans and trucks would not fit through the archway into the enclosure where the equipment was needed and where we had to accommodate the artists in order to keep them within earshot of the action. We hired a number of pick-up trucks to shuttle in essentials and, as far as the caravans were concerned, we had to let the air out of the tyres to lower them enough to clear the top of the arch. All in a day's work.

Although the story ends up tragically it was not helped by the dark and heavy period costumes reminding us constantly of the awfulness of the time. A bit of colour would have helped to lift the gloom that surrounded the set and possibly attract a larger audience that would turn the film into a commercial success, which in the event it was not.

On the plus side, this production was above all educational and gave us privileged access to stately homes that no tourist would ever have a chance to visit.

# 20 Superman IV 1986

## Pay on Time Please

Yoram Globus and Menachem Golan, the cousins from Israel also nicknamed the Go Go boys, stormed into Britain under the Cannon Films banner and hoovered up everything show business that was not nailed down. Screen International, the industry's leading trade magazine, carried pages upon pages of advertising announcing major film projects in pre-production featuring major 'stars' most of whom I understood had not yet signed up. It was largely wishful thinking and a ruse to secure distribution and thus funding. The ABC chain of cinemas previously owned by Thorn EMI was their first major acquisition that, as an add-on, included Elstree Film Studios of Star Wars fame.

A cursory background check could not reveal where all this money was going to come from, even though they had some success with a number of what one would describe as sensationalist releases. A few projects did go into production and, when they managed to secure the rights to Superman IV with Christopher Reeve in the lead, the promise of good Box Office appeared on the horizon.

Their London representative, Michael Kagan, was put in charge of the production. He was, in contrast to his employers, quietly spoken with a manner that made it difficult to turn down any of his requests. Getting him to reciprocate, though, would elicit no response, just a shrug of the shoulders with a gesture indicating that as much as he would like to help he was unable to do so. I am not sure why I liked him; maybe because he seemed to like me too and was, therefore, instrumental in securing me the contract to supply the production vehicles on all his projects including this flagship one.

The film was originally based at Pinewood but, as the Cannon boys had just purchased Elstree Studios, the offices and stages had to relocate there. The production team who were living within spitting distance of Iver Heath (Pinewood's location) did not relish the daily commute to the outlying (pre M25) studios at Elstree. In any case a strong rumour circulated that, although Thorn EMI had sold the studios, they had not been paid for it, which in turn meant that the whole project could collapse before it had even begun. Lack of funds also forced the cancellation of the planned location shoot in New York. It was to be replaced with interior sets to be built on a stage while exterior scenes would be shot on the streets of Milton Keynes. Alex De Grunwald, the production manager, argued that this was not the film he originally agreed to supervise and, therefore, he and his team would resign. The production designer on the other hand managed to renegotiate his deal on the grounds that his job would now involve more designs and construction workers to replace the sets that could have been found on locations in the States.

The director, Sydney Furie, lived up to his name and was indeed furious. He was about to leave the project but then remembered his million pound fee and swallowed his pride. Equally Paul Tucker, the financial controller, had to resign himself to more than doubling the length of his journey to work because he had turned down other assignments which, by this time, had made alternative arrangements and could no longer offer him employment.

Ray Frift, whom I had worked with previously, was brought in to replace Alex and, with a much-reduced budget, the project was green lit. First location was Superman's parents' house in the middle of a remote cornfield that our location manager had found in deepest Hertfordshire less than an hour away from the studio. The scene demanded that the property would be accessible from all sides and, therefore, the unit base with its dozen or so vehicles had to be constantly moved out of view of the camera. To save on wages, I usually release a number of drivers once they have delivered their trucks and recall them as soon as we were ready to move on to the next location. Here, however, much to the producer's annoyance, we had to keep them all on stand-by and on the pay role ready to manoeuvre the vehicles away from the camera's sight line as it panned round Superman's childhood home. A lot of rushing about and racing into cover was the order of the day. When a helicopter shot was scheduled with the vehicles having to leave the field altogether and park up along the main road more than a mile away from the set, innocent motorists were subject to long delays. We even got a mention in the local news and traffic bulletins. Nothing to be proud of.

A week later we were on the road again, this time to Milton Keynes which, because it was some distance from the studio, was, after much argument, classified as an away location. This meant that cast and crew including the drivers were entitled to hotel accommodation and per diems to compensate them for the loss of home cooking and the use of their washing machines. I, too, elected to become a driver for the day, feeling that I would be happier if I supervised the setting up of the base myself and would also be able to take the opportunity to visit my sister who lived in Northampton just a few miles up the M1. We were booked into the Travel Lodge Motel on the northbound service area of the M1 at Newport Pagnell which forced us to drive up to the Northampton junction before we could return on the south bound carriageway to the Milton Keynes exit. Good for calling on my sister, but frustrating when travelling to work.

As Milton Keynes was to double up for New York, we got permission to close off a number of roads and sprinkle them with American vehicles of all shapes and sizes including a dozen yellow cabs, massive trucks and school buses, all driving on the right. The streets, complete with New York sidewalk furniture such as water hydrants, traffic signs and even fake ventilation covers emitting steaming air from the subway, were almost indistinguishable from the ones in the Big Apple. It turned out to be a major production number with a high wage bill and many vehicles that I had to subcontract in.

In order to meet my financial obligations, which required a healthy cash flow, I submitted my invoices religiously every Monday and expected, as had been agreed, to collect a cheque exactly a week later. Unfortunately the Cannon outfit lived up to its reputation for being slow payers and Michael defended the delays by blaming everybody but himself. With three weekly invoices unpaid I had no alternative but to resist his charms and insist on immediate up to date settlement of my outstanding bills. Michael, with his usual nonchalance, promised a cheque "by tomorrow". I had heard this before and when I tried to stand my ground he closed the meeting by stating "don't panic; a delay of a day or two should make no difference."

The next morning on location in Milton Keynes I instructed my camera truck driver to hide around the corner and not move until he heard from me on the walkie-talkie. I then sidled up to Michael by the catering truck. It did not take long before the camera operator rushed up to me to find out what had happened to his truck. "Why are you panicking?" I responded "Ask Michael, he thinks a day or two later should make no difference". Michael, to his credit, conceded that I had made the point and I had my cheque by lunchtime. Incidentally, the cheque had been lying on his desk for days. Did Cannon have a cash flow problem themselves or, more likely, did it appeal to his sense of humour to see how many weeks he could play me along. Very funny!

Cannon Films went on to produce a number of other small to medium sized budget films including Duet for One. Payments were still always late but, with the help of the bank, I was able to allow them a bit of credit. I had to compromise on one of my principles that "My bank would not rent out vehicles as long as I don't lend any money". When the Cannon boys decided to open a studio in Israel they asked Michael to find out if I would be interested in jumping into bed with them. The money, assuming I could verify its existence, seemed right and the weather in the Holy Land could also tempt me to leave Blighty for a more exciting future in the new Hollywood that was about to rise from the rocks of Jerusalem. Fortunately, I woke up in time to discover that they were building a castle in the air that would need me to fund it. Shame! I was looking forward to a life under the sun with my children playing on the beach and my wife doing what she liked best, lying by the poolside working on her tan.

It did not take long and, as suddenly as they had appeared, Cannon -after producing a few more low budget films - disappeared, though Michael stayed on in London where our paths were going to cross again when he was appointed line producer on Robin Hood Prince of Thieves.

# 21 Duet For One 1986

## We Are All Professional Here

Another Cannon Film production that cannot fail! Based on a successful play with wall-to-wall biggish names, some of yesteryear and others yet to be discovered. Julie Andrews in the lead, Alan Bates, Liam Neeson, and Rupert Everett in support. Also rans were Max von Sydow, Catherine Harrison (who?) and Margaret Courtenay. I didn't normally worry about who the actors were, just what trailers they were entitled to.

This one, however, was very different. The producers were so excited to secure Julie Andrews in the lead role that they called at least a dozen times to impress upon me how important she was to the production and that whatever I did, regardless of cost (a first for Cannon), she must get the best of everything. Cost, on the other hand, was an issue when it came to the 'Rest of Them'. So, old-fashioned caravans for them and my top of the range motor home for her. Not only that but could I personally attend to it: "We don't want just ANY driver looking after her". I was not too proud to demote myself from being the boss to a mere driver to please my client who, in this instance, was my boss.

I did, however, have another problem to deal with. They ordered the largest six-position make-up trailer on my fleet. It was due to be returned on the Friday before the Monday it was expected on location for this production. On Thursday afternoon I got a call to inform me that the shoot it was on was overrunning by three days. It would, therefore, not be possible to return it before the end of the following week. Frantic phone calls to find a replacement did not produce a satisfactory result. To describe my subsequent state of mind as stressed would be an understatement. There was nothing to it but to kit out another vehicle that could replace the make-up trailer that had been delayed. We had just a weekend to achieve something that normally would take at least two weeks to complete.

Two strokes of luck! I found a large enough caravan that was used by a circus performer as a mobile home and was still serviceable enough to be towed around with a degree of safety. I also had enough room at the back of my house to park it up so that we could work on it without interruption and with continuous catering supplied by my sympathetic wife. What we did not appreciate was that the inbuilt furniture in the caravan was also part of its structure. This meant that when we pulled out the old cupboards we had to replace them with new supporting beams to prevent the vehicle from imploding.

The shopping list included 6 mirrors with 60 light fittings to surround them, six make-up chairs that had to be purchased and collected from Balham (no fun on a Friday afternoon), long work tops, twelve sets of shelves to fit on either side of the mirrors, six kitchen drawer units to support the worktop, a shampooing basin complete with reclining chair, water heater, tank and pump, electric fuse box and twelve plug sockets, coils of electric cables and an assortment of water pipes and fittings. Added to that were blackout blinds for the windows and a lot of white paint and chrome door handles and taps.

Seven of us went to work, each one with a specific task to complete. Fortunately B&Q stayed open over the weekend and I was the one going back and forth buying the bits and pieces that we had forgotten to add on to the original shopping list. Eventually, lots of tea and sandwiches later and with only an hour to go, it was ready for the off. As we tried to tow it out of my garden the front axle collapsed under the weight our make-up furniture had added to the once lightweight caravan. To the rescue my low loader truck! The make-up trailer arrived on time (just) on our first location in Holland Park on top of my low loader. It did look a bit of a shambles unloading it but I managed to conceal my embarrassment when the make-up designer and hairdresser were able to get on with their jobs without a hint of a complaint either from them or the artists. The location manager was not impressed and, when she advanced to production manager and later producer on other shows, I never got a chance to work with her again. Her loss!

On a subsequent location the stand-by prop driver got out of his cab to check out the space he was allocated to park his vehicle in. Normally he would use his mirrors to judge the distance between him and his neighbouring vehicle and it was this that prompted me to question his eyesight: "Well, I cannot see much without my glasses" he said "Where are they?" I wondered because I had never seen him wearing any since he joined us more than a decade ago. "I lost them years ago" and added "I am perfectly alright without them and in any case they make me look stupid". I disagreed, not about his looks but because he failed to identify a number plate as required by the Highway Code. I told him to go and get a new pair before I would let him drive one of my trucks again. He returned three days later with a pair of new spectacles balanced awkwardly on his nose just in time to move his truck to the next location. As he moved away from the kerb he misjudged the distance to a parked car which he then hit causing substantial damage. The irony was inescapable. After 30 odd years of accident free driving and a clean licence, albeit with poor eyesight, he loses his faultless record as soon as his eyesight is restored.

Back to Julie Andrews. Whatever issues - perceived or real - the producers had with her they did not extend to her presence on the set. I would like to think that my motor home helped her feel at home but even with less pampering I am sure she would have just got on with it. The fact that she was married to Blake Edwards - where private jets and a second home in Switzerland were taken for granted - did not stop her fitting in with us lesser mortals.

On one occasion I had to attend to a plumbing problem under the kitchen unit in her motor home. With her permission I crawled under the sink and, with torch and spanner, worked away while Julie and her dresser chatted on, from time to time inquiring how I was getting on. A few minutes later: "All Done" I declared and crawled out from under the unit. As I stood up my knees almost gave way. In front of me not six feet away stood the iconic, prim and proper star of the Sound of Music, stark naked making no effort to conceal her body, least of all her more private parts, from my gaze. I did not know where to look. Miss Andrews seemed unaffected, thanked me for attending to the plumbing and followed me to the door as if nothing unusual had happened. She then saw me out of the door with another thank you, all whilst momentarily standing in the doorway unclothed in full view of any member of the crew who happened to be passing by. It took me a while to recover but then I thought "what the hell, we are both professionals doing our job". I was attending to the motor home and she simply took her clothes off to change into her costume. Obviously, no big deal!

A few years later I worked on a made for television film, She'll be Wearing Pink Pyjamas. It was shot in the Lake District and featured eight women on an outward-bound survival course. One of the scenes required the women to strip naked as they went for a dip in the lake. When the camera was ready to immortalise the picture the lead actress, Julie Walters, turned round to the members of the crew assembled on the set and demanded that they, too, should undress and carry out their tasks without a stitch on, just as they expected her and her fellow actors to expose themselves and share in their embarrassment. As they all complied, any onlooker (I was, from a discrete distance away, one of them) would have thought they were transported back to the mid sixties when nudism was all the rage. I would like to add, at this point, that scenes featuring nudity or provocative behaviour were usually subject to a closed set with only essential personnel allowed to witness them. This meant that driver and facility suppliers (me) were subject to such exclusions which we often, just for the fun of it, took no notice of.

My old friend, Gregory Dark, recounted another story involving nude female players. He was assistant director on Carry on Emmanuelle's second unit that was tasked with shooting scenes that featured a whole bunch of naked women going about their provocative business. In other words they were unclothed throughout the day in full view of the crew. After wrap, cast and crew assembled in the Pinewood bar for a drink when the very same girls, whose bodies were on display all day, entered the room dressed in mini skirts so short that they almost exposed their knickers. The crew and especially the sparks (electricians) could not hold back their excitement at what they nearly saw. In fact, nearly getting a good look at the undergarments caused a bigger uproar than getting a good look at what these undergarments hid from view.

Unfortunately Duet for One, despite the script that was based on a best-selling novel and the inclusion of well-known and established actors, failed to deliver profits large enough to save Cannon Films from near fatal financial disaster.

# 22 Empire of the Sun 1987

## The Art of Road Building

Chris Kenny, an old acquaintance and one-time client, was about to produce the story of Peter Pan for Steven Spielberg's company when the filming had to be put on the back burner because, as I understood it, Great Ormond Street Children's Hospital, who own the rights to it, were not happy with the terms, the shooting script or both on offer by the production company. Just as he was to gather his possessions and clear his desk at EMI Studios in Elstree, Steven Spielberg's producers Kathleen Kennedy and Frank Marshall brought in another project which they offered him as a consolation prize; after all he was an experienced line producer and, in their opinion, best suited to take charge of crewing up the production team. Top of his list was my friend and mentor, Ted Morley, who took on the job of production manager with special responsibility for the shoot in the UK and Spain.

This promised to be one of the largest and best-funded productions I was contracted to service with facility vehicles. Filming was scheduled to start in the UK, then move on to China and end up in Spain where a massive set was being constructed. It involved building a practical runway for Second World War Japanese planes to take off and land. A life size steam train would move up and down a mile long track emitting large white clouds from its boilers, accompanied by the huffing and puffing of the escaping water vapour and its high pitched whistle announcing its arrival.

Central to the set was a full size detention camp with accommodation blocks, exercise yard and the obligatory watchtowers that, like giant guards, reminded any potential escapee that an attempt to scale the barbed wire fence and seek freedom would be futile. This is where, following the Japanese invasion, a large number of ex-pats from the occupied countries were interned.

To add realism to the scene, the actors were put on a special diet that made them appear haggard, undernourished and unkempt. Among the prisoners was the 11-year-old Jamie Graham who is the central character of the story. This was Christians Bale's introduction into the film industry that led him, a few years later, to become a major Hollywood star. Behind the camera the second assistant director Roy Button, in time, climbed the dizzy heights to head the European arm of Warner Brothers collecting an OBE on the way, while the third assistant Tim Lewis was to co produce several of the Harry Potter movies.

The whole set was being built in the middle of a vast swamp designated as a protected area of natural beauty and was home to a large variety of wild life. How we got permission to invade it remains a mystery only very few of our top brass could shed light on. Must have had something to do with name-dropping and money talking.

By its very nature the site was inaccessible and a new roadway had to be built to carry all the construction equipment, the shooting unit and location facility vehicles to the set. A local company was contracted to build half a mile of road strong enough to support our vehicles that would weigh no more than 17 tons each. Half way through the construction period the road began to subside and I was questioned about the fact that I had specified the 17 ton maximum gross weight per vehicle.

I was confident about the information I had imparted and, therefore, travelled to the site to see for myself what the problem was. As we travelled from the airport to the site along some very narrow roads I noticed a number of large earth moving trucks of at least 25 tons in gross weight coming the other way. I inquired of the driver what they were doing in such a remote area when he proudly replied that they were the ones servicing the road building effort. There and then I diverted to my hotel from where I telephoned the contractors to point out the error of their ways. Fortunately my Spanish was not good enough to understand his excuses. Suffice to say that a revised road-building program was initiated.

Our U.K. construction crew had three months to erect the set and, on arrival, decided that the one thing they needed urgently was an acceptable latrine, the sort they were used to at home. This, therefore, was the first vehicle I sent out. This was not as straightforward as it would be today. It was pre-EU and paperwork was king. Looking after a mobile toilet in a wild life reserve which meant fighting off flies, midges, and sometimes rat-like creatures was not an occupation of choice and my man, Tony Wise, deserved a medal in addition to his pay cheque. In the event it stayed there throughout the construction and the shooting period, a total of six months, just one day short of the time permitted under the temporary importation licence (Carnet de Passage) we had been granted.

Meanwhile filming began in the UK; first location Sunningdale, where we found a house similar to the one our hero's family owned in an affluent suburb of Shanghai at the time of the Japanese invasion. Unit base with all the paraphernalia was ready to receive one and all. Mr. Spielberg, as is his unassuming way, asked for no special treatment and no special treatment British mode was offered. What we did not appreciate was that no special treatment in Hollywood still means the provision of an American motor home. Fortunately I had one available just a few miles away and all was well soon after this misunderstanding came to light.

On the set, one of the camera crew celebrated his birthday and his mother decided to gift him a box of biscuits from Harrods that he duly passed around. Spielberg helped himself to one and either genuinely or out of politeness remarked how much he liked it. Keen to please, the floor runner rushed into the production office and declared that Mr. Spielberg would appreciate it if we could get him some of the said biscuits.

We don't do things by half where our leaders are concerned. A driver was dispatched to Knightsbridge to buy as many boxes of the biscuits in question as possible. Once he returned, they had to be air freighted to Hong Kong where a container loaded with our provisions due for China had to be held back to await the arrival of the sacred cargo. As a result it missed its scheduled departure but, after frantic phone calls and breaths held, it did make it to China in time for the crews' first meal. Surprise, surprise, not one single biscuit found its way to its intended target and the boxes were returned unopened to the U.K.

Back in Spain in the swamps of Jerez the set was taking shape and the unit base was made ready to receive both cast and crew. Unexpectedly, the saga of Mr Spielberg's modesty as far as his trailer was concerned repeated itself but, this time, one of the local caravans seemed to do the trick. However, the producers were looking for something more in line with their prestigious position. No suitable vehicle could be found locally and I was charged with providing a trailer good enough for our nobility. As luck would have it, one of my American motor homes was about to return from Tangiers where it had been used to house Farrah Fawcett Major. I managed to contact my driver and it arrived on the base to be used as an office by the producers. An assistant was dispatched to a garden centre 20 miles away and charged with buying assorted plants and flowerpots that were placed around the vehicle and thus created a colourful garden that reminded the top brass of their tinsel town home.

The unit base did not have to move during the shooting period and I was free to leave my people behind to look after the day-to-day needs of the unit. When I mentioned that I was about to return home, one of our local helpers whom I had befriended during my stay insisted that I pay respect to the touristy sites of the city. She dragged me along to the old Moorish castle, the sherry distillery and riding school; unfortunately for both of us I have little interest in Arab architecture, alcoholic drinks or horses. In the town square, however, I spotted a brand new Kawasaki motorbike. I could not resist being drawn to it and started to examine it in detail. Soon the owner appeared and in unaccented English explained that he was a member of a racing team, here to test new tyres on the nearby racing circuit. In passing he invited us to join him there in the afternoon. As he did not offer to let me ride pillion I turned to my guide who, unbeknown to me was also a motorbike enthusiast, for a lift in her car to the track. From having to feign interest at what she had to offer in terms of tourism we could now share looking forward to an afternoon in the company of racing professionals.

Gerhardt (he was German) welcomed us like old friends and immediately pointed out that these new tyres would allow the rider to lean steeper into a bend than was ever possible before. I have watched grand prix riders who would lean over far enough to scrap their knees along the road surface, which was a worrying sight in itself; now, however, with this new compound it would be possible to reach the ground with their elbows and possibly their upper arm. To see this manoeuvre close up did take my breath away. As far as I could work out, it defied logic and the rules of physics. It would send Isaac Newton back to the drawing board. I watched the bikes complete lap after lap until the team called a halt to the tests, started to pack up their equipment and made ready to leave. Long after we said our goodbyes and thank yous I stayed behind staring at the empty road incredulously replaying in my mind what I had witnessed. Being a member of a crew working for the most iconic filmmaker of the age seemed unremarkable compared to the riding skills whose exponents I had just been privileged to almost touch.

I only had to visit the set on a couple of occasions, more out of courtesy and curiosity than necessity. Then after wrap all my vehicles but the honey wagon, which had to service the de-rigging crew, returned to the U.K. without incident. Eventually when the honey wagon was cleared to leave, it was on the very day it's temporary six months import permit expired. Relief!

# 23 Robin Hood Prince of Thieves 1990

## To the Rescue

They talk about the ups and downs of show business. 1990 was one of the lower points of my career. I had produced a musical for the West End stage that ran for three weeks before closing down leaving me with little cash to keep going. I consoled myself remembering the maxim that in the film industry one is only a phone call away from solvency.

It did not take too long for the proverbial phone to ring. Michael Kagan, ex-Cannon Films which had by now been discredited and had disappeared from the U.K. scene, had been appointed line producer of this major Hollywood number. One of my old friends, Brian Hathaway, was appointed transport co-ordinator. Hard work and happy days were about to make a come back.

I had sold most of my vehicles prior to entering theatre land as an impresario and my fleet was now reduced to only eight trailers and trucks. I urgently needed another tow vehicle. My neighbour, a second hand truck dealer, had just bought a bunch of discarded vehicles from the GPO, forerunner to British Telecom. I purchased the least expensive one. It had a stainless steel tank, an array of pipes and a motor mounted on its back. I did not care for these attachments because my interest extended only to its suitability as a tow truck. It was my assistant, Eric Yoxall, whose curiosity got the better of him and concluded that what we were looking at was a vacuum pump that was most probably used to suck mud out of the trenches dug out to carry telephone cables. It was, in fact, a gully sucker that, with small modifications, could be used to solve the age-old problem of emptying the waste tanks of the mobile toilets and the bathrooms in the artists' trailers. We were able to apply for an official waste disposal licence to comply with the incoming health and safety regulations, not to mention the sensitivities of our more precious clients.

Thus, without doubt, the least glamorous driving job in the film industry came into being. Five star catering may be de rigeur for the crew but someone has to deal with the inevitable consequences - getting rid of human waste. In the early days, one of the prop man's duties included digging a trench, covering it with planks of wood with holes cut out... need I go on? Unacceptable now but commonplace in an age of outdoor privies and general conscription into army service. Individual chemical toilets followed and the privacy with better hygiene were welcomed but the waste remained in the vehicle - the more squeamish should skip the next paragraph.

To dispose of the accumulated waste a number of methods were employed. These varied from emptying it into old milk churns and tipping it into the sewers to towing the full vehicle to an officially appointed waste disposal site. Progress, however questionable, was made when we developed a recycling system. Here the liquid waste was filtered and separated out and, with chemicals added, was then used for flushing the toilet bowls. All this came to an end when we began to employ the newly discovered gully sucker that enabled us to empty the waste in situ and replenish the bathrooms with fresh water. One of the many innovations we introduced that improved the quality of our service and the drivers' lot.

However! When I visited a set on the Pinewood back lot, where our gully sucker driver was on stand-by, I noticed that he was not wearing protective gloves when handling the sucking equipment. Shortly afterwards he was about to join the crew for lunch without first washing his hands. Apparently he had lost the gloves and was reluctant to lose his place in the queue to be served. I admonished him and gave him my spare pair.

I returned in the afternoon when he proudly demonstrated his use of the gloves when uncoupling the waste pipes from the mobile toilet. He then walked across to the catering marquee and grabbed a sandwich without taking the gloves off. "I love them" he announced: "I keep them on, just so I don't lose them". Words failed me, other than to ask the unit nurse to take him aside and explain basic hygiene to him.

Needless to say the gully sucker and the rest of my decimated fleet were contracted to serve the picture. However, to supplement my income, I could act as what is known as the rushes car. This meant that every day once filming was completed I would take the rushes (the exposed raw film) to the laboratories that would develop them. Once they reported back to the producers that the film did not suffer any unforeseen damage (rushes report) I would then return the developed film to the set the next morning for the director and his crew to watch and evaluate the completed previous day's footage.

As this only required my input mornings and evenings I could attend to my depleted fleet during the day and ensure the vehicles remained in good working order. I would leave home in good time to pick up the rushes from the labs in Denham and deliver them to the set half an hour before the unit call (8 am as a rule) to give the projectionist enough time to prepare the material for the screening.

When the crew was working within a reasonable distance from London in Burnham Beeches or the New Forest, I would get going at about 6.00 or 4.30 am and be back in bed by 10.00pm and midnight respectively. Again it was bearable because, I, more often than not, could get my head down during the day while the rest of the crew were shooting away. Once the production moved to North Yorkshire and days were still only 24 hours long, I had to adopt a new routine that would preserve my sanity and my cash flow. Get up at three am; pick up the rushes at 03.45 followed by a three to four hour drive to Newcastle where the rushes were being shown in the crew hotel. A cursory inspection of my vehicles on location at Alwyne Castle and a quick update from my drivers followed by a brunch served by the caterers and into bed back at the unit hotel for a siesta. By 1800 hrs back to meet up with the camera crew who would hand over the rushes and return by midnight at the latest to the labs. Thus my overnight stay at home was reduced to some three hours. On occasion, though, I was too tensed up to get a proper night's sleep or a chance to dream of the riches I thought I deserved.

To reduce the wear and tear on my car that would result from the high mileage I would be covering during this episode, I hired a self-drive car from a Newcastle company that offered an unlimited mileage deal. I was prepared for an unhappy reception once I returned it having covered more than 4000 miles in just a little less than three weeks. Surprisingly the manager made no comment other than to thank me for my custom and hoping to be of service again.

The production on the whole was mismanaged on several levels. The young accountant and his team were totally overwhelmed by the size of the project. On away locations, of which there were several, the cashier would be handing out the location allowances to the crew, including the drivers, without keeping a proper record. In the event the less honest workers, and I am ashamed to admit that it included some of my drivers, doubled and trebled up their demands for pay outs. The scam worked thus. The head of department would go and collect the allowances for his underlings, in my case the charge hand, and distribute them to the individuals on his list. Then other heads of departments would go in with their own list that would include the driver that looked after their vehicle. For example the camera crew would include the camera truck driver as one of their team. This would now be a second payment. Finally each driver would sign for his own individual entitlement which, once handed over, would treble his allowance.

On several other occasions my invoices were ostensibly lost and I had to present copies that were settled promptly. Then my original invoices resurfaced and were honoured without questioning their validity. Being paid twice was not a problem as such but working out which payment related to which bill was something we never quite managed to work out. In the end we had to agree to an arbitrary figure and issued a credit note that would balance our books. It made no sense to the auditors who bombarded us with queries months after the show had wrapped.

Weak management also allowed all-comers to order transport with no regard for the size of the fleet that had to be accommodated on location. Travelling to the New Forest meant that a convoy of more than forty vehicles of all shapes and sizes converged simultaneously on to the M27. Then, when it came to slow down in order to exit the motorway and join the B road into the woods, the backlog it created caused a major traffic jam. Irate motorists summoned the police who should have been given notice of our arrival days earlier. They took over an hour to unravel the gridlock caused mainly by the fact that our convoy contained trucks that were too heavy and too large to access the allocated unit base by the prescribed route and had to find alternative ways to enter the forest. We encountered similar problems at Burnham Beeches where we had to park some vehicles along a public highway where they inconvenienced local residents to such an extent that we had to offer them substantial financial compensation to ease their pain.

On the other hand our artists were well looked after, with the most up to date American trailers at their disposal, and a team of the most experienced drivers to ferry them and their families around. Kevin Costner, the lead actor, had the exclusive use of Colin Morris, one of the top and most popular unit drivers in the business who counted such luminaries as Meryl Streep, Jack Nicholson, Harrison Ford and many others as his regular passengers and who, over time, became his friends. Kevin was on his way to join Colin's illustrious clientele when for no particular reason Mr Costner declared that "familiarity breeds contempt".

It did not need familiarity to spread the contempt that he invited, not just from the drivers but also from most of the cast and crew. When Waterworld, the film he funded out of his own pocket, failed to return a profit very few of us who had met him shed a tear. Schadenfreude.

Sean Connery who, for an outrageously high fee, made a cameo appearance on the set cheered us all up when he entertained the child actors on the set, especially my daughter Sammy who could not understand why James Bond should be meeting Robin Hood.

Unfortunately my man Michael did not win any medals overseeing this somewhat shambolic production and, although the film was a commercial success (something to do with the song?) he did not work as a producer again. Brian, to whom I was eternally grateful, also felt the strain of working with an undisciplined outfit and the difficult locations involved reverted to working as unit driver again.

While working on Nanny McPhee he was diagnosed with the big C and passed away shortly afterwards. He had worked in the industry for more years than anyone could remember (older than me) and was always a loyal friend and good for a laugh. I, and all who knew him, will miss him for years to come. I am dedicating this book to his memory.

# 24 The Camomile Lawn 1992

## Wrong Girl

The Camomile Lawn was a TV mini series produced for Channel 4 and directed by the venerable Sir Peter Hall. Not so venerable in my eyes. Central to the script was a young girl and, having auditioned a number of 11 year olds, the producers felt that my daughter, Sammy, would be ideally suited to play Sophie. Not so our director who, in his unbiased opinion, cast his own daughter Rebecca in the part. I suppose second best would have to do. I am not certain that he had noted my disappointment when, a few days later, we found ourselves standing by the gates of a girls' school and surveying the goings on in the playground he remarked, and I paraphrase: "Isn't it strange that every one of these girls, however plain or simple, is the best looking and most talented in somebody's eyes? This is just the way parents pass judgment about their children". Was he having a dig at me? I just nodded agreement but never found out whether he was referring to me or was he trying to justify the preferential treatment his daughter received?

The main location was a six-bedroom family home on the Cornish coast high above a cliff with a garden bordering on to the coastal way meandering along the rock's edge. The camp of trailers and trucks was set up in a field on a plateau 100 yards or so inland and everything had to be carried to the house via a narrow passageway, past the main entrance to the back of the building and through French windows into the living room which, once dressed with furniture of the period, doubled up as one of the sets.

The show was scheduled to be shot in the summer and our production supervisor, my loyal friend and client whose experience was unrivalled, promised us a sunny and warm summer on the English Riviera. If he was ever wrong, this time was it. It wasn't exactly cold but dry it certainly wasn't. Rain followed rain and it resulted in wall-to-wall and hedge-to-hedge mud. Rubber boots that had sunk ankle deep on their way across the unit base brought wet soil right up to the doors where, as a precaution, they had to be discarded. The cast could then put on their customised shoes while the crew behind the camera spent their days walking around in slippers. It was a strange and somewhat amusing spectacle to watch burley electricians tramping around the house in dainty footwear.

On the field that was home to our unit base the ground began to swallow up the vehicles and we had to commandeer a local farmer with his tractor to stand by and ferry cast, crew, and visitors across the field on a trailer designed to carry bales of hay. He was also invaluable when vehicles that had to leave the site needed a tow out of this quagmire on to the tarmac road. In truth, the main road was nothing but a narrow country lane chiselled out of the landscape and bordered on both sides by huge hedges. Only truck drivers and coach passengers could get a glimpse of the surrounding country side, while sitting in a low slung car reminded one of travelling through a long corridor constantly searching in vain for an escape route to make room for oncoming traffic.

Not many cars appeared head-on but, when they did, it was a question of who was going to give way by reversing into the nearest gap left by a gate to a field. The polite "after you" often resulted in comical confrontation especially when mutual politeness saw both cars reverse and, once it was realised that the road was clear for one of them to pass, both moved forward simultaneously for the whole process to repeat itself. Then there was the occasional standoff with a truck confronting a car that inevitably the larger vehicle survived unhindered. A more frustrating situation occurred when two large vehicles met each other. It then turned into a game of chicken and the loser had to reverse his large contraption down the lane into a gap large enough to accommodate him. This could take a while. Being in a hurry or trying to get somewhere on time was not an option. Driving at night was a lot easier as oncoming traffic sent out a light beam well ahead before it actually came into sight.

Cast and crew were spread over a twenty-mile radius and getting everyone to location on time was always a challenge. The big boys - producers, director and the lead players - came in from the five star (what else?) Carlyon Bay Hotel, others such as Felicity Kendall rented a house somewhere in the middle of nowhere and the rest of the artists and most of the crew stayed in St. Austell. I and the drivers who had to open up the camp in the mornings roomed at a bed and breakfast hotel in a hamlet just five miles away. In spite of the miserable weather and the remoteness of the location, or maybe because of it, we all pulled together and a sort of camaraderie between crew and the 'stars' developed; Paul Eddington of Yes Minister and Felicity Kendall, with whom he appeared in The Good Life, were particularly engaging.

Unusually for a largely philistine bunch of drivers the dining bus turned into a forum of discussion about the Turner prize, which that year had been awarded to Anish Kapoor. Other than that he was a sculptor from India who lived in this country we knew very little about him. What did strike a chord, though, was that our ultimate paymaster on this show, Channel 4, had decided to contribute £20,000 to the prize money; money that would have been better employed in raising the crew's wages. I tried to intervene on behalf of the art world but my arguments fell on deaf ears.

Years later I worked with Stand by Your Man Tammy Wynette on the KLF video of Justified & Ancient. It was shot on the 007 stage at Pinewood studios and was sadly her last screen appearance before she passed away. However, during the shoot the conversation turned to the Turner prize and KLF were keen to ridicule the award, just like my drivers did all those years ago. They came up with the idea that they were going to burn (yes burn) one million pound notes as an event of extraordinary significance and contribution to conceptual art. This, they argued, would have a good chance to merit winning the Turner Prize later in the year.

I could not take their plans seriously until I was tasked with escorting a black long stretched limousine, normally used for funerals, from Barclays Bank in the City to Black Park and was told that it contained the million pound notes that were to be set alight on a bonfire in the woods. However much I sympathised with artistic endeavours this one just passed me by. Arriving in the park two burly dark suited giants emerged from the car and, with the help of bystanders and the drivers, started to count out the money. A bevy of journalists and photographers stood at the ready to record the event. 984,000 notes made it onto the cinders that were to be ignited. 16,000 remained unaccounted for. Thus the event would not quite live up to expectation and the rest of the evening was spent searching for the shortfall with accusations of theft and worse, sabotaging the art event of the century, making the rounds. Needless to say, the money was never found and no postcard from South America provided a clue about its whereabouts. Recently I found out that, undaunted, the burning of the million pounds was staged in total secrecy, at a secret time and at a secret location. Oh, KLF did not even make the shortlist of nominees for the award.

Eventually the unit moved on to Saint Mawes where we continued filming and where we could set up our unit base on a tarmac car park next to the playing fields inland from the sea front. The town spread in single file along the quayside with only a few hotels and bed and breakfast establishments dotted among the residential properties. Members of the crew were allocated rooms ranging from ones offering three star comforts to no comforts at all. In the company's defence, it was not a question of saving money but just a question of what was available. I was allocated a studio that contained a single bed, a lopsided wardrobe and a chest of drawers across the way from my bed. When I discovered that my TV came without a remote control, I had to improvise by using a long bit of timber purloined from the stand-by construction truck and aim it from my bed at the desired buttons on the TV set, thus controlling the volume and changing channels.

On the plus side the rain was, for the first time in weeks, interrupted by short bursts of sunshine which gave us a chance to unpack the summer wear that we had had no use for during the preceding weeks.

A lot of us befriended the local pub regulars and, to pass the time over the weekend, a football match between Saint Mawes United and a volunteer eleven from the film crew was arranged. It was an eye opener, as I had never associated some of our players with athletic prowess. In particular our first assistant director, Rupert Ryle Hodges, Eton educated and very posh who kept goal like a pro. (During a conversation I found out that Eton is the only major public school where soccer as opposed to rugby is on the curriculum). The other revelation was that our diminutive transport captain, Bryan Baverstock, would mesmerise us with his close ball control and vision and was, therefore, without doubt, our star player. I felt I was just there to make up the numbers though the corner I took was met by our weight challenged prop man, Mark Fruin, another surprise, who headed the ball in for the only goal we scored. Fun and aching limbs were had by all and some say the game ended up as a draw. I, however, remember it as a win for our team.

The production wrapped just as the sky finally cleared and we returned home with fond memories and the realisation that, for us at that time, Cornwall bore no resemblance to the French Riviera. Several weeks later, as is the norm, I was invited and attended the cast and crew showing of the finished article and, in my unbiased opinion, my Sammy would have done a better job of Sophie even though Rebecca, the chosen one, went on to bigger and better things.

# 25 The House of Spirits 1993

## The Winter in Shorts and T-shirts

'Favourite Nations' is a contractual obligation often quoted by production managers when ordering artists' trailers/motor homes. Strangely enough, it does not mean that we are dealing with a favoured actor; in fact, just the opposite, in that none of the listed artists can avail themselves of better treatment than their playmates, particularly when it involves the size and interior décor of their trailer. I am not sure where 'nations' came into it. I can only surmise that this refers to their egos or, more likely, to the egos of their agents who pride themselves in negotiating the best possible deal for their clients.

This project was a German/Danish/Portuguese co-production to be shot on location in Portugal that would double up for Chile where the original events in the story took place. For the scenes that required sets to be shot on a sound stage (read sound proof) the production would move to Denmark. The plan was to start filming in the middle of the Portuguese countryside, move on to the studio in Copenhagen and then return to Lisbon for the final weeks featuring the cityscape sequences.

The film was based on the best selling book by Isabel Allende about a well to do rancher and his clairvoyant wife who live a privileged life through the politically turbulent nineteen sixties and early seventies. It is so well written that it counts as one of my favourite books.

What makes the story particularly interesting is that its heroes and their life experiences are based on real characters and events of the time. The young Pedro, a farm worker's son, is a firebrand revolutionary who attracts overwhelming support from a large section of the underprivileged working classes. His character is based on the Marxist Doctor Allende who was the first democratically elected Communist President in the world. The rancher Estaban represents the conservative elite who, unhappy with the democratic process that allowed the socialists to legitimately form a government, seizes power for his own conservative party in a coup d'etat supported by his friends in the army. Allende himself is said to have committed suicide but it was recently confirmed that he was, in fact, assassinated. With life imitating art, civil unrest followed and the Army under General Pinochet was called in to control and take over the running of the country. They did it with extreme brutality and would not tolerate any dissent, with thousands of protesters and innocent civilians rounded up and tortured, never to be seen again.

Eventually Pinochet was ousted from power and, before he could be tried for crimes against his people, he fled the country and found a safe haven in leafy Surrey thanks to a sympathetic Margaret Thatcher. The story ends when Pedro and Blanca, the rancher's daughter, rekindle their childhood friendship and live happily ever after; similar to the citizens of today's Chile who, tired of the turbulent past, have settled into a democratic and just way of life.

Neither Portugal, Denmark or Germany could, at the time, provide facilities suitable for an international Hollywood production, especially American style vehicles acceptable to A list actors with the now famous Favourite Nations clause in their contract.

With this clause preying on his mind, Dieter Meyer, the German executive producer, met me in my yard at Pinewood Studios to view the location vehicles I had available. (The term executive producer normally applies to the person or persons that have been associated with raising the funds to make the film. This time, I suspect, he was described thus to imply a promotion from the lesser production supervisor). His stars Glenn Close, Meryl Streep, Jeremy Irons, Winona Rider and Antonio Banderas, with a cameo appearance by Vanessa Redgrave, academy award winners all, had a list of requirements faxed (remember what a fax machine looked like?) over and my motor homes and trailers ticked all the boxes until it came to Favourite Nations where we had three choices - either five motor homes each with a driver, five American Trailers each with a tow vehicle and driver or a combination of both.

However much it cost to engage our Oscar winners, Dieter's job was to save money wherever he could, with particular attention to transport and wheeled facilities. So it was decided that the cheapest option would be to hire two motor homes that would tow a trailer each and a third trailer that would be towed by a pick-up truck that, on location, could double up as a service vehicle. Some more vehicles such as a make-up trailer towed by a mobile facility generator and a honey wagon were added to the list. As he had rented a room in the unit hotel for the wardrobe department, he would only require a truck to deliver and collect most of the costumes, some from London and others from Rome. Keeping it as a vehicle on location would cost too much. What he did not take into account was that he would need a vehicle to transfer daily requirements from the hotel to the set and that the assistants would have to travel from location back to their base every time an outfit needed washing, drying or ironing. Something that could have been carried out in my truck as it was equipped with a washing machine, tumble dryer and an iron with an ironing board. It could also be used as an office for the wardrobe master, thus keeping him in earshot of the director if and when needed. My suggestion met a blank expression and I did not pursue my argument but decided to await the inevitable. The inevitable occurred once the truck returned from Rome. The vehicle stayed with the unit until the show wrapped three months later.

New Years Eve 1992 was a subdued affair because the first day of 1993 would see me at the wheel of one of my motor homes hitting the road to Portugal. I was hoping that my fellow drivers in the convoy out of my yard had equally limited their celebrations to just one or two toasts to welcome in the New Year (watching their demeanour I had reason to doubt that they heeded my warning the previous night). Dover was just a couple of hours away and during the crossing to Calais they would have a chance to sober up enough to enter France safely. We decided to avoid driving bumper to bumper but left enough gaps between our respective long vehicles to allow faster road users to overtake us one by one. It did not matter if we lost sight of each other as we all had CB radios (remember them?) to keep in touch and to alleviate boredom by calling and talking to other CB savvy truckers in the vicinity.

We reported to the unit base a couple of days into the New Year and set up the circus in an orchard of randomly growing trees that could be harvested for the cork that formed their bark. Our trailers were scattered around the orchard, each trailer under as much shade as possible. This shrouded the base with the casual and relaxed air of a holiday campsite. Temperatures were significantly higher than at home at this time of year and putting out deckchairs in winter was a new experience to be savoured.

Next the artists arrived to inspect their homes from home and it did not take long before they noticed that Favourite Nations was not exactly adhered to. Not wanting to say "I told you so" I busied myself with laying electrical cables at the far end of the site. Dieter, whose responsibility it was to allocate the trailers, went AWOL.
To the rescue our second AD, Tim Lewis with my driver Gary in tow. He, together with our first assistant director, were hired because of their experience in dealing with the Hollywood greats. Something which no one from either Germany or Denmark could be entrusted with.

Just as well. The animated discussions with the various actors especially Glen about who should be allocated which trailer I only witnessed from afar. Unexpectedly it soon turned into benevolent smiles and peace broke out. I don't know how he did it but his diplomatic skills saved the day. No wonder that his career moved on apace and he was last heard of as an executive producer for one of Warner Brother's mega productions.

Villa Nova de Milfontes is a sleepy yet smart seaside resort 125 miles to the south of Lisbon. January to March was a very quiet time there. Most of the crew were booked into the only local hotel that did not shut up shop for the winter, though I cannot imagine anyone but us needing a room there at that time of year. Entertainment was restricted to drinking (very affordable) in the only local bar watching satellite television.

As the vehicles were not due to move for a while I elected to fly back home and return when and/or if needed. I ordered a cab to pick me up at 0600 to get me to the airport in time for my 1100am flight. Timekeeping is not in the Portuguese DNA. The cab turned up after several phone calls at just after 0700 with the driver assuring me that I need not worry. I had heard this before on other southern European locations and knew that, when told not to worry, I would be in trouble. And in trouble I was. I have noticed in the past that many drivers related the speed at which they drive to their prowess in the bedroom. This one was in his own opinion a master lover though I guess it was the opposite, which he was trying to disguise. Staying with the bedroom theme, I deducted from his erratic movements, big yawns and drooping head that he had not seen his bed for some time.

I made him stop at one of the petrol stations open at that time of day and plied him with cups of coffee. I have been to Vietnam and Greece, where reckless driving is commonplace with an unsurprisingly high rate of accidents. Compared to Portugal they are the proverbial walks in the park. It was only a matter of time before disaster struck in the form of a truck overtaking another and heading our way head-on on our side of the road. To my surprise - and thanks to the coffee he consumed - my driver reacted quickly and threw his cab into the ditch missing the said truck by inches. The truck failed to stop but some other drivers did and we all proceeded to push our car back onto the road. My man was furious and, with me back in the car, turned round to chase the offending truck. Naturally my protestations went unanswered and I settled down to watch the road rage incident that was to follow. When we caught up with the truck and forced the driver to stop he turned out to be a giant compared to my height challenged man. A short exchange of words and an inspection of the damage to our car later and we were back on our way to the airport. The incident must have brought him to his senses and he could then be mistaken for a north European road user. As luck would have it the flight on which I had booked a seat was delayed and I managed to board it after all.

More importantly the film, financed and produced by one of Germany' s wealthiest men and based on the said best selling book starring five Oscar winners with Vanessa Redgrave in support as well as a shooting script by an award-winning director, could not fail. But fail it did. In spite of winning a few prizes and proving popular in Germany where some of the population could identify with the happenings in South America, in the rest of the world especially the USA the film did not live up to its commercial expectations. I do not want to appear unkind but maybe the Germans should have stuck to making cars.

During the wrap party I received a frantic call from Branco Lustic, the producer of Schindler's List, who urgently needed another motor home for Steven Spielberg in Krakow, southern Poland. He already had two of mine and the only one I had available was one of the ones being released that evening in Lisbon. I, therefore, had to persuade two grumpy drivers to forgo the celebrations and set off towards our next project in Eastern Europe.

# 26 Schindlers List 1993

## Non-stop across Europe

Steven Spielberg to Branco Lustic, the Producer: "Don't worry about me, any old trailer will do". Music to Branco's ears, whose main raison d'etre was to save money. Filming was due to start in ten days' time.

He only had to order two high spec. (American and expensive) motor homes, one for Liam Neeson and another for Ben Kingsley. Saving money seemed to matter more than providing home comforts, Hollywood style, to one of the most prolific but least demanding filmmakers in the business. Still, who am I to argue even though I had in the past, during the filming of Empire of the Sun, witnessed the panic created when Mr Spielberg similarly declared that he did not require special attention. The fact that he meant no special attention Hollywood style sent the production team into panic mode when they realised that what he really wanted was a standard size American motor home of some 30' in length. In the US, such vehicles are usually allocated to the minor players rather than a star trailer that measures 35'+.

In a repeat performance, the producers dismissed my concern and duly ordered a 3-position trailer with one position allocated to Mr. Spielberg. When he stood in front of it he appeared not to understand what was going on and turned to his assistant to question him about the whereabouts of his motor home. Fortunately it all happened on location in Sunningdale only a few miles from my yard and, less than an hour later, my motor home was set up with heavy traffic blamed for the delay.

This time, however, he was in Kraków some 1500 miles away. The two motor homes were dispatched and my repeated questions about the need for a third one were dismissed as an attempt to increase my earnings. In any case, caravans and 3-position trailers were available locally and, if need be, would be good enough to accommodate our director.

This time it was a member of his family who wondered where his motor home (which they took for granted) was. They wanted to visit the set and needed somewhere to while away the time between shots. It was the Friday evening before filming was due to begin on Monday morning and suddenly it was my problem to provide an additional motor home in Kraków by Monday morning. I got the call during the wrap party of The House of Spirits in Lisbon.

The only suitable vehicle I had was the one we supplied to Glenn Close who was due to send in her assistant to empty it that Friday evening. In order to cover the 2100 miles in 48 hours the motor home had to travel nonstop and needed two men driving alternately taking the wheel. It took all my persuasive powers and an untold amount of overtime pay to get them to forgo the end of picture party and set off as soon as they could get their luggage out of their hotel.

The other problem was that this motor home was equipped to comply with Glenn Close's requirements, which involved taking out the dining table and chairs and replacing them with a make-up position. Naturally Spielberg and entourage had no need for it but expected a dining area as is usual in such a vehicle. The furniture, however, was stored in my yard in the UK.

So while one of the boys was driving the other one had to dismantle the make-up position. At the same time, I dispatched a van and two drivers from London with the dining table and chairs on board to meet the boys from Portugal at a motorway service area south of Paris.

The plan was that the two Londoners would take over the motor home and, while one of them was driving, the other one would install the furniture in the dining area. After a suitable rest, the Portuguese would return with the van that had arrived from the UK to Lisbon to pick up the motor home (Winona Ryder's) which they left behind and then, with the drivers who had recovered from the end of picture party, make their way back home.

Not quite. As my drivers were preparing to leave for home I received a call from Ray Frift who was prepping a TV series All in A Game to be shot in Barcelona. It was loosely based on the time Gary Lineker spent as a player for Barcelona's famous football club. He had just inspected the facility vehicles that were available locally and found that they did not meet the standard his UK crew - and especially the English cast – would find acceptable. His budget did not allow for having to bring in vehicles all the way from the UK, not to mention the cost of accommodating foreign drivers. I managed to wipe away some of his crocodile tears when I advised him that the vehicles he was looking for were already on the Iberian Peninsular, thus saving him substantial shipping expenses. As they say, it was a no brainer and I diverted my drivers to Barcelona where they would spend the following 12 weeks in the company of a lively Catalan/ UK crew.

On one occasion one of them took an evening off to visit the Camp Nou Stadium and, as he looked around the outer perimeter, he was propositioned by one of the many streetwalkers who congregated there. Far away from home and lacking female company he negotiated a fee and brought her back to the crew hotel and up to his room. Just a minute or so later his door was flung open and a heavily made-up male figure with wig in hand stumbled into the corridor and was helped down the stairs with a hefty push that landed him prostrate on the floor of the reception hall in full view of other crew members who were having a drink in the bar. He picked himself up and, running the gauntlet of a mocking crowd, limped out into the night.

It was obvious what had happened. However, the police had to be contacted in case his fellow workers came round to seek revenge for the treatment their colleague had received.

Back on the road to Poland the new crew installed the dining table and chairs and managed to reach Kraków late on Sunday night ready to drive to location first thing Monday morning. There was, however, another matter to attend to. At one of the fuel stops back in Spain the vehicle failed to start and, as it was the only American style motor home that featured a manual gearbox, a small army of helpful bystanders managed to push it and breathe life into it. As a result - and for fear that the motor home would not start in the morning - no one dared to turn off the engine and, therefore, it was parked up all night outside the hotel in Kraków with the engine running. Not exactly eco friendly but a medal or two were awarded for saving the day. For the record the fault lay in a wire, which had come off the starter motor and was reconnected in a matter of minutes.

I visited the location a few days later and not a word of appreciation was uttered and, therefore, I had to console myself by presenting Branco with an eye-watering bill for my drivers' efforts that took his breath away. I now had three vehicles on contract which were being looked after by just one driver, who was made to shuttle them on demand from one unit base to the next. His duties also included keeping them clean and tidy as well as carrying out routine maintenance. As is often the case, at the end of principal photography a raffle was held. Every member of the crew threw a ten-dollar note into the hat with the winning ticket being drawn out by the producer. To Mr. Lustic's credit my driver, Bryan Baverstock, was declared the winner, though it was suspected that foul play led to his well-deserved reward. A reward that thus did not have to be paid for out of company funds.

The subject matter of this film and the proximity to the location, Auschwitz concentration camp, where the most despicable and horrendous crimes were committed, drained away all my lighthearted approach to the situation. My state of mind did not improve when I visited the set in the late afternoon. In front of the railway station the forecourt was filled with hundreds, if not thousands, of crowd artists who had to starve themselves for several days in order to appear like the wretched detainees who were arriving at this very location fifty years earlier and were herded into the nearby concentration camp. The fact that very few survived by being put on Schindler's list could not detract from the fact that the vast majority, that is 6,000,000 (six million), were put to death in gas ovens or worse, if there is such a thing, by unspeakable torture. For the first time in my life, I had to walk away from a live set when I became aware that my grandparents must have made that same journey from which they never returned.

Back in my hotel room, I could picture my grandparents serving customers in their upmarket menswear shop in Stettin and, on the seventh day, putting on their Sunday Best taking a stroll down Main Street (I have a photograph) where they would meet friends for a chat and acknowledge lesser mortals with her nodding and him raising his hat in salute. It sent shivers down my spine to think that they were plucked out of this late Edwardian genteel idyll and plunged into the nightmare, the humiliation and certain death just because they were Jews. I only hope that they managed to bear it all by believing it was all a bad dream from which they would wake up. Tragically they did not.

I did plan to pay homage to the victims of the slaughter by visiting the site that is now a monument to the fallen but, with the horrific images dominating my thoughts and a tightening of my stomach that would at any moment push up yesterday's lunch, I grabbed my suitcase and in a trance-like state left the hotel and drove out of town away from the re-enactment of that incomprehensible era.

I woke up from this nightmare when the fuel indicator light in my car began to flash and I turned into a service area by the side of the road. I was too tired and traumatised to operate the pumps. I, therefore, found a parking space and fell asleep leaning forward with my head on my folded forearms resting on the steering wheel.

Hours later cramp in my foot woke me up and after a short walk and a modest breakfast I returned both physically and mentally to the safe and happy world I was lucky enough to inhabit.

When I now read about the atrocities that still take place in far away places I have to remind myself that, with a shrinking world, they could soon be arriving on our doorstep. Ironically the very people (Germans) that carried out the genocide of yesteryear are the ones who are the most welcoming hosts to the victims of the massacres that we can hear, see and read about today.

# 27 The Remains of the Day 1993

## Curry on Unit

Ismail Merchant and James Ivory spent some twenty years together producing films, largely with an Indian theme for a niche audience, until they finally hit the big time with A Room with a View. They had secured the rights to E.M. Forster's novel some time ago but it took all of Ismail's money-raising skills several years to secure the funds needed to go into production. James, his partner and director-in-waiting of the film, expressed doubts about taking on the project because he thought that it would not find an audience big enough to return a profit. Eventually, with a script by their old friend, Ruth Prawer Jhabvala, filming did go ahead. Maggie Smith, a young Helena Bonham Carter and a supporting cast that included Daniel Day Lewis, Judi (now Dame Judi) Dench and a handful of notable Shakespearian actors were recruited even though it has remained a mystery to this day how they were all persuaded to sign up to this production. Perceived knowledge was that an E.M. Forster story would neither be a popular subject, nor were Merchant Ivory Films well enough funded to afford the fees such a cast would command.

In the end the film received outstanding critical acclaim winning three academy awards (Oscars) and produced a healthy profit for its investors. Basking in their success Ismail and James immediately embarked on their next project, Howard's End, another E.M. Forster novel, again with a script by Ruth Prawer Jhabvala, James directing and, needless to say, Ismail credited as the producer. This time even bigger names including Anthony Hopkins, Emma Thompson, and Vanessa Redgrave joined Helena Bonham Carter in the cast.

Even though Howard's End did not attract the critical acclaim of its predecessor, it still returned a respectable profit and, on the basis that one would wait for a bus for ages and then three would turn up at once, there was no time to lose before Merchant Ivory, with another script by the trusted Ruth, would embark on their next venture, The Remains of the Day.

When characterising a producer he is often said to be careful, very careful, or even too careful with money. Ismail Merchant is, without doubt, the best-qualified exponent to hold a master class on the subject. It is even rumoured that, when principal photography wrapped on The Bostonian in the USA, the production manager was left behind to finalise outstanding matters but with no funds to settle any of the bills. He and his co-ordinator had to leave town - with creditors chasing them all the way from Boston to New York for payments - before they managed to catch a flight home leaving several unhappy people behind.

By the time they launched The Remains of the Day their reputation for squeezing suppliers was well established and most potential contractors, including myself, approached them with caution. It was their appointment of Joyce Herlihy as the production manager that persuaded me to tender for the job. Joyce was the grand old Dame of the film industry. Her credits included Chariots of Fire and Agatha in a career stretching back over forty years with an unblemished reputation for straight dealings.

The cast read like a Who's Who of British acting talent; Anthony Hopkins, Emma Thompson, James Fox, Hugh Grant (before Four Weddings...) and many more. Christopher Reeve before his tragic accident would play an American that, it was hoped, would help attract an international audience. Unlike previous projects, during which the producers got away with supplying lesser facilities, this time Joyce insisted that as long as she was in charge the actors were going to be treated with the respect and care they deserved. She also, I was assured, had enough money in the budget to hire and pay for the appropriate vehicles. If the truth were known I would have worked for her at any price but in the event it was not necessary and a deal was struck.

Anthony Hopkins loved his curries and Ismail Merchant, our producer, loved to cook them. As a result Ismail regularly took over the catering truck and served up curries of all shapes and sizes to all comers. Though he received high praise for his efforts from most of us, it was on these occasions that drivers were sent out to secretly visit takeaway establishments in the area for anything other than curries for the members of the cast and crew not partial to Anthony's and Ismail's tastes.

A few weeks after he had played out his main scenes the director asked Anthony to return to the set for an additional day's work near Plymouth. He was by then working in Shepperton Studios on Richard Attenborough's Shadowlands. He was given time off and I was charged with taking him and his make-up artist, Chrissie, after wrap down the M4/M5 to his hotel in the West Country, ready for an appearance on set the following morning.

En route he mentioned that he had not had a chance to eat before we left the studio and that he fancied, yes, a curry. It was getting late but I was confident that we could find an 'Indian' in Marlborough just off the M4. Disappointingly, no luck. A diversion and a search around Swindon and no luck again. We gave up and decided to make do with a snack at the Leigh Delamere motorway service area. So the famous one with the two of us at his side gingerly entered the restaurant which, by now, was about to shut down for the night. On enquiring as to what was on offer we were told that the only dish left was, unbelievably, curry. Autographs and a minor commotion later it was happiness all round.

Back on Remains of the Day Joyce ran the show with military precision. No wonder, as we later discovered at one of the many manor houses we visited. There the lady of the house entertained us with tales about Joyce when she was a non- commissioned officer in the army back in the fifties and was giving the recruits like herself a hard time.

On another occasion we were filming in the gardens of almshouses near Richmond. The old age pensioners, who lived therein, curious as they were, came out to watch the action. It was a strange and yet amusing sight when we realised that Joyce who was, on paper, older than most of the spectators, was directing the 100 or so crew who, without question, followed her instructions.  She did, however, occasionally reach for a discrete pick me up from the inside pocket of her coat where she had safely stored a bottle of gin. When she was nominated and won the First Women in Films Award the opening sentence of her speech, in front of a hall full of feminists, acknowledged the help she had received from her male colleagues in the industry.

This time the film had to contend with just one award, that of a BAFTA for an actor in a leading role, Anthony Hopkins. The modest critical acclaim was followed by smaller takings at the box office, which was explained away as a temporary setback that would soon be forgotten.

The Golden Bowl proved an attempt too far to produce another period piece by the same director, producer and writer, albeit with a new set of actors, Kate Beckinsale, James Fox, Angelica Huston, Nick Nolte, Uma Thurman and others. Filming was scheduled for London, English Manor houses and, in an attempt to replicate their earlier success, Italy.  I should have heeded the warning when a relative newcomer had replaced my trusted Joyce Herlihy.

The other shot across the bow was that a young Paul Bradley, who served his apprenticeship as an assistant to Ismail, was appointed line producer with the obvious brief that he should be even more careful with expenses than his boss, if that were at all possible.

In spite of the financial constraints imposed upon her Sarah Bradshaw, the new production manager, extracted a tolerable deal out of me. Fortunately she did appreciate the financial sacrifice I made - and noticed my crocodile tears - when she helped to dry them off by becoming a loyal and fair client on future productions.

There are very few people in this industry whom I have caught red handed granting contracts after accepting questionable inducements from suppliers. When Sarah, as the associate producer on Syriana, employed one such person as her transport co-ordinator and asked me to tender for the supply of vehicles, I explained that I would be unable to work with him and, therefore, did not want to service her production on that occasion.

This did not go down well and once my emails went unanswered we lost touch. A few weeks ago we chanced upon each other and judging by the enthusiastic reception I got, I sensed that my time in exile might have come to an end. As much as I believe in holding on to my principles, I did regret losing someone with whom I was hoping to forge a long and lasting relationship.

# 28 Braveheart 1995

## The Battle Plan

My old friend and mentor, Ted Morley, was to manage this film and another old friend, Paul Tucker, was put in control of the finances. I had better do a good job because I would not want to unfriend either of them.

**The** Mel Gibson was to produce, direct and star in this epic project assisted by his long time co-producer, Bruce Davey, and a hands-on executive, Stephen McEveety. Other top brass were Dean Lopata and the legendary Alan Ladd Jr. To please all of them would be a challenge to which I had to rise. There were hints that our American and Australian cousins did not trust us to get the job done to the standard they were used to back in Hollywood.

Freddie Chiverton, 6', 18 stone, monosyllabic, half Irish half Jewish gentle giant from the East End of London, was already on board as a general-purpose unit driver, later to exclusively look after Mel Gibson. In the meantime, however, he recruited one of his moneyed and star struck friends, to cover for him by temporarily chauffeuring Mel. It was his first introduction to show business and he misguidedly went out and bought a white Bentley to impress his charge. When Mel left the production office that evening our newcomer proudly ushered him towards his new and shiny carriage. "I am not getting into this" muttered Mr Gibson and promptly turned to Fred who was parked alongside in a Range Rover, got in and left behind the poor shell shocked novice. Next day the Bentley was sold and was replaced by an Audi, which joined the fleet of unit cars and remained with us for the rest of the production run.

A few years later, after a stint as a transport co-ordinator, that same driver invested heavily in cars and light vans and became a major supplier of self-drive vehicles to the industry.

It soon transpired that this was a project that would require many more vehicles than I could supply from my own resources. This meant that, if I were being asked to be the 'preferred' contractor, I would need to hire in equipment from a number of other operators. Under normal circumstances I would do this and add a handling charge to my invoice. This time, however, it was agreed that it would be mutually beneficial if I were put on the company's payroll as a transport co-ordinator. I would thus supply my vehicles at 'arm's length' matching the rates of other suppliers and hiring in vehicles and services from competitors at 'cost' which would then be billed directly to the production company.

It was clear from the earlier incident with the Bentley that the powers-that-be wanted to avoid giving the impression of being extravagant. No limousines, just cars of lesser standing than a Mercedes, should be engaged as unit cars. This would present no particular problem in Scotland where we were going to rent self-drive cars and employ local drivers. Not so easy in Ireland, though, where most of the established unit drivers drove Mercedes cars that they owned and, more contentiously, they enjoyed the protection of their trade union.

As far as trailers were concerned only Mel should have a large one where he could be made up, hold meetings and get his head down if time allowed. The rest of the cast would be accommodated in basic yet comfortable caravans or sections of the multi cabin American style trailers (3 positions). The crowd would have to make do with marquees, which would be well heated and furnished. A total of 24 trucks and facility vehicles would carry props, cameras, costumes etc and would be parked at the unit base with a fleet of 4x4's and quad bikes shuttling cast, crew and equipment to and from the set.

On one of my first scouting trips I arrived in Inverness on the night sleeper. I was going to hire a car to go and inspect possible unit bases and assess the difficulties, if any, of accessing them by our circus. As I exited the station I noticed to my right a car rental office. Just what I needed! A very helpful couple ran it and, once I had sorted out the paperwork, I casually asked about renting four-wheel drive Land Rovers. Their faces lit up when they explained that their son Michael ran a company called Sharp's Reliable Wrecks that did just that. Not only would he be happy to oblige but, as he had on several occasions worked with film and TV companies, he understood their modus operandi. One problem solved. I am not sure what happened to him once we left Scotland but Michael Sharp was next heard of as a location manager in Rumania and recently as unit production manager of The Fantastic Beasts, a sequel to the tales of Harry Potter.

Finding a large enough area for a unit base close enough to the sets near Fort William was more difficult. The car parks in the narrow valley were not only too small but were also reserved for the tourist trade and had to be kept open especially at weekends. Eventually our flamboyant location manager, Paul Shersby, who did not shy away from chartering a seaplane to fly with assorted dignitaries to and from luncheon venues along the lochs, charmed the local forestry commissioner into creating a clearing in the woods that we could access from the main road and was large enough, with hard standing, to accommodate our unit base. When I returned to pace it out a couple of weeks later it was as if it was meant to be there. In fact, it would be designated as a new visitor's car park once we left.

Fort William can only offer a limited amount of hotel rooms so the location assistant and I had to tour a number of smaller lodgings to judge their suitability for our crews. Most landladies had on previous occasions hosted film units and were particular about which members of the crew they would prefer to welcome into their establishments.

It seemed that drivers were particularly unpopular because they tended to spend little or nothing at the bar while the sparks (electricians) for the opposite reason headed the popularity list. Not sure who won that lottery; suffice to say that I managed to get myself booked into one of the only two proper, if only three starred, hotels.

It was rain, rain and more rain when we started to film and the 4x4's were churning up the ground with mud flying everywhere. Each day we had to redirect the cross-country vehicles to an alternative route in order to prevent the topsoil from sliding down the valley. Soon straightforward Land Rovers gave up and we had to resort to hiring in so-called 'Gators'. These three and four axle all wheel drive machines, used mainly by mountain rescue teams and remote crofters, were the only ones that could cope with the muddy terrain and thus allowed us to carry on filming in the appalling conditions we had to cope with.

We prayed and prayed but HE did not listen. Days later the weather relented and the sun appeared. So did the midges though. They came out of the woods in such big swarms that they blocked out the sunlight.

All the shops along the lochs to Inverness that were stocking beekeepers' hats with nets to stave off the blighters sold out within hours, as did all sorts of lotions and creams. It left the bulk of the crew with no protection and frantically waving their arms to keep these insects away. Fires were lit to discourage them but to very little effect. Our London contacts were ordered to search for and corner the market for these silly hats and rush them up to us on the overnight train. Only the smokers, of which Mel was the most prolific, escaped the worst onslaughts and showed little sympathy to those who were badly bitten. "Rain come back, all is forgiven" became the new anthem. It came back a few days later and stayed with us until we wrapped the Scottish location but not without causing part of the set to be swept away by the raging waters that broke the banks of the stream that flowed alongside our make believe village.

When we flew on a private charter from Inverness to Farnborough the cabin crew asked Mel if he would mind posing for a photograph with them. He agreed on condition that they let him smoke during the flight. After consulting the captain the deal was struck. Mel chain smoked on the plane and after landing posed for pictures on the aircraft steps, his arms around the uniformed hostesses with the two pilots in the background looking on.

For my part Ireland, our next location, beckoned. I left Bryan, now our transport captain, in charge and embarked on my first scouting trip to Dublin and beyond. A unit car picked me up from the airport with a very chatty driver, trying to find out how we were getting on in Scotland and more importantly what we were planning for Ireland. He was an owner-driver and extremely proud of his car, a Mercedes. I did not comment but made vague approving noises. The bad news could wait, especially as I was unsure of how to handle it.

When I checked into the unit hotel, the Westbury, the receptionist confirmed my booking remarking that I would be staying for 88 days. Under my breath I repeated incredulously: "88 days?" But said nonchalantly "that's right", pretending that I fully expected it. I was given a choice of rooms and opted for a second floor one overlooking the pedestrian area in front of the building.

At one point Sheila and my daughter, Natalie, came to visit and, coincidently, that same night Westlife stayed in the hotel with hundreds of screaming fans gathering under our window in the hope that they would catch a glimpse of their idols. Cheekily I went down and pointed at one of my drivers, Bob Lilley, in his people carrier and announced that he was one of the group's uncles waiting for them to come down. The poor man was mobbed immediately and just about managed to get away when his real charge, the venerable Alan Ladd Junior, appeared. The sixty something old had to fight his way through the screaming teenage crowd to the amusement of the other drivers who were there waiting for their own passengers to emerge from the hotel.

On to our production office where I met our Irish production manager, Mary Alleguen, and, in an office tucked away at the end of the corridor, our location/unit production manager, Kevin De La Noy. I knew that he was going to be there from our meeting back in Shepperton Studios during the pre-production days. What I did not know was that he was the proud owner of one of the first laptops on the market. I made the mistake of asking him about the advantages this gismo had over our old and tried methods of communicating face to face, by telephone or by written memos or letters. As the order of command goes he occupied a senior position to me and, not only that, he had by this time already spent several weeks in the country and had familiarised himself with the local conditions that we would encounter. This meant I had better listen. I only understood a fraction of his lecture but the bottom line was that he would be able to produce a document that would contain everything every crewmember needed to know every day and every alternative procedure for every unforeseen circumstance. Every possible situation was thus covered in writing in advance of the film crew's arrival.

This A4 half-inch thick 'Battle Plan' was distributed to everyone who may or may not be affected. Nothing was left to chance and there would be no reason to ask further questions because the answers were all to be found within the dozens of pages in the printout. In fact, the American powers that be - and especially the production designer - were so impressed by his detailed and thorough piece of work that they put him forward to supervise their next productions. Today his credits include such epics as Titanic, The Dark Knight, Ali and Saving Private Ryan.

Our first location was on the 5000 acre Currah where the Battle of Stirling Bridge was going to be re-enacted. It was scheduled to be shot over a period of six weeks and would involve some 1600 Army reservists as extras. Make-up artists and wardrobe assistants would have their work cut out and, with military precision, they would usher the crowd through a long tunnel-like marquee where each player would be allocated a hook on which to hang his civilian clothes. He would then join one of several queues to receive his costume, then on to get hold of his spear and finally on into make-up where some 40 make-up artists would apply the war paints. From arriving at the site in their civvies to being battle ready took a total of 4 hours each day. It meant an early start and a staggered arrival timetable to avoid a gridlock.

Although strictly speaking it would be my responsibility as transport coordinator to take charge our leader Kevin, in conjunction with the military command, had it all under control as described in 'Battle Plan'. I could, therefore, turn away to attend to my other concerns. I toured the various centres of operations such as the armoury, artists' make-up, wardrobe and catering marquees and paced out the areas we would need to access and park up our circus and where the allocated unit cars could stand by without interfering with the through traffic. At the same time they needed to be in visual contact with the assistant directors who would be calling on them to transfer artists to and from the set. Fortunately we were operating from a large field where space was aplenty and, therefore, I did not have to compromise on freedom of manoeuvre. In any case the battle plan foresaw my requirements and all we had to add was metal tracking to avoid vehicles getting stuck in the mud bath that would result from the inevitable rain.

I made contact with a couple of local car rental companies which would supply cars to the crew members who elected to drive themselves from their hotel to the set. I was also introduced to our local facility vehicle supplier, Gerry Fearen, who would double up as my assistant. I raised the question about the No Mercedes unit cars and offered to discuss the matter with the drivers' union representative during my next visit.

In the meantime, the animatronic horses were ready to be shipped from UK to Ireland and we had to decide how to do this efficiently and safely. It was one thing loading them on to semi-trailers crossways side by side but we also had to accommodate 30 ft long tracking on which these horses were pushed along by hydraulic rams. In the film they were placed among the real horses, which were unharmed, while the artificial ones suffered the unspeakable cruelty the audience witnessed. We managed to load it all, albeit rams separated from the horses, on to three 40' trailers. When the side curtains of the wagons were drawn back the make believe horses lined up side by side stared out at me poised ready to jump out as they did in Butch Cassidy when, with riders astride, they resumed the chase of the outlaws. Fortunately they were tied down and the rams that would push them along had not yet been assembled.

Back to Scotland where we began to ship props, costumes and other miscellaneous items that were wrapped early to Ireland via the ferry from Troon to Larne, Northern Ireland and then by road to our location west of Dublin. The big push was going to be at the weekend when the whole unit was due to move all at once. The convoy would consist of 24 mainly long vehicles so, in order to minimise inconvenience to other road users, we consulted the constabulary who suggested we split the circus into two, one travelling via Stirling and the other via Loch Lomond. Ironically, we thus caused long delays to the traffic on both routes.

To be able to deal with unforeseen breakdowns and to ensure that all arrived in time for the allocated sailing, each line of trucks was tailed by a heavy breakdown truck with two mechanics on board. After only a minor holdup due to a stuttering fuel pump we boarded the ferry and on to our first Irish location.

We had a heated discussion about the use of Mercedes cars mainly because the drivers feared a loss of income if their cars were not being used and would, therefore, only be paid a driver's wage. I had to follow strict instructions from our executive producer, Steven McEveety, who was more concerned about appearing frugal rather that actually being so. However, saving money would always be welcome. Another meeting convened by our Irish producer ended with a compromise whereby the drivers would drive self drive cars that we would hire in and, because their own cars would not suffer wear and tear, they would reduce their rate to halfway between the standard drivers' pay and the full rate for a Mercedes unit car.

The only driver who insisted on carrying on with his own Merc had to be kept away from the set and stood by to run errands for the accounts department which was housed above the transport office on the first floor. One day a gang of three youths stormed into the accounts office and ran off with its safe. Gerry and I heard the screaming of the girls upstairs and, as we ran onto the front of the building, we caught sight of the robbers ripping open the door of the Merc, dragging the driver out and, with the engine screaming, making their getaway. However, before they could exit the property they had to speed past Gerry and me. I picked up a stone and threw it at the windscreen, which shattered immediately causing the car to swerve and hit a tree head on. Gerry, with me in pursuit, ran towards the damaged car but, before we could reach it, the boys got out and ran away. The very car that we had to keep on the payroll was now damaged beyond a quick repair and the driver was forced to join his colleagues in a rental car. In spite of police roadblocks and tracker dogs the culprits were not caught. Ironically it transpired that the safe they had carried off was empty.

Six weeks on the battle scenes were in the can and we were ready to move on. The large crowd was dispensed with and replaced by a normal size cast and crew with straightforward demands to satisfy. This gave us all a chance to savour what Ireland - and particularly Dublin - had to offer. What surprised me most was the quality and friendly service of their eateries. Before we left, though, we had another incident to deal with. Alan Ladd Jr's driver, the ex-motor bike racer Bob Lilley, was rushed to hospital with a suspected heart attack. We held our breath for a few days and were relieved when he was released having been diagnosed with indigestion. However, our producers could not forget the concern he caused and dubbed him from that day on as Bob, Heart Attack, Lilley, which is how his name appears in the film's credits to this day.

# 29 Evita 1996

## Palms Grow in Budapest

I was particularly pleased to secure the contract to supply location facility vehicles for this show, especially as I would get the chance to meet Madonna, then one of my favourite performers, and Alan Parker who was and still is my most admired director. I count Midnight Express as one of my top ten movies of all time.

As a bonus Antonio Banderas was cast to play Che Guevara. I met Antonio on the set of The House of Spirits where we often exchanged non-PC observations about some of the female cast and crew. We also shared an admiration for Winona Ryder who relieved all comers, especially the drivers, of their living allowances with her card playing skills. We forgave each other for this laddish behaviour and ended up somewhere between friends and acquaintances.

Budapest was new to all of us; it had only recently come out of its communist past and had embraced the capitalist system with no shame. Everyone seemed to be 'on the make.' We checked into our hotel, the Hilton, which felt like any other Hilton and were asked to report to reception where we were going to receive our per diems to cover our living expenses, mainly evening and weekend meals. However, our local representative who owned the casino next door offered us the choice of either the money or gambling chips to twice the value of the dining out allowance. In any case, he argued, if we visited the casino we could enjoy a free meal. A no brainer so I opted for the chips which I lost on the roulette table in spite of the system I employed that, I was assured, would beat the bank.

Budapest represented Buenos Aires and had to be dressed accordingly. Most of the facades featured retro baroque, Catholic ornaments similar to the ones Spanish architects placed there to remind them of their homeland. The only thing lacking in Budapest was the warm climate with its fauna, mainly an abundance of palm trees.

Show Business is often called upon to mimic reality and, in no time at all, the art department designed and produced artificial palm trees that could be wrapped round the lamp posts along the street that was to be a South American avenue. From the middle distance and thus on film they were so realistic that I overheard an American couple wondering why, if palm trees could grow in Budapest, they had not come across any others on their journey through Central Europe. In any case, why did the guidebook not mention them?

Some years later I worked on Full Metal Jacket directed and produced by the legendary Stanley Kubrick. Like my wife, this burley larger than life character was terrified of flying and was determined that when his time came he would not be in a crashing plane. The Story was set in Vietnam with the battle scenes re-enacted at the derelict Beckton Gas Works that were due for demolition. It was an ideal site for letting off explosions and filming house-to-house warfare. The only missing link was the lack of indigenous trees. According to the art department palm trees would do the trick, but unsurprisingly none could be found. Mr Kubrick, who did not much care about his personal unkempt appearance, did care about what appeared on his films. He, therefore, insisted on importing fully grown palm trees from Africa and planting them randomly in and around the set that turned out to look like a credible location for a Vietnamese war zone. As expensive as this exercise was, it tuned into a profitable venture when all these mature trees were subsequently sold to the residents of the up market St George's Hill and Wentworth who welcomed the opportunity to feature these ready made exotic plants in their gardens.

We parked up the motor homes and the other facility vehicles in a side street that was cleared for us off the main drag. Unusually, Budapest provided electric power points on nearly every street corner, very much like we would expect water hydrants at home. This meant that we could plug in directly to the mains supply without running up our generators that could interfere with the sound effects and speech on the set.

Madonna arrived first for her make-up call and seemed pleased with her motor home. Neither did her make-up artist, hairdresser or wardrobe mistress find any fault. We would always hold our collective breath on the first morning because there was bound to be something that needed changing, fixing or was missing. Just to make sure my driver knocked on the door and, on entering, introduced himself to the star and her assistants. He was well received, a sort of rapport developed and he soon became part of her entourage.

I was not witness to what was said or done but some risqué banter must have taken place because, once we wrapped and said our goodbyes, he was given a pair of Madonna's knickers with the remark that his dream of getting his hands into them had come true. Very funny! I, on the other hand, had to make do with a signed photograph.

Alan Parker immersed himself in the project and got quietly, as far as I was concerned, on with directing the show. I did once or twice extract a smile out of him but otherwise my hope of engaging him in a conversation or sharing a drink - of which he had plenty – remained an unfulfilled ambition.

Neither did my relationship with Antonio reignite itself. After all, he comes from Malaga where I had just bought an apartment and I was looking forward to discussing with him the merits of the local nightclubs and eateries. He was being trailed by his wife, Melanie

Griffith (God, she did not look well), who made sure he behaved himself and that she would be the only one allowed to appreciate his charms and good looks. No roving eye, suggestive remark or sidling up to another female. Poor chap, I thought, and then "is that me, when my wife takes the reins?"

Jonathan Price, the third lead, buried himself alternately in his hotel room and his trailer and either managed to enjoy socialising with friends out of sight of the crew or made do with just himself for company.

A couple of my drivers boasted about a system that would beat the bank and, to everyone's astonishment, they did walk out of the casino and into the hotel bar waving a bunch of notes for all to see. All included a glamorous blonde whose profession was clearly one of the very old ones. She sidled up to them and, a drink or two later, I was invited to join them to help negotiate a deal that would benefit the three of them. They were keen to re-enact a scene from a pornographic film they had watched on the adult channel in their room. It involved two guys like themselves having a sexual experience with a girl (more woman) like her. I had to ask the barman for a pen and paper to illustrate what they had in mind. We all saw the funny side of this encounter especially when each one of us in turn re-drew the picture and adjusted the various positions of the forthcoming action. She wanted more money than the boys were willing to shell out and they naturally held out for a better deal.

At one point it was suggested that if I chip in the difference I, too, could have a bit of fun with them. When I declined with an excuse that I had lost all my allowance on the roulette table the youngish lady wondered if, for a reduced contribution, I would want to come up and just watch the performance. A lot of giggles and another round of drinks later a bit more money changed hands and the three of them disappeared into the lift that would take them up to the theatre of their dreams. I never knew her name. She may have been the only one to receive an early reward for her efforts but was soon followed by an army of wealth seekers from every trade and enterprise in the city.

Like most tourists and working foreigners we were bombarded with promises of financial gains if we entrusted them with our money. From cab drivers - licensed or not - nightclub doormen to more respectable professionals like lawyers and wholesalers, they all saw a chance to live on streets paved with gold, just like the ones we walked on back at home. In the event I responded to an approach from a company serving the local film industry which led to a mutually beneficial future. Among other projects, we later co-operated on an Eddie Murphy film and on several commercials that were shot in Hungary.

I to'ed and fro'ed from Budapest on several occasions during the shoot and later when I tendered together with my local partners for other projects. In spite of my limited success there I always enjoyed 'touristing' the place with the majestic Danube transecting the town and the company of what now have become friends. The local eateries vied with each other as to which one of them could dish out a goulash that would stand comparison to the one my Hungarian aunt would serve up. One or two of them came pretty close. I avoided the ever-growing number of gambling dens that seemed to dominate the city centre and was, therefore, rich enough to overnight in some of the more distinguished hotels in town. I particularly remember the Boscolo, Autograph Collection, which dates back to the $19^{th}$ century with its Victorian (Austrian, Hungarian) elegance that, at the same time, offered its guests the air-conditioned comforts one would expect from an up-market, modern establishment.

By far the most enjoyable experience I had in the town was when I, on another occasion, visited the open-air theatre on Margaret Island. My daughter, Sammy, was appearing in The Rocky Horror Show that was touring Europe. This was one of the venues on their schedule and, like any doting dad, I made sure I was there to witness the performance. Unlike any other doting dad I did not get the feeling that my presence during this explicit musical embarrassed her. On the contrary she proudly introduced me to the rest of the company of players who assured me that she was the best thing that happened to them and that she significantly contributed to the success of the show. That may not be exactly what they said but that is exactly what I heard.

Six weeks on, Evita returned for location work to the UK. We had just three days to complete the move that, having to cross six borders (into Austria, Germany, The Netherlands, Belgium, and France then from Calais to Dover) with the countless documents to be stamped up, was a challenge. We set up the base in front of the Officers' Mess in Halton near Tring in Hertfordshire where the interior of the building would feature in the film.

I tried again to meet up with Antonio and Alan Parker but they had better things to do. It was a matter of so near yet so far. And, as far as Madonna is concerned, I have since found other idols but have nevertheless kept her signed photograph to remind me of what could have been. Dream on!

# Greece

Patras. Make sure you are on the right boat.

Corinthian Canal. Doing the touristy thing

# Danish Adventures

Greenland

Slaughter of whales

I am the Greatest !

Not the M25

Will Smith: I am Ali

# Spy Game

Photo: Keith Hamshere

Robert Redford and Brad Pitt off screen.

A Real Thing for a Make Believe Show

# Moroccan Days

Its Going Nowhere (Jewel of the Nile)

Jason Looking for the Pub (Good Luck!)

Costume Truck

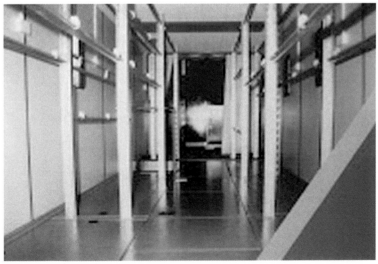

Costume Truck Interior

Units Cars

Truck Mounted Generator

# Latvia

Riga

Rundale Castle

# Lithuania

The Dunes

Vilnius Winter

# Goal II

Madrid

The Barnebeau

# The Willie The Wheel Award Winners

Jon Chu

Heather McKay with Monster

David Rosenbaum

Mark Dilliway

Patrick Totatopolous

Some of my new friends Paul, yours truly,
Brian, Barry , and Martin

**Phil Allchin with Katerina Ruskova (1) and Marik Kalawski(r)**

**Jasmine Mitchell**

# 30 Smilla's Sense of Snow 1997

## Frosty Reunion

The last time I worked with this production team was in sunny Portugal during the making of The House of Spirits. This time it was to be freezing Denmark and even frostier Greenland in winter. The welcoming party included Berndt Eichinger, the moneyman, Dieter Meyer, now promoted to line producer, and Billie August, the director, with his Danish crew. Other than Guy Travers, the first AD, I did miss the British assistants who were replaced by their Danish counterparts who, back in Portugal, were the assistants to the assistants and were now assistant directors in their own right.

The story of Smilla, an Inuit, follows her instinct that both a father and his son were murdered and, therefore, did not die accidentally. She used her intuition to solve the mystery by travelling from Copenhagen to Greenland where one of the suspects was working as a scientist. The book was a bestseller and, as with The House of Spirits, the producers hoped that with a star studded cast it would return a good profit. Again, it eventually attracted a respectable audience in Germany and selected European countries but failed commercially in the most important American market place. Other than Vanessa Redgrave there were no Oscar winners in the cast this time. Jim Broadbent was awarded one later, Tom Wilkinson had been nominated and Gabriel Byrne was a Golden Globe winner while Richard Harris was to liven up procedures from time to time.

The home of the Little Mermaid and Hans Christian Anderson had been overtaken by The Tivoli Gardens as a 'must visit' site. Not because of the gardens themselves that housed an impressive funfair but because of the surrounding quarters that apparently spawned the first legalised pornographic industry. Live shows of depravity and sexual deviation were the main attractions that raised most of my men's blood pressure. There was no stopping them spending their not so hard earned money on these dubious pleasures. They were then able to walk away with a bagful of related magazines as souvenirs to remember the day by and to be used as evidence that they had had the good fortune, if fortune it was, to witness these unique performances. For my part, gynaecology is not my favourite subject. I, therefore, had to see no evil, hear no evil and speak no evil when the subject came up in conversation.

In the event, except for the said Guy Travers, we were the only crewmembers from the UK. In addition to our normal vehicles we brought with us one of our double decker buses that had been converted to a mobile dining room by removing all the seats and replacing them with tables and benches. This provided not only a shelter and warmth during meal times but also a safe haven from the cold when permission was granted to take a break from the set.

To avoid inconveniencing the good citizens of Copenhagen a police escort would lead the way from one location to another. It also, in those pre sat nav days, helped us reach our destination by the shortest and quickest route. The convoy of production vehicles consisted of an assortment of some 12 vehicles including motor homes, trailers and the soon to prove to be our Achilles Heel, mobile diner. This well-meaning arrangement backfired when the police outrider, unfamiliar with the height of our bus, tried to lead us under a low bridge. Fortunately Bryan, the driver, spotted the height restriction in time and stopped in mid flow there and then with the rest of us piling up behind him. The red-faced policeman got off his bike and tried single handedly to clear the roadway to allow the bus to reverse away from the overhead obstruction.

A comedy of errors ensued as some motorists obeyed his instructions but others decided that they knew better and tried to edge past the stranded bus, only to find themselves facing an oncoming vehicle head on with no room to allow it to pass. In the meantime others followed the culprit thus blocking off a possible retreat. Chaos, accompanied by protestations and continuous horn blasts, ensued. The cool Danes were cool no longer. Eventually a van full of uniformed helpers arrived to restore order. It was only then that we managed to reverse and take an alternative route that saw us on set an hour later than expected. As a result, it was decided that in future we would dispense with official guidance. It would be up to the drivers themselves to check out the roads for hazards before embarking on the journey to their next location.

Strictly regulated working hours, as they are all over Scandinavia and the lack of daylight giving rise to very short days, meant we could enjoy more leisure time than was usual in our industry. Again I was not needed for much of the time so I restricted my presence to short visits. My drivers, however, honed their skills of ten-pin bowling and surfing TV channels. Their usual pastime on location of visiting bars and eateries was heavily curtailed by the high costs of alcohol and food in what must be one of the most expensive cities in Europe.

One or two drivers were more fortunate when they befriended local talent. This, in turn, helped to pass the time with less costly and better quality entertainment. In one case, it led to a more permanent relationship that was followed by setting up home in the UK. They were to live happily ever after though 'ever' lasted just a couple of years.

On set the director was looking to add a ship's cook to the cast. The boat in question was an old rusty trawler with a crew that one would not want to meet not just in a dark alley but also anywhere in bright daylight. Unkempt, scar faced with ripped clothing and an aggressive stance, our 6'3" Tiny, with his 20 stone bulk and permagrease outfit would, with only a little help from make-up and costume, fit the bill perfectly. Much to the amusement of his fellow drivers he stepped on to the stage and followed directions like an old pro. Applause on 'Cut' and a small fee as a reward made him a star for the day. Unfortunately it only lasted a day because the relevant frames ended on the cutting room floor.

Some of the scenes demanded snow and, as Copenhagen only provided ice and a frozen sea, reliable snowscapes would only be found inside the Arctic Circle. Money no object, we all packed up our equipment and flew up north. If the mountain would not come to......The drivers left their vehicles back in town and were handed skimobiles to move cast, crew and equipment to and forth. To say they had fun was an understatement. Racing over miles and miles of snow egging each other on was an unforgettable experience. Shame it only lasted for a few days. Like all good things it had to come to an end.

Back in Copenhagen we packed our bags and made ready for the return trip to Blighty to a warmer clime and a chance to thaw out, yet we did leave a bit of our proverbial heart behind.

Our love affair with Denmark and some of the local film crew came to an abrupt end when we were asked to service their next project, Barbara, to be shot on the Faroe Islands. Apart from the awful crossing from Peterhead, our arrival coincided with one of the most horrifying local customs, the mass slaughter of pilot whales rounded up and driven on to the beach. The waters turned red with blood and our Danish friends were looking on like spectators cheering on matadors at a bullfight. A sickening sight does not begin to describe our feelings and it took all the drivers' self control to last the distance. No more Danes for them.

Years later when working on Wallander in Southern Sweden the crew included a number of Danes whom we either knew from yesteryear or with whom we shared common friends. It is a strange human characteristic that one only remembers the good times while less enjoyable experiences fade away. It was great to reminisce and the renewed friendships have lasted to this day.

# 31 Oktober 1997
## The High Point, Literally

Some of the scenes in this mini series were set in the Alps and, after many location scouts covering most Swiss and French mountain peaks, the production settled on the Aiguille du Midi in the Mont Blanc massif. It is 3,842 metres high and can be reached by cable car from Chamonix. I had visited Chamonix many times during my ill-spent youth when special weekend trains ran from Paris on Friday nights and returned on Monday mornings. The idea was that one slept on the train (en couchette) on both outward and return journeys and in the carriage, which sat on a siding, on the Saturday night. This gave me the chance to go skiing, après skiing and do the unmentionable, French style, over the weekend.

I was now looking forward to revisiting my past but, before I could do so, I had to get my fleet of production vehicles there. As luck would have it, the French lorry drivers held a weeklong protest by either staging a go slow along the motorways or blocking them altogether. This meant we had to travel the long way round via Belgium, Germany and Switzerland eventually crossing into France near Geneva - simple, not quite! Switzerland is not a member of the EU and we needed carnets (transit documents) to cross the border. It was essential that these carnets were stamped on entering and signed again on leaving the country. Failing to do so could result in being made liable for import duties and a fine. I had great faith in my drivers but, just to make sure and because they were not familiar with this procedure, I waited for them at the border post in order to assist them if need be. It all went to plan except that there was no sign of our electricians.

We were due to be ready the following day and management decided not to take a chance and ordered emergency electrical equipment at great expense as cover for the missing items. I left the border post and arrived that evening at Chamonix early enough to notice that it was no longer the place I had left behind all those years ago. It had turned from quaint mountain village to a densely populated city, from a one-horse town to, and I am not exaggerating, a floodlit conurbation. Apartment buildings vied for roadside positions with hotels of every size displaying plaques with anything from five stars to no stars.

The restaurants, coffee shops and boutiques would not have been out of place anywhere in any town in the Western hemisphere. The only giveaways were the odd shops displaying ski equipment and the signposts directing the visitor to the countless cable cars and ski lifts in the area. The streets were stuffed full of vehicles that, in the French tradition, were parked at odd angles bumper to bumper without an undamaged panel in sight.

The electricians arrived in the early hours having driven through the night. Like rebellious teenagers they resented the fact that we did not trust them to make it in time. In any case they got held up at the border - really?! And, more credibly, they had lost all their running money. On examining their tachometer disc it appeared that they had taken a detour of some 80 miles, coincidently exactly the distance to and from the German Gambling Spa of Baden Baden to the Autobahn, which had been marked out as a direct route from UK to Chamonix.

A unit base had to be set up as close to the lower cable car station as possible from where all the shooting equipment could be carried into the cabin that would take us up the mountain. A lot of paperwork (fortunately my schoolboy French came in handy) and the inevitable fees later we managed to secure the section of the car park closest to the entrance, forcing the public to go the long way round.

After a couple of scenes shot at the entrance to the departure point it was up to the top with the camera kit and all the other bits of equipment destined for the restaurant/viewing terrace overlooking the rocky and snow covered mountains of the awesome Mont Blanc massif. Over 3,800m above sea level the air gets pretty thin and breathing normally is an acquired skill. The crew, unaccustomed to these working conditions, soon started to feel unwell. As a precaution we had oxygen bottles at hand that helped some of the crew to carry on. Others, namely our leading man Stephen Tompkinson and the electricians, believed that alcohol in the blood would do the trick and promptly self medicated.

More seriously our DOP suffered a suspected heart attack and the unit nurse and two of my drivers, who helped with the props, were overcome with nausea. They elected to descend back to the base where I got ready, together with a couple of paramedics, to replace the sick that had left the set. During the trip up the medics revealed the secret of how to get used to the 'High Life'. When reaching the mountain top station, step out very slowly and climb the 50 steps up to the set at an even slower pace. It seemed to work and I stayed up there for the rest of the day occasionally moving a table from one corner to another and at one point helping the focus puller to measure the distance from the camera to the object in shot. We left most of the gear up there overnight and for the rest of the shooting week at the end of which the equipment was brought down and loaded back on to the trucks without my help.

Our locally recruited crew, mainly minibus drivers and charge hands, guided us to various eateries and bars strewn across the town where new friendships were formed. I remember in particular a Norwegian blonde who seemed very keen to show us the sights and who, I think, was looking for more than just a driving job. Someone must have obliged because in the morning she was spotted bleary-eyed stepping out of someone's hotel room. Next stop Geneva!

The script took us to a five star hotel on the shores of the lake. We parked our circus in a car park across the road along the water's edge and touristed for the rest of the day ready for a night shoot. My itinerary included the Reformers Wall with its statues of the four main preachers, Guillaume Farel, Theodore de Beze and the more familiar John Knox and Jean Calvin of Calvinist fame. Other worthwhile sites to visit were the Place des Nations with its sculpture of the Broken Chair that symbolises the fight against anti-personnel mines, of which Princess Diana was a prolific advocate, and the giant fountain just offshore in the lake facing our unit base.

Switzerland - and especially Geneva - is famous for its prices so the only person who could indulge in the local offerings was our leading man. He obviously enjoyed it so much that he did not realise the effect it had on his ability to stand up and report to the set. Caution to the wind and to hell with the expense, coffee - and seemingly gallons of it - had to be employed to get our man onto the job. In spite of his diluted blood stream he delivered his lines faultlessly.

It was Friday and our last night on location. We got what sleep we could get before setting off back home to report to Pinewood Studios on Monday morning for the remainder of the shoot. The truckers' dispute had been resolved and we could travel straight through France to Calais where we would catch the ferry to Dover. The problem was that large vehicles, of which we had a few, had to clear the country before midnight to escape the weekend driving ban that was being enforced throughout the continent. This meant driving non-stop which, in turn, would break the driving hours rule that required regular rest periods and specified maximum driving hours. These restrictions did not apply to the lighter vehicles or the motor homes. We thus could stretch the law by juggling the drivers around by letting them at intervals change over from heavy to light vehicles.

It all worked out except again for the electricians who refused to co-operate and decided that they deserved a break in Paris for which they could claim another day's wages and living allowance. The producers had to double up on the missing equipment and filming resumed with the replaced equipment and a new set of electricians.

The series received great acclaim but in the back of my mind I wondered if all the effort was worth it as, in my humble opinion, the photography did not do justice to the magnificence of our mountaintop location. Still it was an enjoyable, interesting and, above all, profitable excursion into my past.

# 32 The Man in the Iron Mask 1998

## Late? Explain!

It was a pleasant surprise to hear from old clients/friends Ariel Levy, with whom we had fun and games in Egypt on The Sphinx, and Rene Dupont, who gave me my first mega job on Silver Dream Racer. Rene was the co-producer and about to start shooting The Man in the Iron Mask with Ariel as the unit production manager. Antony Studios, 10 miles south of Paris, provided the stages on which the set for the interior shots would be built, while filming exterior scenes would take place on locations within easy reach of our base, no further than 50 miles away.

The local French contractors had brought along their motor homes but they were deemed not good enough for the leading artists, Leonardo DiCaprio (before the release of Titanic), Jeremy Irons, John Malkovitch, Gabriel Byrne and, making his directorial debut for the big screen, Randall Wallace. It was allegedly gifted to him as a reward for writing the script of the box office hit that was Braveheart. Gerard Depardieu, who broke onto the international scene by appearing in Green Card, had now turned into a patriot and dismissed my American trailer as decadent. He opted to slum it in a locally kitted-out contraption. Ironically, just a few years later, his patriotism gave way to his political convictions (or need for publicity) and he exchanged his birthright for a new life in Russia. I suppose being Putin's friend beats a career as a traitor in his own country or an also-ran in Hollywood.

To their disappointment, not to mention annoyance, the indigenous companies were reduced to a supporting role while we were leading the charge to look after the stars. We dispatched three motor homes and two trailers of matching quality, a make-up trailer and a costume truck and parked up in front of the studio building, which lacked suitable dressing rooms and workspaces ready for immediate use. Three drivers stayed on to keep an eye on and maintain the vehicles. They were booked into a nearby hotel and used the pick-up truck to commute and run errands. Soon they befriended the French crew and the initial resentment petered out.

On several occasions additional trailers were required and I took the opportunity to visit Paris by undertaking to deliver them myself. On my first such trip I called on one of my oldest friends (my best man) who lived on the fourth floor on Victor Hugo in the 16eme (very posh) arrondissement. I did not know him to be a keen gardener and was surprised to notice, looking up from the street below, a couple of flower boxes full of plants. On closer inspection my suspicions were confirmed. He was growing his own smoking matter and it was not tobacco. Strangely enough it was typical of him to challenge convention with no fear of what may result. For my part, I would not have had the cheek or courage to risk the consequences. On every one of my following visits I drove along the street to check on the flowerpots that adorned his windows and was relieved to notice that they were still there. This meant my friend continued to enjoy his freedom and his homegrown weed.

Back at the ranch things proceeded to plan except that the director and the producers no longer saw eye-to-eye, not to mention the public rows that ensued. Something had to give and it was Randall, our director, who ended up on top. Consequently a change in leadership was afoot. Rene and Ariel stepped down and were replaced unceremoniously by Paul Hitchcock, the former financial controller and a leading light at Warner Brothers, as co-producer and Steve Harding as UPM (unit production manager), with whom I had worked several times before when he was still an assistant director. Both were UK based but neither had up to that moment employed my services - for some unknown reason they preferred to engage one of my competitors on their projects. This time though they had little choice as the artists had settled down well into my vehicles and they had enough on their plate taking over a production half way through shooting with a director who had solidified his status and artists, especially DiCaprio, about to hit the very big time.

Still, we were on trial. I was handed a chance to demonstrate our professionalism and convince my erstwhile enemies that we could handle location facilities as well or even better than any of my competitors who had previously enjoyed Paul's and Steve's custom. Sadly, we did by all accounts do a good job but did not succeed in prizing them away from their usual suppliers. Still we lived in hope.

One of the locations was the Chateau de Vaux-le-Vicomte 65 kms from the studio bypassing Paris through its southern suburbs. Our drivers were given a movement order, i.e. detailed directions with a time scale. It allowed for one and a half hours of travel that involved crossing several main arterial roads that led in and out of the capital. While the crew departed from their town centre hotels and travelled against the morning rush hour traffic, the drivers had to crawl along country roads and were held up for what seemed hours every time they had to cross a main thoroughfare.

Inevitably they took more than two hours to reach their destination and were welcomed by an irritated crew and unhappy producers. I trusted my drivers when they assured me that they followed the movement order to the letter. In order to shed light on their failure to turn up on time, I decided to make my way to the set and have a face-to-face meeting with them. I arrived in the afternoon (flight to Charles de Gaulle and hire car) and, after a short conversation, I asked the assistant responsible for the movement order to show me how he managed to cover the journey in the time he allowed for the trucks. Gung Ho he led me to the main gate of the chateaux and, handing me a crash helmet, swung his leg over the top of his motorbike and announced: "Allons y", "let's go!!"

I just stood there dumbfounded. There was nothing I could do but turn away and, without a word, I walked back to my drivers and reassured them that, as far as I was concerned, all was well. When I tried to explain that morning's incident to the producers they were otherwise engaged. In any case it had all happened many hours ago and, as the show was back on track, nobody seemed very interested. I left it to the drivers to educate the culprit. Needless to say he disappeared never to be seen again.

Away from work Sheila and I, together with another couple, often enjoyed a weekend break at a European destination. Paris was on the list and we decided to visit the city when an opportunity arose to mix business with pleasure. After an obligatory walk up and down the Champs Elysees we passed a restaurant that advertised Alsacian dishes. I am partial to choucroute (sauerkraut with a selection of boiled meats) and had little difficulty in convincing my wife and friends to sample it. The long walk called for a comfort break. We took it in turns in order not to lose our table that we were lucky to secure in the lunchtime rush. Lynn, my friend's wife, admitted to having a weak bladder and hence went first.

When she returned ten minutes or so later I hardly recognised her. She was hyperventilating, with her pale complexion even paler. She was reaching out for her chair and, as we helped her back on to her seat wondering what had happened to make her lose her composure, the story unfolded. Once she settled down she had noticed an unusual commotion in the cubicle next to hers. When, however, a pair of men's trousers fell to the floor and crept under the elevated partition into her space, it occurred to her that she might have wandered into the male section by mistake. No big deal, she would wait until he finished, then leave in a hurry and just shrug her shoulders if challenged.

Just as she was coming to terms with her situation, both female and male groans began to fill the air. The well brought up lady from the right side of the tracks froze. Her buttocks stuck to the seat and she was unable to move for fear of being discovered in close proximity to a performance that in her world should have been confined to the bedroom. I tried with the support of her husband to explain that this is France. Here sex is nothing to be ashamed of and, unlike someone who has lived a sheltered life in a leafy suburb, the Parisians are far less inhibited where lovemaking is concerned.

She was not convinced. She could not get over the fact that it all happened an arm's length away from her. When the food arrived and the plate contained sausages laid out in a suggestive manner, she lost her appetite completely. On leaving the restaurant she spotted the offending couple at a table near the exit. She froze again when they acknowledged her with a knowing smile. Her embarrassment was palpable and, even though it did not take us long to laugh off the incident, I can still make her blush by reminding her of the meal that she did not eat.

The film received a Royal premiere and I was allocated four tickets, with money going to a charity, for the event in the Odeon Leicester Square. I took my wife and two youngest, Adam and Natalie, and as we walked on the red carpet surrounded by celebrities Adam, in his Sunday best, was mistaken for a VIP. He enjoyed the attention and began to play to the gallery responding to the screams from the crowd with elaborate gestures. I just about managed to stop him from signing autographs.

# 33 Ronin and Plenty 1998 and 1985

## Know Your Place

I have always considered myself to be well mannered, respectful of my fellow men and tolerant of the shortcomings of colleagues. John Frankenheimer is none of these. If one adds shouty, rude and opinionated then one would get close to summing up his character. I don't like to speak ill of the dead but it is important to understand the atmosphere that dominated our time together. The fact that we shared an interest in tennis and agreed that Robert Mitchum was one of the best actors of all time only rarely lightened the gloom under which we worked.

I was invited to an interview by Derek Kavanagh, the production manager, whom I knew quite well as we went back to the Pink Panther franchise and, more recently, The Jewel of the Nile. The production offices were set up at the Saint Denis Studios north of Paris on the top floor of a building that had seen better days many years ago. I was met and then ushered into a large open space with desks randomly laid out and occupied by timid youngsters buried in paperwork. I felt like a headmaster entering a classroom to make sure the pupils were all busy with their studies. Normally, such an office would be a buzzing beehive with old and young moving about chatting and balancing plastic cups around the room. Not here, just gloom and a fear of letting the side, or more accurately the boss, down.

In the far corner was a cubicle where I was to meet my counterpart. I didn't know who was more relieved; me entering a welcoming water hole or Derek seeing an old friend who reminded him of the cheerful and easygoing times we shared on previous workouts. It appeared that Frankenheimer thought that France - and Paris in particular - owed him total obedience and that anything he needed to realise his vision had to be made available, irrespective of the chaos and inconvenience it may cause to its good citizens. After all, he put the country on the international map when he shot The French Connection II in Marseille and Grand Prix, which won three Academy Awards, in and around Clermont Ferrand. A standoff ensued. The French film crew, who were concerned about their jobs, lobbied the City Authorities. They were mindful of the repercussions a traffic gridlock would cause and would not relent. "Who does this man think he is?" was the administration's initial reaction "We are not going to dance to this American's tune, however famous he may be" (loosely translated from French). It was said that Frankenheimer literally stormed into the Mayor's office, dropped a few names and agreed to part with an outrageous amount of cash. The bullyboy, pleased with himself and branding the location manager as useless, got a permit to close off a section of the Peripherique to stage his car chase.

As far as the location facility vehicles were concerned he only cared about a luxury motor home for himself and an equally well-equipped trailer for his leading man, Robert De Niro. Everyone else would have to make do with what was available locally i.e. basic and, more importantly, cheap. I did wonder why Derek tolerated such instructions but, as he explained optimistically, if the French equipment was not good enough for his cast and crew he would, when the time came, threaten to resign if he did not get clearance to order more suitable vehicles. He did resign.

It was left to me to provide the said motor home and trailer. The only problem was that I only had the motor home ready to go and had to sub-contract the supply of the trailer for De Niro to an owner-driver (later to become a major supplier). The shoot went ahead on schedule and the director, with his impossible demands, had the French crew running around like headless chickens, stopping traffic, diverting pedestrians and putting up with horns blasting and insults flying. My drivers just stood there watching with amusement the ensuing rage of the inconvenienced citizens and the hair tearing out of the poor assistants. Schadenfreude is a great pastime.

The mood lightened up a bit when Robert De Niro found a diversion from the constant shouting that, though it was never directed at him, he still wanted to escape from occasionally. It came in the form of a couple of allegedly professional ladies of the night whom he indiscreetly paraded around the set. Not only that, but he made no effort to conceal them when he returned in their company to his hotel where they stayed until the early hours. On the other hand they could have been old friends or innocent and excited fans who happened to be staying legitimately in the same hotel at the same time. It did, nevertheless, attract the attention of the media who jumped to the worst possible conclusion and a scandal was brewing. It took friends in high places to minimise the damage to his reputation.

Eventually the production left Paris for the South of France where the unit base was set up on the back lot of the Victorine Studios in Nice. The owner-driver of De Niro's trailer decided that he would promote himself to the position of personal assistant to our leading man. It transpired that he was what we would call 'star struck', something that among the crew was deemed unprofessional. He spent his time finding excuses to walk in and out of De Niro's trailer, engaging him in conversation and constantly offering to be of service. It came to a head when Robert's wife and mother-in-law visited the set and he decided to introduce himself as if he was an old friend. Embarrassment all round and I was summoned to the South of France to diplomatically prize him away from the set. Initially I seemed to have succeeded but found out later that he indeed managed to befriend our star. He even agreed to build a bespoke trailer for his exclusive use on future assignments.

Not so lucky was one of my other drivers who looked after Johnny Depp's trailer on Sleepy Hollow. Again he went out of his way to attend to Johnny's every need, virtual and real. On completion of principal photography Johnny Depp, as was his way, thanked him and complimented him with a remark about how much he would appreciate it if he could have such a good assistant back at home in Paris. What the driver thought he heard, however, was that he was being offered a job as an assistant to the Depp family in France.

His first duty would be to deliver a motorbike to his house just outside the French capital. To be able to do this he needed to borrow a truck that I gladly let him have. When I heard about his 'life changing' opportunity, I tried to persuade him that he must have misunderstood the remark. After all, how could he be of any use if he could not speak the language? Nothing would persuade him. He even believed that a translator would be hired to overcome this temporary difficulty until he had learned enough French to stand on his own feet. Misguided does not begin to describe his plans. I lent him a truck and, accompanied by his wife, (at some point Johnny Depp remarked that he would love to meet her) he set off. On arrival he pulled up outside Johnny's house, knocked on the door and soon afterwards someone enquired from a first floor window as to what he wanted. "I have come with Mr. Depp's motorbike" but, before he could add that he expected to start a new life there, the voice responded: "Thank you, just leave it in front of the garage" and disappeared back into the building and out of sight. So there he stood lost for words with his dumbfounded wife by his side.

I don't think he ever recovered and neither did Johnny Depp forget the incident because, when he next worked in the UK, he specifically stated that he did not wish this particular driver to attend to his trailer again. Just a lesson about knowing one's place!

I must admit that I did once break the rules about not allowing a member of the public to address and meet the stars. We were working on Plenty with Meryl Streep. An English couple that had settled in the Dordogne engaged me in a conversation about life in general and particularly about the film industry. Gordon's pride and joy was his collection of film posters, of which he apparently had several thousands, and Jennifer, his wife, seemed to know everything there was to know about the French impressionists. When I mentioned my favourite artist, Modigliani, her vocal floodgates opened. A quarter of an hour into her lecture her eye line shifted from my face to something she spotted behind me over my shoulder. As she pointed to whatever captured her attention, she began to hyperventilate. I turned around only to realise that Meryl Streep had just got out of her car and climbed into her trailer.

A few minutes later Jennifer recovered her composure and wondered if she could ask Ms Streep for an autograph. Apart from looking after my trailers I am also expected to protect the artists from unwanted attention. This time, however, against my better judgement I promised to liase with the girl from publicity after wrap and have an answer in the morning. Jennifer and Gordon turned up as expected the next day armed with a poster for Kramer v. Kramer. Meryl was briefed and she graciously agreed to meet my new, soon to become my grateful and lifelong, friends. She signed their poster before she got into her car that made off to the set. Once they recovered from their Meet the Star experience Jennifer fetched another poster from her car and handed it to me as a present. It was the poster for 19 Montparnasse, the 1958 film about Modigliani starring Gerard Philipe, Anouk Aimee and Lilli Palmer. I was touched and have added it to my own collection of memorabilia from the Belle Époque. It only goes to show that it occasionally pays to break the rules, especially when an unassuming and sympathetic celebrity is involved.

After France the schedule took the unit to Tunisia. Although I did not join my drivers on this location I recall the story told by Meryl's driver, Colin Morris. He was handed a rental car, ostensibly the best available locally. By all account it was a wreck with none of the dials on the dashboard giving out a correct reading, a suspension with worn out shock absorbers that resulted in an up and down motion similar to that of a small fishing vessel battling a rough sea. It was accompanied by a constant rattle from the interior fittings that had worked themselves loose over the twenty or so years since it left the factory.

At one point the shoot in mid desert wrapped but, as the crew needed some time to pack up their equipment, Meryl and her co star Tracy Ullman decided not to wait until everyone could travel in convoy back to the hotel. They jumped into their car with Colin at the wheel and made their way through the sandy landscape that stretched as far as the eye could see. The petrol gauge showed Half Full. It was, as were all the other gauges, faulty and the car rolled to a halt in mid desert with no living soul in sight. Colin's charges did not seem too perturbed because they knew that sooner or later the crew buses would pass through on their way back from the location. Half an hour later they espied sand clouds whirling up from where they expected the film unit to come from. "Can you put on a cassette, Colin?" Meryl asked.

Naturally he complied and, as soon as the music started to blare out, our muses got out of the car, climbed on to the roof and started to dance wildly with thumbs up attracting the attention of the oncoming traffic. The sight of these two mega stars gyrating on top of a car in the middle of the desert stays with him to this day. His biggest regret is that he was unable to immortalise the scene by taking a photograph of the incident. (It was, of course, before mobile phones would oblige). Naturally the unit vehicles stopped and gave our girls a lift while Colin had to stay behind in these god-forsaken surroundings. After the longest hour of his life help, in the form of a jerry can full of petrol, arrived. Nobody blamed him when he refused to carry on driving this contraption and he was given a ride back to civilisation in the private jet that was hired for the use of our powers that be.

# 34 The Tenth Kingdom 1999

## Ted's Swan Song

I met Ted Morley back in the mid-eighties when the restaurant at Pinewood Studios played daily host to the men and women of the film industry's production managers in waiting. Waiting for the phone call that would turn them from seeking a job to holding a job. A job that would mean that they would be giving jobs to technicians that make up a film crew and, most importantly, deciding which suppliers would be contracted to service the project.

Lunch went on all afternoon and was always a jolly, dare I say, inebriated affair with lots of anecdotes making the rounds. From time to time I joined in, not just for the laughs but also to engage in some networking. After all, someone at my table may soon manage or supervise a production and, with a bit of luck, I would be first in line to be offered a chance to supply the necessary facility vehicles.

It was on one such an occasion that I met Ted and, sharing a sense of humour, we became friends well before we did any business together. Our bit of business was done when he supervised the making of several episodes of Remington Steele, the TV series.

It was the first of many of his projects that I serviced and climaxed when he took charge of this production. As with our arrangement on Braveheart, I took on the responsibility for supplying vehicles from my own fleet at 'arm's length' (matching competitive rates) and contracting in additional trucks from related suppliers, not to mention helpful competitors if and when needed. The deal with Ted was, as usual, non-negotiable. He handed me a cross plot detailing the vehicles and the drivers he would need with the price he was willing to pay alongside each item. Naturally it was not as much as I hoped for, but he knew that I knew that he knew that his offer was a fair one. Only a twinkle in his eye betrayed the fact that he had a contingency in the budget that allowed for additional payments to cover unforeseen circumstances and bonus payments for the drivers that allowed me to motivate them with a carrot rather than a stick.

This mini series told the story of the heroine and her father travelling into the nine kingdoms of the popular children's characters of Snow White, Little Red Riding Hood and Cinderella where their kingdoms were threatened by trolls, ogres and goblins. They eventually reached The Tenth Kingdom where everyone would live happily ever after.

With a budget of $44.000.000 for five two-hour episodes the production was scheduled to shoot on quite a few locations. It would take us to Austria for four of them and then to France for another four sets. In the UK we would travel to half a dozen locations as well as shoot some scenes at Pinewood Studios. The establishing shots in New York would not involve me other than having to arrange for airport transfers for the cast, crew and their equipment. The production designers in conjunction with the directors (there were two that alternated between episodes) visited and settled on all the locations except for the set that was to feature the castle central to the story. Time was running out and, because I had previously worked in Austria, Ted asked me to accompany him and the designer to search the country for a location we could all agree on.

The brief was to find a castle or palace overlooking a river from a great height, the sort of fortification a robber baron would occupy. We spent two days driving along the Danube from Vienna to Passau and rejected every castle-like structure on her embankments. I then remembered the location used on Where Eagles Dare at Werfen, South of Salzburg. Schloss Hohenwerfen stands 100 metres high above the town of Werfen on the banks of the river Salzach. That was it! A castle in good condition (not a ruin) with a river below and a history in the film business. The only snag would be accessibility. The cable car would be too expensive to operate in the off season and, therefore, we would have to use small pick up trucks to ferry equipment and personnel up and down the narrow path carved into the rock face. Fortunately we could source a few of them locally without drawing out cold sweat from Ted's brow, who would otherwise have to rework the budget to fund the rental of such vehicles from as far away as Vienna.

Nothing worth reporting occurred during our journey to Hallstatt, our first base in Austria. Our scenes were going to be shot high above the town in a salt mine, which contained a subterranean lake. Spectacular by any standard. It had to be reached via a cable car that carried all the necessary equipment, crew and cast to the set. This meant that once we parked up we, the drivers and me, could sit back and enjoy the scenery. At one point we took out a boat and fantasised about raising the Nazi Gold that was rumoured to be languishing at the bottom of that very lake. As clear as the water was it was too cold and too deep for a diving expedition that would give away its secrets. We tried to console ourselves with a spot of fishing that, unsurprisingly, bore no fruit either.

Next, a lake of a very different kind. The mountain reservoirs of Kaprun 2000 metres above sea level where the water is held back by a dam that is over 100 metres high and half a kilometre long. Vehicles could be loaded on to the platform of an eight hundred meter long elevator, the tallest in Europe, which would be dragged up the incline over iron rails by a wire cable. The problem was that it could only accommodate one truck at a time which meant that getting our five essential vehicles up there took nearly two hours. That's a total of four hours out of our working day which we had not allowed for. Consequently we spent a day longer there than planned with our Ted rolling his eyes to the sky while working out where he could save money to make up for this unexpected expense.

I, for my part, could not get enough time to wonder at this huge structure with its record-breaking features amidst the alpine mountainscape. What did affect me emotionally, though, were not the architectural merits of this project but the fact that it was built using Jewish slave labour.

Apart from his concerns about the budget Ted also worried about the dog that was central to the story. At this point I would like to add that Ted and his wife Alison are prolific animal lovers who, among others, look after abandoned donkeys in the field behind their house. Would it be able to perform in comfort at high altitude? It fell upon our transport captain Bryan to take the dog up the elevator for a test run. Although Bryan did not relish walking a dog, the dog seemed to relish his outing in the fresh mountain air.

Having visited the breathtaking Schloss Hochwerfen during our scouting trip, stunned by the subterranean lakes in the salt mines and overawed by spectacular structure of the dam at Kaprun, I did not think that I would be impressed by what was to follow.

The thousand feet high waterfalls at Krimml thunder down the rock face with such force that reminded me of how powerful and untameable nature can be. How insignificant digging out mineshafts or erecting monumental structures is compared to the crushing weight that pounds down through the air and on to the riverbed below, relentlessly from time immemorial to eternity.

We stayed for a couple of days in the village of Krimml where some of the crew and drivers found friendly female company whose traditional Dirndl costume is worn over a tight corset. It squeezes their midriffs and lifts their bulging bosoms, which are scantily covered, up towards their chins leaving little to the imagination. Many were seduced into finding out what lay beneath the revealing outfits and some, I understood, did succeed in freeing the maidens from their constricting underwear and were rewarded for their efforts. In fact, one of my boys was so taken by the experience that he jumped ship and decided to live the dream from that day on. It is rumoured that he married his erstwhile friend and is now clad in a pair of Lederhosen, working as a tourists' guide.

My favourite set was the castle at Werfen. It stands high up on a solitary rock with just a narrow roadway chiselled out of its elevation. It was a long way down to the river below, not a place for sufferers of vertigo. Needless to say, only the essential camera equipment, loaded on to a pick up truck and a minibus shuttling the cast and crew up and down, would be allowed into the castle yard. The rest of us parked in the village below twiddling our thumbs while all the action took place high above.

While there, I often recounted a story about a young lady I had met in the early sixties who, apart from being extremely good looking, was great fun to be with. She worked - as far as I could remember - in the Goldener Hirsch, an upmarket hotel in Salzburg. Ted and a couple of others showed some interest in my stories and we all decided to pay the place a visit. I remembered her well, though I had forgotten her name, and I feared quite rightly that if she were still there she would be, as she was then, my age. Secretly I feared she would be quite old and ravaged by time. I was prepared and spent the journey listening to the ribbing I got about going to meet her grandchildren, some of whom may be mine.

In the event all that was left was the Goldener Hirsch itself; after all it was built in 1400, some 600 years ago, so the fifty years since my previous encounter were just a drop in the ocean and insignificant. My unrealistic expectations turned out to be unrealistic and Heidi, as we christened her, will remain forever the young and beautiful girl from my distant past. So I bought a very expensive round of drinks and, after a short stroll along the pedestrian zone of this historic city, it was back to our hotel deep in the valley upstream.

Next on the schedule was the Alsace Region of France. The journey took us on the Autobahn via Munich to Strasbourg where we crossed the Rhein River and then south into the Alsace proper where we stayed in the town of Mulhouse, the birthplace of the legendary Bugatti motorcars. Unfortunately, cars were not the reason for our visit. We set up the production office in the hotel and travelled in convoy, minus the mobile office, through the vineyard-covered countryside to our first location.

Unlike the rest of France the streets here were hoovered, the buildings whitewashed and the gardens immaculately presented. Walt Disney would have been proud to associate himself with such a spotless landscape - must have something to do with its German heritage. The Alsace changed allegiance from France to Germany on several occasions in history, the latest Germanisation lasted from 1871 to 1918 and, to this day, they pride themselves in their culinary skills that feature sauerkraut and boiled ham served with the regional white wine. Love it.

Before we all reached Mulhouse we had to cross the mountains of the Black Forest where the autobahn covers some steep inclines. All but our dining bus managed the ascent and the even slower descent in low gear. The dining bus, a converted single decker that had served London commuters some twenty years previously, struggled and eventually rebelled and stopped. The driver, Tiny a 6'3" 20 stone man in permanent blue overalls and with a voice audible at 500 yards, was in his element. Nothing excited him more than attending to a breakdown and spending time under a truck dripping with oil and handling greasy matter. He rejected help from all comers and six hours or so later had the bus rolling again albeit very slowly. Suffice to say that he checked into the hotel in the early hours and, being a pro at heart, did not go to sleep before he delivered the bus to the location ready for breakfast. It was only then that he collapsed and we had to get him back to the hotel to recover. We covered some other equally tidy and pristine locations in Kayserberg, Riquewihr and the Ecomusee in Ungersheim before we left the continent for the rest of the shoot back at home.

Next stop Pinewood for some interior shots and then to Bourne Woods. We had no problems to speak of getting back to Blighty. Our leading lady, Kimberly Williams of Father of the Bride fame, was at the time dating Pete Sampras who, having just completed his stint at Wimbledon, visited her on the set in mid forest. I admire most actors but my heroes are without doubt the high achieving sportsmen and women. Even more so tennis players who are closer to my heart because my son, Adam, is a tennis pro and has often explained the finer points of the game. Pete Sampras is, according to my third born, the most complete of all the competitors. I sidled up to him as he joined the queue that had formed by the catering truck but could only manage a wry smile which he returned as nothing emerged from my mouth, I just dried up. I hardly recognised myself, as I am not often known to be short of a word or two. "Pull yourself together, what would Adam say when he finds out that I stood next to 'the Man' and returned without recounting a snippet of conversation I had with him". When he got into his car to leave I managed to stick my head through the window and told him that he was my son's hero. "Oh" he mumbled, "Give him my regards" and off he sped. I spent the rest of the day regretting my inability to grab the chance I had to engage the great man in a conversation that I could recount to my son. What a hero I would have been! My daughter Sammy, who is a choreographer, fared a bit better when a folk dance was scheduled for a scene at a country show. Neither our director nor Kimberly were familiar with the required routine and Sammy was hired to direct the necessary movements.

The show wrapped soon afterwards and Ted, to all and sundry, emerged as the most admired if not loved production supervisor any of us had ever had the pleasure to work for. Unfortunately his popularity caused some resentment in the accounts department, a husband and wife team, who forever forecast gloom and financial disaster caused by Ted's handling of the production. Little did they appreciate that what Ted did not know about running a show was not worth knowing and in the end a successful and critically acclaimed series saw the light of day. Sadly the accountants' constant long faces and criticisms got through to the producers and Ted was never again asked to manage one of their future projects, even though he served them loyally for many years and on countless productions.

Even sadder is the fact that, before Ted could be hired by another producer, he passed away after a short illness. It is a mark of the respect and the admiration he enjoyed that the funeral parlour overflowed with mourners with standing room only for the latecomers. For my part I am dedicating this book to his memory.

# 35 Enemy at the Gate 2000

## The German Revival

Unlike the German industrial recovery after the Second World War, its film industry remained in the doldrums that befell it following the end of hostilities and division of the country into the West and East zones. The film Das Boot was, in over forty years, its only notable contribution to world cinema. It was shot in the Bavaria Studios near Munich that are home to commercials and unremarkable lowbrow productions similar to our Carry On films.

On reunification Babelsberg Studios, which were the mainstay of pre-war film making, developed an ambitious programme to re-establish themselves as a home for international large-scale productions. The studios occupy a 100-acre site with large sound stages and supporting workshops, prop storage buildings, costume department and offices that offer the Hollywood trained film maker the facility and infrastructure to satisfy his needs. The only drawback was that the whole site dated back to the earliest days of cinematography with additional structures erected during the Third Reich in the totalitarian style. It was like stepping back in time, yet still workable. Its plans were - and still are - supported by generous subsidies from both the central German government and the Federal state of Brandenburg where it is located. Government subsidies that support local industries contravene EU Laws as they give an unfair advantage to the recipient over his competitors in fellow member states of the Union. Nevertheless, the administration introduced a roundabout way of using tax credits to circumnavigate these restrictions. Not to be left out, many other members of the EU such as Great Britain, Belgium and, more recently, the Baltic States have introduced similar schemes and thus exposed the futility of such Laws.

Enemy at the Gate was one, if not the first, international big budget production to benefit from these tax breaks. It set up offices in Babelsberg and found a suitable location for the largest part of the shoot in a disused barracks complex some ten miles away on the outskirts of the city of Potsdam. These barracks were a monument to past German military might, order and discipline. One entered the site through double width ornate cast iron gates onto a half-mile long tree lined avenue with three storey accommodation blocks set back on either side. The parade ground at the far end was large enough for at least four football fields with a grandstand to hold some 100 dignitaries. In front of it stood a raised three-foot high platform where the commanding officer would stand to take the salute from his square bashing troops. To the right - and separated by a line of trees - were the workshops and the compound for the motorised units. To the left more accommodation blocks and, beyond, the munitions stores and an administration block which stood beyond the parade ground, again out of sight. The exercise fields with lots of muddy ditches overlooked what I imagined to be the punishment block covered with small barred windows that indicated that these were prison cells.

What must have once looked like a well-tendered garden city had been abandoned after the Berlin Wall came down some ten years previously. The brickwork was still in tact and amazingly the windowpanes were unbroken (no vandalism?) As for the rest, it was all overgrown and in places the weeds reached man height with trampled paths where wildlife made its way; deer, wild boar and an assortment of foxes, wild cats and stray dogs populated the grounds, not to forget the hoards of rats. The parade ground and all the other paved surfaces were cracking up leaving large potholes that had to be manoeuvred around carefully or traversed very slowly.

Although most of the buildings were erected during the thirties some of them dated back to the 1860's. This was when the legendary Prussian Army set out to invade France and helped the even more legendary Bismarck to consolidate the German Reich under Kaiser Wilhelm I, grandfather of the infamous Wilhelm II. The central officers' mess was obviously hastily whitewashed and, out of curiosity, we scratched the surface to discover communist slogans all over the walls. Deeper scratches brought Nazi propaganda into sight. There was no stopping us now and soon we uncovered army memorabilia from the First World War which, in turn, hid the names of heroes who passed away in the nineteenth century serving both the emerging German army and the preceding Prussian garrison, for whom these barracks were originally built. So here we were ready to transform this historic site into Stalingrad that was razed to the ground during the bitter fighting on the eastern front and which served as the backdrop to our story.

When the project was first mooted the producers were under the impression that the entire crew and facility vehicles could be sourced locally. It only later transpired that key personnel had to be brought in from abroad. When the second AD, who came from the UK and who would be responsible for looking after the artists, inspected what was available in terms of trailers, make-up, costume and the usual additional requirements - including drivers who were experienced enough to assist him - it was decided to call in the circus that formed the unit base from the UK. I managed to beat off competition from other suppliers and strike a deal.

Willies Wheels' convoy of 15 vehicles created a bit of a stir if not an obstruction on the autobahn where cars were rocketing past at 100 mph and more. Soon we were pulled up by the local police and advised to split up and carry on with no more than four vehicles at a time. We all kept in touch via our CB radios (remember them?) with constant repartee with each one of us trying to upstage the others with stories that were getting more risqué by the minute.

We pulled up for an overnight stop at a service area near Hanover where we slept in the artists' trailers and, in the morning, took in a German breakfast of sausages and cheese – a first for some of us. We arrived in Babelsberg Studios the following afternoon from where we were directed on to the unit base at the back end of the barracks. There we found an area of hard standing on which to set up our base. It was going to be our home for several weeks so cables and pipes could be laid out neatly to set an example to our German helpers on how things should be done. Even if I do say so the onlookers, especially the German transport co-ordinator and the location manager, were impressed.

It was not all work and no play; after all we were only 10 miles from Berlin. My motley crew showed no interest in its historic sites but made for the seedier venues that the city had to offer. One was a nightclub with burlesque floorshows as in the film, Cabaret. Another was a restaurant that served up food and drink in total darkness, which was supposed to enhance the taste buds but more likely gave plainer good time girls a chance to find a sponsor for the evening. Under normal circumstances such visits would be strictly rationed by the limited amount of spending money (per diems) handed out, but fortunately Heinz, our transport co-ordinator, was well connected and would negotiate substantial discounts that made regular visits to these dens of iniquity affordable.

Next on the list was one of the most awesome locations I had to access. It was an open-air mine/gravel pit several kilometres long and three hundred meters wide with walls to a height of a hundred meters either side. A narrow roadway was carved into its elevation to allow the earthmoving machines to climb in and out of the bottom. The works were now abandoned and the hole was filling up with water. The effect was to create a deep canyon with a forty-meter deep and seventy-meter wide lake. The set was to represent the Volga flowing through Stalingrad with refugees on flimsy boats crossing the river to escape the fighting. The landing craft reminded me of large soup bowls with shallow bottoms likely to capsize at any moment. In deep waters, not exactly a safe enterprise.

Firstly we had to get these floating death traps, 10 m wide and 15 m long, to the set from 300 km away on the Baltic coast. Fortunately someone located an old Russian tank transporter with a driver who was willing to undertake the job. Had we not found one it would have fallen on me (my license entitled me to drive it) to take charge of this unwieldy road train. All we had to do was to get the necessary permits to move it along the autobahns and then, more delicately, down the slope of the quarry to the water's edge. Two to three days on the road at nought miles per hour followed by a suicidal crawl down a near vertical dirt track was not something I was going to relish. In the event the trip took a full week. Then the 'powers that be' decided one boat was not enough to do the unfolding drama justice. Fortunately money was not too much of an issue and we were able to persuade the same driver to undertake the journey twice more.

When it came to shooting the scene the boats with their human cargo were packed to the rafters. They were floating across the river swaying to and fro and landing on the nearside shore. Munitions were exploding overhead and flares were lighting up the night sky. The action was so overwhelming that it made us appreciate what these people must have gone through in real life. I did not see it but I understand that some extras did fall off the boats and the frogmen, who stood by, had to rescue them. Just as well our trailers featured central heating. The unit nurse was also kept busy with minor cuts and bruises that needed attention.

Three nights on and we wrapped the show and, just as we got ready to leave, another project hit town. Around the World in Eighty Days, a remake of the old classic, was scheduled to shoot some major scenes in and around Berlin. Jackie Chan headed the cast with Steve Coogan as his master, each of them contracted to have a motor home at their disposal. Arnold Schwarzenegger would also need a very special trailer when he turned up for a cameo part. The German transport department, which did not include Heinz our laid-back previous manager, displayed all the insecurities of young fans about to meet their idols. I did try to reassure them that the artists were all professionals and that the trailers we had on offer would be just what they would expect. To calm their nerves I had to agree to stand by when the actors first turned up and personally deal with any complaints they may have.

Jackie Chan wanted to know where he could find a broom because he liked to sweep out his trailer himself. "Its therapeutic" he explained. Steve Coogan shook my hand "I am Steve" he said and when I replied that I am Willie he told me that it was good to meet me and climbed into his home from home. When he did not reappear for fifteen minutes I concluded that he was happy in there and I passed on the responsibility of looking after him to one of my drivers. Arnold Schwarzenegger walked up to me grabbed my hand with a German accented Hello, gave the trailer a cursory look and, with a "Good" that sounded like Gut in his mother tongue, walked off towards the make-up truck ignoring the anxious looking transport manager who was now breathing a sigh of relief. My job done, I made my way to the airport. I visited the set a few times especially when I was able to witness the hot air balloon taking off from the Gendarmenplatz, a square in midtown Berlin. It is surrounded by French and German churches and these, as well as the Konzerthaus (concert hall), have been restored to their pre-war splendour after they suffered heavy damages during World War II. It traditionally houses a market, parts of which had to be cleared, paying heavy compensation for loss of trade to the stallholders. Incidentally, this is the very market square where recently a terrorist mowed down innocent bystanders with a stolen truck.

More film productions followed and local enterprises, one headed by one of my ex-drivers, began to supply similar facility vehicles to the local industry and I slowly retreated from the German scene.

# 36 Spy Games 2000

## Good Planning Blown Apart

The film, starring Robert Redford and Brad Pitt, was to be the most ambitious production I supplied for many years. It was to be shot in Israel, Budapest and London.

First of all logistically we had to get all our equipment to Israel where principal photography would begin, with priority given to the motor homes for our lead actors. Having inspected and rejected most of what was available locally, it was decided to ship over other vehicles such as a costume truck, a make-up trailer, a mobile toilet and two three-position artists' trailers for the supporting cast. In addition the stand-by trucks would include a couple for the prop department, one for the construction team and another kitted out as a mobile workshop for the special effects technicians. (They liked the local camera truck). All in all, including the tow trucks for the trailers, some 14 vehicles made up the unit I was contracted to supply.

The easiest route took us across to Calais then through France, Belgium, Germany, and Austria to Ancona in Italy. There we would board a ferry for the overnight voyage to Patras in Greece and then by road again to Piraeus from where a roll-on roll-off combined truck and passenger service would cross the eastern Mediterranean to Israel. At the same time three shipping containers loaded with miscellaneous props, costumes, camera and grip equipment would be hauled to Marseille from where they would travel unaccompanied by sea to meet up with the crew in the Israeli port of Haifa.

Space on the various boats was limited and costumes and other bits and pieces could only be readied for shipping in stages. This meant that the delivery of the production vehicles would have to be staggered. First to leave were the motor homes, the make-up trailer and the honey wagon. As planned they travelled through Europe and arrived in Israel ten days later. Five days behind were the rest of the facility vehicles, led by my son Jason, that stood by in Piraeus waiting to board the boat that would take them on their final leg to the film location. The shipping containers had just arrived in Marseille ready for their onward journey with an estimated time of arrival four days later.

The production office in Israel was located in Jaffa, a suburb of Tel Aviv, overlooking a busy street market. With everything going to plan there was nothing else I could do here at home; my next mission was to clear the vehicles through Israeli customs where I anticipated lots of formalities before they could enter the country. I got my air ticket and packed ready to leave the next morning.

That very afternoon a bomb went off in full view of our office staff. Although they were not physically injured the carnage they witnessed affected them to such an extent that they, without looking back, hurried to their hotel and on to the airport insisting on immediately leaving the country for home.
Filming in Israel was suddenly no longer an option. The powers that be met in Shepperton Studios and, within a couple of hours, rescheduled the shoot to start in Budapest, then move back to London and finish up in Casablanca. Here the Moroccan Film Commission was going to do all in its power to accommodate us even though some of our dates clashed with Ramadan. A potential working holiday in sunny Israel turned within the hour into a logistical nightmare.

Budapest first. Instead of having weeks to move the circus from UK we now only had days. A lot of running about and raised voices later it came together except that some of the props in a container in Marseille also needed to get to Hungary. A posse of prop men was flown to the French port to reload the necessary items on to a lorry that travelled overnight with a second driver, and rendezvoused with them by the quayside. They then would have only 24 hours to complete the journey to Budapest. The handling of the load was like the proverbial walk in the park compared to the paperwork and permits required that allowed us to interfere with a sealed container already cleared to leave the country. It was to the credit of our local freight agent - and the two drivers who drove non-stop through the night - that filming would eventually start on time.

We now had a couple of weeks to set up the UK location with largely the equipment that was still in Israel and Athens, as well as what was left in the container in southern France. No panic here other than a script change which required the two remaining containers to travel directly to Morocco. Paperwork did not allow this to happen so it had to travel back to be formally imported back into the UK. Only then would it be cleared for export and temporary import to Morocco. The only problem was that, from experience, I knew that importing anything into the port in Casablanca could not be guaranteed to proceed smoothly. Stories of containers being held back for weeks were commonplace. Therefore everything, however cumbersome, had to be shipped by road through Spain and cross the Gibraltar Straights from Algeciras to Tangiers. It was the vehicles from Budapest that had to carry out this journey while filming in London took place. Again, lots of paperwork later, the journey was completed, not without unofficial payments that had to be made on arrival in Tangiers.

Not all went to plan. Most of the hand props (small) and light construction tools as well as camera equipment were air freighted from the UK to Morocco. However all flammable matter such as paints and white spirit used for cleaning the brushes had to be shipped over land. I laid on a suitable truck that was duly loaded with the relevant bits and pieces. Just as the driver was ready to lock up the back of the van he received a message that the set decorators urgently needed a few rolls of barbed wire. All the paints were standing on the floor single file thus allowing the prop men to place the rolls of wire on top of the assorted cans. The paperwork was soon completed and the vehicle embarked on its lone five-day journey to Casablanca.

Two days into the trip my man crossed the border into Spain and proceeded along the motorway to Bilbao where he had to turn south and climb up the Pyrenees towards Burgos. Several drivers in cars that overtook him gesticulated at what he thought was a problem with the back of the truck, but all he saw was a lot of billowing smoke covering his rear view mirror. The truck was not one my best ones and the driver assumed that the steep incline he had to take had caused the engine to emit more smoke than usual. Then, after a short warning that there was a problem with the brakes, it came to a sudden stop. In disbelief the driver witnessed flames engulfing the whole cargo area and miraculously a fire engine pulling up behind him ready to fight the blaze. Having blocked the motorway, the ensuing chaos made the local news. The truck was towed to a garage where, after a cursory inspection of the damage, all was revealed. The spikes on the barbed wire had pierced the tops of several paint containers and, as metal rubbed against metal, a spark ignited the flammable materials that led to the floor catching fire. As long as the truck was moving the smoke from the fire appeared to the driver to be dirty exhaust from the engine and only when he came to a halt would the fire rise vertically and engulf the whole cargo area. The fortuitous appearance of a fire engine was due to the fact that passing motorists had alerted the authorities to the impending incident.

Other than the fire damage to the rear of the truck, the only other problem was that the heat melted the brake line under the floor and thus brought the vehicle to a halt (air brakes automatically activate if the connection from the wheels to the brake pedal or compressor is interrupted). Replacing a brake pipe involves a minor repair and, less than 12 hours later, the truck would be roadworthy, albeit with a scorched rear end, and able to return home under its own steam. The driver, slightly shaken by the experience, remained in my employ for several more years and lives to tell the tale.

Some years earlier the headline in the Dorset Evening Echo read 'Lucky to be alive' and featured a photograph of one of my double decker dining buses with flames shooting out of its rear engine compartment in spectacular fashion. It happened during the making of the TV drama of Stretch. The bus had just been serviced but, because it was due to leave for a night shoot, it had left the workshop prematurely before our fitter could check the fuel line for any leaks. Such checks are routinely made and very rarely require attention. Therefore no undue concern was raised. They call it Sod's Law. This time tiny drops of fuel made it on to the exhaust manifold and, while the bus was moving along the motorway at speed, the flammable droplets evaporated before any harm was done. However, once the vehicle slowed down on the A road that led to its final destination, the hot exhaust ignited the fuel and flames quickly spread and engulfed the vehicle in spectacular fashion. The driver was indeed lucky to escape.

Another less serious yet even more spectacular incident unfolded when an unnamed artist balanced a cigarette butt on the edge of his bedside table in his trailer while he made his way on to the set. It was not difficult to foresee the consequences. The cigarette overbalanced, dropped on to the carpet that started to smoulder. With no one to witness and contain the flame the blaze took hold and the whole 40-foot long luxury RV (Recreational Vehicle) burnt to a cinder in a matter of minutes.

Back on the location of Spy Games the local runners soon directed our set designer to a shop that stocked paint and metholated spirits that would replace the ones lost on route, while the local police force obliged by gifting the barbed wire that was needed to dress the sets.

In Casablanca we parked up in a secure pound which became our base and from which artists, crew and equipment were shuttled in local vehicles to and from the sets. Because our schedule coincided with Ramadan we were asked not eat within sight of passers-by during daytime hours. For this purpose we had to bring a dining bus all the way from home. We would then position it near the set with blinds drawn and the air con at full blast.

At one point I had to hire a car as a runabout for my drivers and the owner of the rental company gave me a lift to his base to pick it up. Casablanca is awash with beggars who approach cars at every set of lights. I then noticed that my companion stored a whole bunch of change in the tray between the driver and passenger seats. Every time a beggar approached he reached into it and tossed a coin out of the window. The beggar then gratefully acknowledged this gift and proceeded to accost the next vehicle in the queue. Good tip, I thought, and followed his example on every street corner at which I had to stop.

As there was no significant movement of vehicles planned I was free to leave for home but not before I celebrated a reunion with my old friend, Patricia, with whom I had previously worked in the South of France and who now co-ordinated all the travel arrangements for this show. She was the one who, following the making of The Jewel of the Nile, married Joel Douglas and, as often happens in show business, she was now divorced and in need of work to pay the bills and retain her self respect.

There was another memorable moment during the making of this film. When shooting in a dance hall with its Edwardian decor in south London, for some reason I walked on to the set only to spot Robert Redford on his own sitting in a corner engrossed in a book. With dozens of technicians and actors busying themselves in the noisy breaks between takes there was one of Hollywood's royalty unperturbed and apparently at ease with himself with just a book for company. There was no one to fuss around him, as he was able to leave his entourage back in his trailer half a mile away.

# 37 Captain Corelli's Mandolin 2001

## Make Believe

The screenplay for this film is based on Louis de Berniere's best selling book of the same title. The story is set on the Greek island of Kefalonia, which has been invaded during World War II by the Germans as part of their campaign to conquer Greece. Once they secured their positions they asked their Italian allies to assist them by landing and occupying the island while they would go on to subjugate the rest of the country.

The three protagonists in this film are the doctor's daughter, Penelope Cruz, a young local fisherman, Christian Bale, who joins the resistance movement that is attached to the Greek underground forces and a major, Nicolas Cage, serving in the invading Italian armed forces. The fisherman is engaged to the doctor's daughter who, in her fiancé's absence, falls in love with the mandolin playing major. It also featured John Hurt, the doctor, under whose sympathetic eye the action builds up to its climax. It is sparked off when the Germans, unhappy with the easy-going Italian expeditionary outfit, ruthlessly begin to impose their own rule of terror. The drama unfolds when the major has to decide where his loyalties lie. Is he going to betray his people or abandon Penelope and lose the love of his life forever?

With nine producers of all shapes and sizes and five members of the crew credited as unit production managers, post production executive, production supervisor and executive in charge of production, a decision was made to move the whole production team to the real life location where this tale of fiction was set.

No question of Make Believe by choosing a more accessible place to shoot the movie. The story simply could not be told without featuring that very island's landscape and fauna. No alternative location in the whole of mainland Greece would do it justice and, as it was not for the likes of me to argue, I settled down to prepare for the logistical ramifications that this project would throw at me.

Kefalonia's main port of Sami, which is central to the action, was completely destroyed and razed to the ground by the earthquake of 1953 with no photographic evidence surviving. It was also bereft of an infrastructure that would allow us to make use of local stores and workshops that would cope with the basic demands of a film production company. Even nails and simple electric cables had to be imported. This presented a challenge on many fronts particularly where transport, ready availability of construction materials and equipment, as well as period costumes, props and street furniture were concerned. Everything had to be brought in either from the mainland, Italy or the UK.

On one occasion a truck loaded with urgent props pulled into a service area a few miles into Germany. When the driver returned after his meal break the engine would not restart. He was stuck. During the phone conversation that followed, our mechanic concluded that it was a faulty lift pump that was the cause of the trouble. We had a spare one in stock and, in order to save time and keep the problem 'in house,' he would tend to the problem himself. He loaded his tools and the new pump into his van and was ready to leave; all he had to do was to ascertain the exact location of the stranded vehicle. The driver insisted that he was near a town called Ausfahrt, while our man back in the yard insisted in ever-louder tones that he could not locate it on the map. "It must be quite a large place because I have passed at least three exits pointing to it" repeated our man from the foreign shores. "No it can't be, it's definitely not on the map!" The argument continued with no end in sight until the shouting match from the workshop alerted me to intervene. May be a linguistics test should have been included in the job interview. (For the record Ausfahrt in German means Exit). When my nine-year-old son made a similar observation on one of our journeys to Austria, we expressed our admiration for his ability to make such a deduction but an adult driver failing to do so just proves that he would have difficulty joining Mensa.

Working for a film company often involves panic management which, in my case, means getting materials to location as fast as possible, something that poses its own logistical problems when shooting a major movie on a remote island with scheduled flights to Athens only. Not much use if one is in a hurry to get home or to any other major destination. The other window to the world is the Port of Sami, which is the main ferry terminal for an overnight crossing to Patras. To reach Patras we had to cross the Adriatic Sea from either Ancona or Bari that involved spending more than 20 hours on board a ship. In turn, travelling by road from UK added another two days to the journey; in other words few urgent deliveries could reach the set in less than five days. Foresight and detailed planning became the priority.

On one occasion a truck was sent back to the UK and, while queuing up in Patras for the boat to Ancona, another driver on his way from Patras to Kefalonia spotted his colleague and, as he had some time to kill, pulled up alongside him for a chat. Both trucks were British registered and, to the uninitiated, were both heading to Italy on their way home.

In due course the homebound driver started to board his ferry and the Kefalonia bound driver pulled away and boarded his boat that was leaving from another quay. On arrival in Sami strange noises were heard coming from the back of the truck and, when the cargo doors were opened, a dozen or so men jumped out. The poor blighters thought they had arrived on mainland Italy. They ran out of the port and disappeared into the town. Police soon caught up with them and it transpired that they came from Macedonia and were hoping to make it all the way to England. Some of us wished them better luck next time.

A lot of the local population were recruited as film extras to be dressed up as Italian soldiers when it was discovered that the wardrobe department had not received the army boots that were an essential part of their costumes. They were ordered from a supplier in Rome but, for one reason or another, had not been dispatched. I, as is my way, volunteered to pick up the footwear in one of my trucks. Driving in Rome is, at the best of times, a hairy experience while parking anywhere near my pick-up point was nigh impossible with a car and definitely impossible with a truck. My Italian is not good enough to win an argument with parking attendants, irate drivers that insisted on their rights to get past me or other truckers that would double-park when attending to their loads. Eventually I decided to raise my voice in English and, though no one understood what I said, they all got the gist of my frustration and I was allowed to treble-park, causing untold chaos which, I believe, is what the Romans constantly live with and begrudgingly tolerate.

I got back to Bari that same evening in time to catch the ferry to Patras and then on to Kefalonia. I got the impression that it was all my fault that the original uniforms did not include the boots and that it was high time I made up for my mistake. I was dumbfounded but remembered that it is a long-standing and safe option to blame the driver for any shortcomings of the production team. I took it on the chin and followed my mantra: 'don't get mad, get even'. The invoice that followed eased my pain.

One of the reasons for giving the cast high spec trailers to while their time away whilst on call was so that an allocated driver would be able to keep an eye on them, giving them no opportunity or excuse to wander off. They could enjoy all the home comforts, attention, and privacy they wished for until required to make an appearance on set.

Nicolas Cage, our lead actor, occupied the largest trailer on the unit base and spent his free time locked up in the villa that the company had rented for him. He was not a great communicator and hardly ever spoke to any member of the crew, not even to the guy who looked after the bathroom in his trailer. 'Unhappy at best and miserable at worst' would sum him up. Even his trip, at untold expense, in a private jet to visit Madonna for lunch on the island of Corfu did not seem to cheer him up. Not surprisingly the reviews for his performance did not meet his expectations and consequently he has removed most references to his involvement in the film from the industry's directories.

Meanwhile Penelope Cruz, not yet the star she was going to be, was full of smiles and good humour, excited to be acting opposite a Hollywood 'A Lister', and a couple of easygoing professional actors who protected her from Mr Cage's worst outbursts. She, John Hurt and Christian Bale had to make do with smaller but no less comfortable trailers, all parked on a unit base as close to the action as practicable.

So far so good until John Hurt decided to explore the island. Having spent days in his trailer waiting to be used without a call coming, he felt that his absence would go unnoticed. He slipped away, hired a scooter and off he went. As is often the case on such occasions, just then the call went out for him to come on to the set. Panic ensued and headless chickens ran about trying to find out where he was. To add to the confusion word came that he had actually fallen off the bike and grazed his arms, knees and, more alarmingly, his face.

The search party returned with him on board about an hour later and, after a bit of attention from make-up, he put on his costume, reported to the set as if nothing untoward had happened and delivered his lines faultlessly. A true professional! When the film was released the critics unanimously praised his performance above all others.

The production envisaged a number of scenes to be shot in the streets of 1940's Sami that, as explained, no longer existed. The art department had to invent what they believed the town would have looked like. They proceeded to recreate and construct the fronts of buildings along an imaginary road. After all, filming is the art of make believe. It looked authentic enough and happiness reigned.

On leaving the island the crew assembled in the airport terminal to await the arrival of a charter plane that was to take us home. While rummaging around the news/souvenir stand we noticed a postcard featuring our street set with the caption 'Sami as it was before the earthquake destroyed it!'

We are often accused of rewriting history. Good to witness that at least the entrepreneurial people of Kefalonia can profit from it.

# 38 Ali 2001

## A Rumble in more ways than one

Mohammed Ali's life hardly needed dramatising. A world champion boxer, a conscientious objector to the war in Vietnam, a convert to Islam, a witty communicator and voted the greatest sportsman of the twentieth century by BBC audiences. His story has been told dozens of times and another version would not, by all accounts, shed a new light on his exploits. Michael Mann, one of the most prolific producer/directors, disagreed and decided that Ali's background and run up to his fight with George Foreman, also known as the Rumble in the Jungle 1974, warranted a fresh biographical dramatisation. It would cover the ten years leading up to the event in Africa with particular emphasis on his fights with Sonny Liston and Joe Frazier. It was also Ali's last encounter before he was banished from the sport because of his 'Un-American' protestations against the Vietnam War and the general political unrest that dominated the USA at that time.

They say in Tinsel town: "What Michael wants, Michael gets", not only because many of his films were box office hits but also because, as the heir to a vast retail fortune, he wants for very little where money was concerned. By reputation he was an obsessive filmmaker who, when working on set, did not know when to take a break. I am told that, when his crew suffered from exhaustion, it egged him on to work them even harder, always leading from the front.

To add to my reluctance to get involved, my vehicles and drivers would have to report to a location in Mozambique, a country in deepest Africa with an unstable government engaged in a civil war. The good news was that my counterpart was the unit production manager, Kevin de la Noy. I had known Kevin as a location manager on several shows and he always impressed with his thorough preparation and detailed analysis of every task to be undertaken, together with a list of alternatives if or when Plan A hit a snag. All of it presented in writing to all crewmembers and outside contractors so that no one was left in any doubt of what was expected of them.

When we worked on Braveheart this document was almost an inch thick and appropriately named The Battle Plan. I had every confidence that, whatever happened, Kevin would have anticipated it and would have an answer to any dilemma in which we may find ourselves.

Apart from Michael Mann and the not insignificant Will Smith, the lead actor, his numerous helpers, bodyguards and other hangers on, we had to provide facility vehicles good enough for another 12 producers and/ or support artists who would visit the set from time to time. We had four weeks to prepare for the journey and, as we were about to wrap the London based production of High Heels and Low Lives, a number of my vehicles would be laid up while waiting to be shipped out to the set of The Rumble.

On the Thursday, the day before the last day of filming which was a night shoot on a Friday, I got a call from a former client in Bratislava who explained that their leading artist was very unhappy with the caravan they had rented for him locally and could I urgently send them one of my motor homes to be on set first thing Monday morning. As much as I would have liked to help and, of course, make a profit, I had to turn down the request because it would have taken us a day to clean and service the motor home and a further two days to travel to the Slovakian capital. In other words, I could not promise delivery before Tuesday. She hung up and we agreed that if she could not find an alternative she would call me back.

In the evening I got a call from one of my competitors inquiring about the availability of a motor home. There was nothing unusual about such a call as we often had to cross hire vehicles to cover a shortfall. He needed it urgently and agreed to pick it up from the location as soon as it came free on the Saturday morning, then clean and service it himself. I had no reason to connect his request with the job in Bratislava.

On Monday morning one of my trucks was returning from Budapest via Vienna. The driver called me to tell me that he was being delayed by a recovery operation involving a motor home being pulled out of a ditch and it looked just like one of the ones we operated – "Are you sure it is not one of ours?"

It was not long before I received the news that indeed it was my truck that had left the road and crashed into an Austrian field. Keen to win a medal, my competitors had agreed to get our Slovakian clients out of trouble. They decided to push their luck by asking the driver to cover the thousand miles non-stop in twenty-four hours. Unsurprisingly, tiredness overcame him and he ended up in the ditch, fortunately unhurt but with a vehicle that was so badly damaged that it had to be written off.

My competitors were fully insured on a new for old basis but, as I needed to replace the vehicle before it was due to leave for Africa in less than four weeks, I could not wait for the formalities to be completed. A few phone calls later I found a suitable replacement for £51,000.00, which I bought ready for The Rumble in the Jungle. When I contacted the insurance company with my news they rejected my demand explaining that they would soon make me their own offer. A few days later I received a call wondering if I would accept £61,000.00, £10,000.00 more than I had originally requested. When the cheque arrived I waited for it to clear and then, out of curiosity, I rang the insurance company wondering why they had offered me so much more than I would have been happy with. They explained that they do not accept a demand from a claimant, however reasonable, but make their own assessment of the damage for which they are responsible. In this case they contacted the official importer who would retail such a motor home for £68,500.00 and the offer they made me reflected a 10% discount off the retail price. It was the first and only time I ever benefited from an insurance claim.

Eventually we dispatched two motor homes, a costume truck, make-up trailer, honey wagon and a pick-up truck, each towing a trailer, to Felixstowe from where they were to be shipped on to Durban in South Africa. As a precaution the convoy was trailed by a mechanic in a breakdown truck that could, in an emergency, either attend to any repairs or, in a worst case scenario, tow the damaged vehicle to the docks so that at least we could get the vehicles on to the first leg of the journey half way around the world. No problems so far and the breakdown truck returned with the delivery drivers back to base. It would take an estimated two weeks for the boat to make land in Durban and the drivers would then fly out to meet it. With Kevin in ultimate charge, clockwork was the word. We were met off the plane by a fierce looking bunch of men who introduced themselves as our bodyguards who would ride shotgun with us out of the country and into the wilderness of Mozambique. When I say shotgun I mean, literally, shotguns!

Back at home we used a barn on an ostrich farm in Woking (now the headquarters of the McLaren factory and racing team) as an overspill truck park. There we befriended Johan Nel, a South African farmhand who, in addition to his fearless handling of these aggressive birds, was a proficient welder and mechanic. He had since returned home and, having contacted him, he joined us as our own in-house local expert and maintenance man. One of our drivers was an ex-army man who took it all in his stride while the rest of us were not quite so confident about this unusual trip. Gun toting macho men were not our company of choice. Relief a couple of days later when we arrived at our rendezvous and were greeted by the unflappable Brian Hathaway, our transport co-ordinator, who had previously worked in Kenya on Out Of Africa and, even though he carried no weapon or because of it, we felt safe again.

Unsurprisingly filming under the direction of Michael Mann went ahead and continued relentlessly - 18 hours a day, seven days a week was the norm. The drivers who managed to get some sleep between takes did not seem to mind as every extra hour on set was bookable as overtime. Brian assured me that all was well and I returned home with nothing else to do but issue outrageously large invoices, all of which were settled weekly as agreed.

Once filming in Mozambique wrapped I got a message of appreciation from Michael's assistant and another thank you in the form of a signed autograph from Will Smith. The unit then moved on without us to Ghana where I understood we were sorely missed. Even Kevin could not justify the expense of letting us trek across the African continent for the sake of a few days granting some home comforts to his charges.

Back in Durban the vehicles met their boat home, the drivers boarded their flight and, two weeks later, it was all over. I breathed a sigh of relief and notched up another job well done. On reflection we had all enjoyed the experience and I even contemplated setting up an office in South Africa to service the burgeoning film industry there. Johan Nel, however, whom I would have chosen as our local fixer, decided that the United States of America were where he saw his future and my plans had to be put on the back burner where they still languish.

# 39 Mindhunters 2002

## Beyond the Call of Duty

Filming in the Netherlands had so far always taken us to Amsterdam, one of the most picturesque and unique locations to work in, though not the easiest in which to manoeuvre or to park up production vehicles. On the other hand, it is rightly famed for the availability of smoking matter and other recreational powders, illegal everywhere else. On previous occasions, especially on Rough Cut with Burt Reynolds and Lesley Ann Down, enough quantities of such substances were collected to send a significant amount back home. I suspect that, for good reason, I was not informed that this particular consignment was stored in the trailer I was bringing back.

At Customs I routinely drove into the 'Something to Declare' lane, mainly because I am not privy to what may or may not have been left in the vehicle by either members of the cast or the crew. Usually there are personal effects in suitcases, which I discretely leave unopened and which, more often than not, are cleared without question. A cursory inspection and I was waved through this time. On my return to the yard, one of the unit drivers greeted me with a message that he was to collect the suitcases and deliver them to their owners. I was more than surprised that, when he entered the trailer, he proceeded to unhinge the light fittings in the ceiling and bags of white powder emerged. He had stored the illicit substances there because apparently the sniffer dogs are led along the floor and under the furniture during searches but are unable to detect matter that is hidden above head height. The driver, fortunately, was smaller than me so the physical confrontation that followed did not expose me to too much harm. Suffice to say that, realising the consequences I would have endured had the border controls been more thorough, I found it difficult to retain my composure. The driver escaped with a few packs while I threw the rest into the nearest skip. (No, I did not profit from them! Maybe I should have done).

This time, however, our unit base was nowhere near Amsterdam. The list of locations covered almost everything that is worth visiting in the Netherlands; Nordwijk with its wide sandy beach and the host of an international tennis tournament, Utrecht with its old university, Delft of china fame and Zandvoort where the Dutch Grand Prix used to be run.

The forest clearing near Amersford, where the bulk of the film was being shot, did not make the list of worthy tourist destinations. It was an abandoned satellite and missile tracking station 50 miles to the east of the metropolis. The action is supposed to take place in the USA and the locations mimic the actual places in this fictional story. It is set on an island that has been rigged up by the FBI as a training facility for its newly recruited agents with video cameras and hidden technology; this enables the supervisors to monitor the actions of the guinea pigs when confronted by stressful and dangerous situations. We were also aware that one of the subjects was a murderer and all is revealed Agatha Christie style (it's the good looking young one) in the end. Although the Netherlands has a thriving indigenous film industry its infrastructure was not geared to service international projects, especially as the needs of cast and crews from around the world have to be satisfied.

The film was directed by Renny Harlin with a cast that included Val Kilmer, Christian Slater, the very good looking but not so famous Kathryn Morris, LL Cool J and a handful of actors from across Europe and the USA. The crew, other than our Finnish director, consisted of a mixture of Dutch and UK technicians. To keep everyone happy I was charged with providing the artists' trailers and supporting equipment, such as the mobile toilet, costume truck and a mobile make-up facility. The schedule allowed for 54 shooting days of which 45 were to be shot at night.

Cast and most of the crew either lived or stayed in hotels in Amsterdam, which, in spite of the distance from our location, was the closest town that could accommodate us all. Exceptions were some of my drivers who used the artists' trailers to sleep in during the rest periods. I did not normally condone this but the production management approved this arrangement because it saved on hotels and night/daytime security. I, therefore, could not object. Two of my drivers, a male and a female (I am saving their blushes by not naming them), were comfortable sharing one of the trailers, so much so that nine months later the inevitable happened. In Beckham tradition (who named his first born after the place he was conceived) we nicknamed the boy Prowler, the make of the said trailer. Ha, Ha.

At the weekends most of the drivers could not resist the temptation to visit the dens of iniquity in the red light district of Amsterdam. They could not take their eyes off the ladies young, old, pretty and not so pretty in various states of undress sitting like mannequins on display behind full size windows, beckoning the passing menfolk to join them for a bit of fun. Once one or two of them plucked up courage to opt in and agree a price for a session of carnal pleasure, the curtains, most of them red, were drawn and the promised action took place out of the sight of their less courageous and curious friends. The other not to be missed pastime in town was a visit to one of the dozens of coffee shops, not for the coffee, for which in my younger days they were famous, but for the perfectly legal indulgence of smoking a substance that is illegal back at home. What struck them was the choice of various types of weed on offer, especially as they thought that one crop was like any other. They wanted to be thought of as men of the world and, without much ado, pointed at one of the seven large pots laid out on the counter.

I was later told that it was the best afternoon they had ever spent on location and that, if another project in Amsterdam came up, they would volunteer to work on it for a much-reduced fee. I would have taken up their offer but no such opportunity came along. May have something to do with the commercial failure this film turned out to be.

The night shoots presented a special problem transport-wise. Each evening our transport co-ordinator, the normally indefatigable Bryan Baverstock, had to arrange to get the cast from their hotels to the location out of Amsterdam in the evening rush hour. Traffic varied from slow to standstill and it fell upon him to predict the night before (pick-up times had to be notified before wrap the previous morning) how long the journey would take. Impossible to get it right; if he called them early to allow for unforeseen hold-ups that sometimes never happened, the artists would complain that they could have stayed on in town for another hour or so and would still have arrived on time. If he asked them to get ready without factoring in heavier than usual traffic, they would often arrive late with Bryan tearing out his virtual hair (most of his real hair was shed long ago). Meantime our second assistant director, Matthew Sharp, whose duties included getting the actors ready on time, was wearing out the soles of his shoes pacing up and down the unit base. Being involved in the morning rush back after a night shoot was equally frustrating with our two heroes taking the blame again.

Other than Willies Wheels, a great deal of the industry - and especially our director – were fuelled by alcohol. Shortly after the end of principal photography he was meeting friends in the bar of a London Hotel. It all went swimmingly until 11pm when the bar staff declared that they could only carry on serving drinks to hotel guests - disaster! Without wishing to generalise, a lot of Finns need more than just one drink before they can function properly. I don't know why me, but shortly after 11 pm I got the phone call: "Where can we get served now?" I tried spelling out the names of a numbers of establishments I knew of but, from the responses I got, it was obvious he was either unwilling or unable to leave the bar and make his way across town to another venue.

A brainwave! I rang the hotel and, as luck would have it, they had a vacancy. Easy now. I booked him in and asked the night porter to pass on the good news to the barman.

Days later I got a budget breaking bill that I recharged to the production company. It turned out that it was just as well he had had a reservation because in the early hours he was incapable of finding his way anywhere other than upstairs to his room and then only with the help of the staff arriving for the day shift.

I awarded myself a medal because nobody else ever did!

# 40 Extreme Ops 2003

## Extreme Action Required

The Extremists, which was its original title, was appropriately named as it featured extreme skiing stunts which to me meant working in and around a winter sports resort. As a keen skier it promised extreme pleasure. Unfortunately from a financial point of view it produced extreme stress and disappointment.

Initially the deal was to supply four high quality dressing rooms. Easy! Two American motor homes towing an American trailer each to report to Seefeld in Austria, coincidently one of my favourite resorts at the time, half way between Munich and Innsbruck. The journey would take us on the German autobahn to just short of the Austrian border and on to our destination a mere 20 minutes away.

We were ready to leave when we received a distressed phone call advising us that the Austrian authorities would not allow trailers into the country in the winter. First bombshell. Disregard the trailers and add two further motor homes which also meant finding two more drivers willing and able to spend five weeks away from home without having received reasonable notice. In the end we found one driver and I volunteered to drive the fourth vehicle with the understanding that, on arrival, I would fly home and leave three drivers to look after and shunt the four motor homes as and when required. Naturally this new arrangement came at a price and a revised deal had to be negotiated. After watching the line producer shedding tears I relented and agreed a compromise on condition that I would be paid weekly without fail.

I visited the set a couple of times, on both occasions clutching copies of my unpaid weekly invoices, and both times watching a big man (Michael Sheel the producer is 6'5") cry but, with hand on heart, promising to settle up in a couple of days. I went uncharacteristically soft, largely because I could get in a bit of skiing and a few heavyweight Austrian meals and cream cakes. Uncharacteristically I ignored the rumours about the financial shenanigans the producers were up to. Getting cash for fuel and a living allowance was like pulling teeth, something that I should have recognised as a shot across the bow.

Once the production completed filming in Austria, it moved to Germany and the studios in Babelsberg. Here they released three of my motor homes but worryingly they still had failed to settle my outstanding invoices. Again reminders only met with empty promises. Eventually after several phone calls it was agreed that I should fly to Berlin and meet up with the producers who would hand over a cheque to cover all the outstanding payments.

I arrived in the late morning when Herr Sheel explained that he was just the line producer and that I should meet up with the main co-producers who would show up before lunch. Lunchtime came and went, as did my appointments at 16.00 and 17.00 hours with no-shows. Bloody rude, I thought. Letting me fly in and not even having the courtesy to keep an appointment. I was no longer being taken in by the crocodile tears shed by the line producer and his assistants in the production office. If I wanted to be paid, extreme action was needed.

Principal photography was due to wrap the following evening. This meant that, to have any effect, I had to make my point now, before the powers that be disappeared back to their home country of Luxembourg.

I waited until the evening and, when there was still no sign of my debtors, I asked my driver to get into the vehicle and drive it out of the studio to a safe and secret location. The director had left his laptop, some personal documents and the unedited tapes of the film behind (lucky!). This would give me some leverage when negotiating a settlement to our dispute. I took the last flight home and in the morning waited for the phone call.

What happened when our temperamental and now irate French director realised that his computer, together with an untold number of private documents, had disappeared must be left to one's imagination. What is certain is that all hell broke loose. I was still in bed when the phone rang and on the line was an old acquaintance, the French production manager I had worked with in the South of France, Bernard Mazauric. He explained that, though he was not directly involved, the producers were good and honourable friends and would like to resolve our differences urgently as the director was, by now, completely out of control. He hinted that I should not have taken his possessions but immediately retracted the alleged accusation when I suggested I could throw them out of the motor home onto the street.

A short discussion about the outstanding payments and the discourteous behaviour the previous day followed. Then; how could he get the director's possessions back as soon as possible? Simple; just get the money transferred and I would ask my driver to return to the studio; not possible because "today is a public holiday in Germany."

If I had been made of sterner stuff I would have replied that it was too bad and that they must have known it the previous day when they gave me the run-around. I compromised and agreed to accept a personal guarantee from him and the producers, which they could fax over to me. Protestations galore, they had never had to give such guarantees in the past but then I had never had to take away a motor home in the past. An hour later the fax arrived and we returned the motor home to the studio where it was unloaded and later released.

I heard a few years later that the producers had defaulted on other payments and had been declared bankrupt, while Michael Sheel had also been taken to task for other unrelated misdemeanours. Nice people to do business with.

On another occasion an Indian film production company shot a movie in London and rented a fleet of vehicles from me. Again I had great difficulties getting my bills paid. I was sent from crew hotel in Slough to their temporary offices in Ruislip, to location in East Dulwich and the producer's friend's house in Holland Park to collect the non-existent cheque. Principal photography was about to be completed and I was now offered payment in cash. When I arrived at and took the steps up to the accountant's office I was met by our security men coming down the staircase with broad smiles on their faces. They had just been paid and it would be my turn next. No such luck! Apparently paying the security team exhausted their funds and there was no more money left to settle my invoices. I would now have to wait until more funds materialised from India.

The hour-long trip from Ruislip to the location in Dulwich did not help me to overcome my rage. I waited until the end of the day's filming and intercepted the rushes that were on their way to the laboratories. I then placed them for safe keeping in my fridge at home (they have to be stored in a cool place). Many rows and threats later the money in cash appeared and, having settled the account, I handed the rushes back to the producers who had nearly got away with it.

As a matter of interest, the company that rented them mobile phones and walkie-talkies had to take them to court in India but did eventually get paid. The hotel in Slough, ever optimistic, is still waiting for its account to be settled.

The third and last time I had to take the law into my own hands was when one of my drivers removed, without permission, one of my trailers from the yard and sold it to a coach operator who was going to sell it (handling stolen goods) and share the proceeds with the said driver.

Before I could report the theft, the police called me to say that my trailer was spotted being towed erratically on the A13 towards Southend. On several occasions I had subcontracted work to a coach operator in that area and I also knew that some of my drivers had befriended him. I put two and two together and made my way round the M25 to deepest Essex. Sure enough there was my trailer about to be pushed into the paint shop to receive a new identity.

I called the police who, having discussed the matter with the owner of the coach company, informed me that he had actually bought it and that it would be a civil matter to be decided in a court of law. Nothing I could do, as he was bigger than me and had a bunch of even bigger men to back him up. As I turned the corner to head home I noticed one of his coaches parked up by the roadside without a driver in sight (the driver, in fact, was summoned back to the yard to join his colleagues that made up the reception committee that confronted me). I pulled up and, as I climbed into the unlocked bus, I realised it was my lucky day because the keys were in the ignition and the engine was running. There was no stopping me now and off I went heading towards home. A few miles on, I stopped at a service station and called my adversary with the news. He was desperate for me to return his vehicle, which was due to depart on a trip to the continent. No problem, then. Just hook up my trailer and, as soon as it was delivered back to my yard, I would let him know where to find his coach. We agreed on how to solve the details of the exchange and he lost me as a client and I lost him as a sub contractor. I am sure neither of us has missed each other since.

To have served on over two hundred productions having such bad experiences on just three occasions did not upset me too much.

# 41 The Da Vinci Code and Revolution 2003

## The T-Shirt Saga

Based on Dan Brown's best selling book about a mystery murder that is being investigated by the fictional character of Robert Langdon leads to the discovery of a religious enigma. The book is, in my humble opinion, a good read but the over-complicated route it takes to solve the mystery would in real life just take a phone call to reveal the answer. Still, seven producers, one of whom was the director Ron Howard, who could not live down his role in Happy Days, managed to recruit Tom Hanks to take on the lead. Hollywood's best deserved the best I had to offer and, just to make sure, Todd Hallowell, the hands-on producer and second unit director, together with Nigel Gostelow, the unit production manager, asked me to bring my top of the range trailers to Shepperton Studios where they would inspect and, hopefully, approve them.

They were looking to hire four identical looking trailers with each having to undergo minor interior modifications to suit its designated occupant. Different table arrangements, cooking facilities and above all, for Brian Grazer, a fully adjustable fast action climate and hot water control system had to be provided. In the event Mr. Grazer only visited the set a couple of times and, to the best of my knowledge, never used his trailer, Tom Hanks seemed happy with the original set-up and made no additional demands, nor did Todd or Ron Howard hold any meetings that needed a larger table than the original one to accommodate their visitors.

A few years earlier in 1984 on Revolution, a drama that played out against the backdrop of the fight for independence of the American colonies, I encountered a similar problem. The director was Hugh

Hudson who was riding high after the success of Chariots of Fire and could insist on a Favourite Nations clause in his contract. With Al Pacino, Donald Sutherland and Natasha Kinsky it meant providing four identical motor homes. In those early days American motor homes or trailers were few and far between. I only had two that would meet the required specifications and the producers could only locate one other matching vehicle to join my two. Solving this dilemma became a priority with the preparations for the actual shoot taking second place.

The biggest name in the cast, Al Pacino, came to the rescue by agreeing to accept a motor home with fewer gadgets than the ones of his fellow players and his director. Not only did he save their blushes but also regularly alleviated stressful production issues by treating the crew and his fellow actors to light hearted show business related anecdotes that were fuelled by alcohol and gourmet meals. One of the main recipients of his largesse was his motor home driver, Phil Allchin, who a few years later reached the dizzy heights of becoming one of the most popular transport co-ordinators in the industry. His credits include most of the Bond pictures and more recently Into the Woods, Wonder Woman and Mary Poppins Returns where he won the Willies Wheels Award for best Transport Leader of 2017.

Unfortunately high spec facilities do not guarantee success and, although the movie received an award and several nominations, it proved to be a financial disaster for the promising British Film Industry. The famous prediction "the British are coming" at the Oscar ceremony did not materialise.

The bulk of The Da Vinci Code was shot on the stages in Shepperton and Pinewood yet, in some ways, it could have been described as a road movie as, at one point or another, we travelled to Paris where we shot on three different locations, then to Lincoln where the Cathedral stood centre stage before we upped sticks to

Burghley House near Stamford. In and around London we filmed at the Temple Church in Holborn, Winchester Cathedral, Biggin Hill and Shoreham airfield. Other locations used were in Malta and Scotland. However my favourite outing was to Dunsfold Aerodrome near Guildford that was the home of the Top Gear production team. It housed its famous test track and aircraft hanger where the show would be recorded. There I would spend hours imagining me racing around the very same route that the celebrities take in the 'Reasonably Priced Car'. Once a boy always a boy!

For the uninitiated, the 2nd unit - as opposed to the main unit - is usually employed to shoot scenes of lesser importance where the main artists are not required or where doubles can be used to stand in for the leading characters. Such a unit has its own director and crew and concerns itself with what are regarded as establishing or long shots, again where the audience can easily be made to believe that what they see is the key players acting out their scenes.

On the Da Vinci Code one of the producers doubled up as the second unit director and, on completing his tasks, decided to reward his crew with a commemorative T-Shirt. The said T-shirts, with a suitable image imprinted, arrived in three boxes and were delivered to the director's trailer.

At this point I would like to explain that often the producers and other luminaries employ assistants who are usually young hopefuls related in one way or another to a friend or a family member and are given a chance, in spite of their inexperience, to get into Show Business. Unfortunately, because of their connections, they take up their positions without any relevant training either at film school or as trainees. So it was that the director's assistant found herself distributing the T-shirts "just one each per member of the crew".

Jump forward: she has run out of T-shirts before everyone has received his/hers and, without delay, it was concluded that someone must have taken the contents of a whole box without permission. I remember the words stolen or robbed being bandied about. It had to be a driver and I, as the main transport contractor, was summoned to investigate. In the absence of a lie detector I tried to explain that, although I was willing to question my drivers, I knew them well enough to trust them, otherwise I would not have employed them in the first place. Unfortunately, our director was so incandescent with rage about what he regarded as "an invasion of his privacy" that nothing I could say would appease him. Our main unit had just travelled to Malta for some important scenes to be shot. These needed a great deal of input from our unit production manager whose attention was being diverted by constant phone calls from our injured party. As far as he was concerned the search for the missing shirts was not a matter of life or death but, quoting Bill Shankly the ex- Liverpool football manager, "it was more important than that". Certainly making a movie had to take a back seat until the mystery was resolved and the culprit could be sent to the gallows or preferably to the electric chair. Naturally nothing like this would ever happen back home! Really? No crime in LA?

Still, I carried on with my investigation, including watching hours of CCTV of Pinewood Studios car park where the vehicle was left overnight and questioning the drivers. One or two of them were so upset by my suspicion that they refused to have anything else to do with the production and left me high and dry to find replacements without any notice.

I returned to the scene of the crime with my motor home driver who witnessed the distribution of the now infamous T-Shirts and reconstructed the events of the said day. It turned out that, once the first box was empty, the driver placed it upside down on the bed at the far end of the vehicle. This was the very box which our producer's assistant discovered to be empty, not realising that it was she who had handed out its content earlier in the day.

It also transpired that several heads of department collected T-shirts not just for themselves but also for members of their crew. And so it was that, for example, the driver of the camera/grip truck received four T-shirts, one from the focus puller who collected the shirts for the camera crew of which he was regarded as a member, one from the key grip whom he helped out from time to time, one from the transport manager, who was going to distribute them to all the drivers and one he collected for himself. At the time he was naturally unaware of the drama unfolding back in the director's trailer and gratefully received the additional shirts believing them to be a generous gesture by his superiors.

Similar doubling up happened in the special effects, construction, and prop departments. 'Just one each' was observed but inexperience, not to say ignorance, led to the perceived shortage. Our second unit director would have none of it. He had already apportioned blame and nothing but watching someone – anyone but his American girl - on death row would bring him back to his senses.

As Bob Dylan proclaimed "the times they are a changing" and the biggest change in the industry was the appearance of laptops in every production department. It reminded me of the prediction George Marshall, the accountant, made when we discussed the development of the paperless office some years ago. Rather than paper mills going out of business he suggested we buy shares in them as these computers would lead to an explosion in demand for paper. I did not follow his argument at the time, but had to give him credit for his foresight when I was forced to allocate a whole truck to deliver reams of the stuff on a weekly basis. When the production moved to Scotland for the final scenes to be shot we loaded a truck with more than three tons of it to satisfy the demand of the production team. For the record, on previous projects, the total office supplies and equipment would fit into the boot of a car or worse, into a small van.

# 42 Alexander and Black Hawk Down 2004

## Behave Yourself!

The key to success is often good and thorough preparation. I had recently moved my operation into the Pinewood Studio complex; this allowed me to consult my clients and carry out their wishes practically in-house. My workshop was big enough to accommodate four large trucks with a pit to inspect the underside of long vehicles and two ramps that could lift regular cars. Living on the premises of this iconic film factory gave me unsurpassable credibility and a unique status in the industry. On the other hand every man and his dog working there would approach me for little favours concerning their own motoring issues. Could I check the oil levels, arrange for an MOT or carry out what they thought were going to be minor repairs? In the beginning I complied with their requests but it soon became apparent that servicing my own trucks, which after all provided me with a living, took second place. I started to turn away the favour seekers and paid the price by denting my saintly reputation.

The production offices for Alexander were also based in the studio though most of the film was going to be shot in Morocco with only a few interior scenes to be set on the famous 007 stage which was originally built to house the submarine base featured in The Spy Who Loved Me. This time it was turned into the interior court of Alexander's palace with its light blue façade, circular pond and exotic fauna; the art department created one of the most elaborate and splendid sets I had ever seen.

The Moroccan location that would feature the battle scenes was based in the middle of nowhere, some twenty miles outside Marrakech. To accommodate the crowd, two marquees, each the size of a football (soccer) pitch, dominated the unit base, one to provide an assembly and dining area and the other one to house the thousands of battle dresses and paraphernalia for the hundreds of extras who were to alternately represent the Persian and Greek armies. The cast of Colin Farrell, Angelina Jolie, Val Kilmer, Anthony Hopkins and a large assortment of 'Faces' and day players were to be housed in the city of trailers which we had to supply from the UK.

With my old client, dare I say my then friend, Sarah Bradshaw, in charge and Ian Smith producing, I was awarded the contract to supply the production vehicles for the show. The controversial but highly regarded Oliver Stone was to direct it and his crew were aware that a lot was going to be expected of them. This, of course, included the kitting out of their allocated vehicles.

Again, the flip side of being stationed just around the corner from the production offices and stores was that, every time one of the technicians thought of a modification he would like to his vehicle, he could pop into the workshop and put in his request. It was going to be a large and potentially very profitable project and, therefore, I had no hesitation in granting them their wishes even though it increased my set-up costs and deprived us of valuable prep time. Regular such visitors were the camera crew who needed a larger darkroom, a fridge and a silent generator to keep their batteries charged, the wardrobe department that could not do their best work unless the clothes rails were repositioned and the washing machine was moved from the middle to the bulkhead of the truck. Additional alterations had to be performed to the make-up trailer, the special effects truck and prop stand-by vehicle. In fact, on occasions my men had to work through the night, booking an untold amount of overtime. We were nearly ready to leave when it transpired that the project was not yet 'green lit'.

The line producer was putting a brave face on it assuring me that the funding would be coming through any minute. Nevertheless I felt I needed to emphasise the urgency of the situation; after all the cast and crew and even some of the basic camera equipment could fly out and be ready on location in a matter of hours but not so the transport department. We had chartered a large roll-on roll-off ferry to stand by at Southampton and get us lock, stock and barrel to Tangiers from where we were going overland to Marrakesh. Whichever way we looked at it we needed at least a week to get to the set. With that in mind I put it all down in writing and impressed upon the powers that be that, unless the show received the green light within 24 hours, I would not be able to comply with my side of the bargain.

We had more than 30 assorted vehicles ready when we got the go ahead but, before we could leave, the second assistant director (who was responsible for the wellbeing of the actors) produced a supplementary wish list which comprised five more trailers of the three position type of which I had none left in the yard. Many frantic phone calls later I managed to locate some in Birmingham and I ordered them to report to Southampton the following morning without having the opportunity to view them first, something I came to very much regret later. Another last minute request was that we load office equipment on to the mobile office bus immediately. At the time it was on its way to undergo a thorough check-over of its air conditioning system. We couldn't do both so we had to send it on its way with an unserviced unit. Again something I was going to regret later.

Whenever expenditure was an issue the production company had to keep a close eye on costs. So when our freight agent proposed, as the cheapest option, chartering an old Russian ferry to sail with our vehicles across the Bay of Biscay, it was immediately agreed to commit to it without allowing either myself or the transport co-ordinator to take a closer look. It was only when we arrived at the docks in Southampton that we discovered that the vehicle deck did not have enough head room to accommodate four of our tallest trucks. Hurriedly we had to divert these to travel via Dover and Calais, through France and Spain and on to the ferry from Algeciras to Tangiers. There they would meet up with the rest of the circus. Needless to say it resulted in unexpected expense covering drivers' wages, living allowances, fuels, tolls and ferry charges. As they say 'Penny wise…'.

Eventually the charter, laden with our vehicles, docked in Tangiers where the drivers, after greasing the palms of several genuine and some fake officials, were let out of the docks and made their way to Marrakech. These we delivered the trucks to the unit base and checked into one of the most luxurious hotels I had ever stayed in. Suddenly I was on holiday, albeit not for long. The defective air con unit in the mobile office became a major embarrassment for which I was not going to be forgiven however much I grovelled. The drivers of the trailers from Birmingham dumped their vehicles in a random fashion all over the base, refusing to line them up neatly side by side as one would have expected from a more professional outfit. What should have been a couple of rows of neatly lined up trailers and motor homes with the motorised office at the head of the base looked like a ramshackle selection of caravans discarded on an unkempt campsite.

It was too late to rearrange the set up by the time I arrived because some of the artists had already settled into their trailers and the production office was already manned with electric fans as a poor cover for the ineffective air conditioning unit. I tried to explain my predicament of having had no chance to properly prepare the office facility and the last minute request for the additional trailers but did not receive a sympathetic hearing. The show had to go on and, quite rightly, there was no point looking back on what could have been done better.

The Moroccan drivers had no regard for the roadworthiness of their vehicles. In fact, at one point one of them, when checking out a suspension problem under the front bumper, got run over by his own truck which rolled over him because the handbrake did not work properly. The word was that he was fatally wounded yet none of his colleagues seemed to come to their senses and, when I suggested they have their brakes serviced, they assured me contrary to the recent evidence that there was no need to miss work because of one accident. It reminded me of a meeting I had had some years ago with an Egyptian stunt man who took unspeakable risks and who explained that life is a gift from God and it is God's will if he lived or died. He need not take any precautions because his fate was predestined whatever he did. It was and is hard to argue against such conviction and I can only hope that he is still alive and well, unlike the poor driver who had just met his maker.

The heat and the ready availability of substances illegal at home, as well as a number of confrontations among crewmembers, did not enhance the atmosphere. Trouble culminated when the costume truck driver complained about the food. This was followed by an eyeball-to-eyeball stare-out between the caterer and the driver that resulted in the driver slapping the caterer who then – I must admit, like a little boy - ran to the production office with tears running down his cheek. A grown man crying was not something we encountered every day. It was to the credit of our transport co-ordinator, Bryan Baverstock, that my man was not sent home on the next plane and that a peace, albeit a tense one, was brokered.

Black Hawk Down was due to start filming in Rabat, the Moroccan capital, a couple of hundred miles down the road. Our old friend of Schindlers List fame, Branco Lustic, was in charge. Without notice he turned up on set to see which vehicles he could rent without paying for them to travel all the way from UK. Unfortunately he visited that part of the base where the trailers from Birmingham littered the place. With no further ado he decided that they were not good enough and ordered a whole circus from my unmentionable competitors. A chance meeting later - and the fact that he needed more vehicles than he ordered - gave me the opportunity to at least supply him with three trailers and a driver from my own fleet.

My main problem in Morocco remained the behaviour of the drivers who now proceeded to entertain the local sex workers of which there were plenty. These girls had a subtle way of making the boys believe that it was love that motivated them first of all and that payments were a gesture of kindness once they recounted their hard luck stories. In one instance one of the boys was so incensed once he saw through the deception that he threw the TV out of his hotel window followed by the hapless girl who just managed to summon help hanging from the windowsill.

Another driver on his return home recounted his adventures to his neighbour over his garden fence while his wife was listening from the window above. Divorce followed and he was last heard of back in Morocco living in a caravan.

# 43 Archangel 2005

## The Capital Revolution

Latvia, unlike Hungary and Poland, has been an integral part of the Soviet Union and, even after independence in 1990, was home to a large number of Russians who chose to remain in the country even though they were largely treated as second-class citizens. Together with the indigenous population they had gone overboard to embrace capitalism.

We arrived in Riga, the Latvian capital, just 14 years into this new world order where everything western would be welcomed and accepted unconditionally. On the other hand, one could not escape its recent socialist past with housing estates reminiscent of the worst kind of prefabricated constructions common in UK in the mid-sixties. Discoloured and dirty grey concrete high rise buildings that were regularly demolished at home as no longer fit for human habitation provided the mainstay dwellings there. I also discovered that most of these buildings required families to share toilet, bathroom and kitchen facilities with their neighbours, as there was only one of each on each floor. Older buildings showed signs of long-term neglect with peeling paintwork and rotting window frames and doors.

On the plus side, there seemed to be an abundance of the most stunning looking females everywhere and most under 25-year olds spoke English, which had replaced Russian as the first foreign language they were taught at school. The crew, especially the heads of departments, came from Lithuania that, though it is one of its Baltic neighbours, has its own separate culture, history and distinctive language. I was surprised to find out that, to communicate with each other, Russian was the language of choice. The old ways, however much disliked, had retained their usefulness.

Tourism was the short-term fix and a quick way of attracting foreign currency to finance an economic recovery. Riga is an old city with impressive historic sites, lots of churches dating back to the times when it was a member of the Hanseatic League. Modern hotels Scandinavian style and casinos had quickly taken hold along the wide Daugava River that flows through the city, a natural divide between old and new.

The studio base was in Jurmola, a seaside township some twenty miles south out of town. It was a popular holiday resort for well-to-do Russians and featured row after row of dachas, some renovated and lived in by Latvians who commuted to work in Riga, others dilapidated beyond repair and one converted into a film studio of sorts which became our base. Jurmola is a closed community and, to enter it, a toll has to be paid at a cash point by the roadside but, without a barrier, we foreigners did not realise it until we were stopped and put to rights with an appropriate fine.

We were all booked into the Raddison Blu Hotel on the banks of the Daugava that, at this point, is some 150 m wide and would regularly freeze over in winter. It was winter but we preferred to use the bridges rather than step on the thick (never thick enough for us) icy surface of the river to cross over to the old city.

It was a four star hotel with the appropriate facilities and the added bonus of an adult channel which had to be paid for. However, as a teaser, you could watch it for about two minutes before the charges clicked in. It did not take long before some of the crew, mainly drivers and sparks, were running from room to room watching two minutes of free porn as they switched on the TVs consecutively. Apparently they managed on several occasions to view a full-length film without being charged for it. I suppose it beats drinking and/or gambling in the casino next door.

The film, a television 2 hour long drama commissioned by the BBC, was based on a novel by Robert Harris. His previous works included Enigma, which was turned into a feature film of the same title and was shot in France with my peripheral involvement (see chapter 11). The screen play was written by the iconic and prolific partnership of Dick Clement and Ian La Frenais who, between them, created such classics as Porridge, Auf Wiedersehen Pet and are credited with dozens of other TV shows and feature film projects. The leading man was a pre Bond and pre star trailer Daniel Craig who played a university professor seeking to uncover Joseph Stalin's, the Ruthless Russian Dictator's, secret legacy. The story is largely set in Moscow (shot in Riga) and the Siberian like remote town of Archangel that with its stark surrounding and unforgiving winterscape was everything that reminded me of what a frozen Russian hell looks and feels like.

Our normal heating system was powered by propane, which we drew out of gas bottles, one of which was placed next to each trailer. However, the low temperatures solidified the gas and prevented it from feeding the central heating boilers. We had to employ diesel powered blow heaters to gently (gently being the key word as the a sudden burst of heat could cause the bottle to explode) thaw out the gas bottles before they could be used. Unfortunately, diesel tends to wax up in icy conditions. We, therefore, had to add ordinary two star petrol to create a fuel mixture less likely to solidify. This was a trick I learned in my youth when, on a trip to Sweden's arctic circle, I observed truckers pouring petrol into their tanks to be able to keep on going. Again great care had to be taken because not only does this mixture omit an unpleasant smell but reduces the efficiency of the motor and could also do irrevocable damage to the engine (no need to bore you with the why and how).

Although we found ourselves in a world far removed from our own, both in economic and climatic (far too cold) terms, getting there was fairly easy. All we had to do was drive across Germany (autobahn all the way) to Travemunde from where we boarded a roll-on roll-off ferry for the 36 hour crossing to Riga. Our only mishap was a failing clutch on the costume truck which we managed to tow onto and off the boat without suffering much of a delay. An overnight visit to a local garage on arrival and we were able to report for work on time.

The temperatures we encountered deserve another mention. One of the locations was just across the river with minibuses running a shuttle service for the crew from the hotel over the bridge to the set. We had positioned the vehicles on the unit base the night before and my drivers made their way earlier to fire up the heaters and start the generator that supplied electric power to the circus. Thus they were ready to receive a shivering crew and try to cheer them up with shelter and warmth. As I heard nothing to the contrary I assumed that they had encountered no real problems and, therefore, there was no rush for me to get on to one of the crowded buses. I decided to walk (it would do me good) the half-mile or so to the set. I did wonder why the streets were bereft of other walkers; after all it was in the middle of the morning rush hour. Still, I stepped outside wrapped in thermal underwear, shirt, two jumpers and weatherproof anorak, crossed the road and headed for the bridge. However, before I managed to reach the pavement on the opposite side of the carriageway with my hoody up and scarf in a strangle hold around my throat, mouth and nose, the tears in my eyes had begun to freeze up and fogged up my vision. Rubbing them produced a crackling sound. Could the breaking ice with its sharp edges damage my retina? Too scary to contemplate.

I instantly understood why no one else had dared to step out of the building. Hurriedly I returned to the hotel where I waited my turn on the shuttle bus to the unit base. I remembered a quote from one of my Finnish friends when we worked in similar conditions in

Helsinki : "There is no such thing as freezing weather, just inadequate clothing". Wrong!

The last scenes to be shot were set in Vilnius, the Lithuanian capital. The Lithuanian members of the unit were looking forward to going home and the local crew would be left behind and replaced with technicians local to our new base. We bade our goodbyes and hit the road into yet another Eastern European country. Vilnius, however, was a very different city from Riga. It spans a few hills, unlike its flat northern counterpart and, with less industrial developments on view, it exuded the welcoming air of a provincial town. The well-attended university added a young flavour to the many bars and coffee houses that lined the medieval streets of the old quarters. It was also, before the Nazi occupation, an important Jewish cultural and commercial centre. Sadly the old ghetto had all but been razed to the ground with only one of its many synagogues rebuilt and the cemetery buried under a concrete monstrosity of a crumbling sports arena.

On the other hand one would be hard pushed to cross a road without being confronted by a church. Its largely Catholic population has retained, against the odds, its faith throughout its socialist past and is now proudly displaying more Houses of God per square mile than any other city in Europe, if not the world.

Our line producer and his production company were also based there. Gary Tuck, whom I had briefly met back in the days when he worked as a production manager in London, had relocated there and made it his home. He also felt that he, as an ex UK resident, would be able to attract further international clients to these shores. They would in turn make use of my vehicles if I based some of them on the local studio lot. I agreed and he was right. Wallis and Edward, Elisabeth I, The Palace, and others followed and I became the proud owner of a new operating centre.

# 44 Eliabeth I 2005

## Virgin Queen in Virgin Country

The film studios in the Lithuanian capital of Vilnius were seeking recognition in the international film production world after the lost years of Russian domination. Following a number of TV shows of minor significance that were hosted there, now came a couple of bigger ones. Company Pictures' first project to be shot there was Wallis and Edward starring Joely Richardson in the title role and Stephen Campbell Moore as Edward VII who gave up his thrown to marry the twice divorced Mrs Wallis. From a production point of view, barring some accounting problems that had nothing to do with me and for which I unusually did not have to take the blame, the provision of facility vehicles by my good self (no need for modesty) was appreciated and lauded.

Next, Company Pictures were commissioned by Channel 4 in conjunction with HBO of America to produce a TV mini series about the reign of Queen Eliabeth I. They re-engaged Gary Tuck, the director of Baltic Film Services, to oversee the project. The main set consisted of a near life size castle complete with turrets, inner courtyard, and period cityscape. The positive experience of working in Vilnius on their previous venture and the fact that construction materials, especially timber, were considerably cheaper in the Baltics would have been a motivating factor for the production to base itself there. In addition, local labour costs were low and could be reduced further by bussing men in from neighbouring Belarus. Also available locally was an army of seamstresses who were able to put together the large number of period costumes required. It was up to the indigenous craftsmen to prove that their skills stood equal if not higher than those of their Western European or American counterparts. Needless to say, they passed this test with flying colours and received critical worldwide acclaim.

A few years later the BBC commissioned a mini series entitled The Palace that involved recreating the interior of Buckingham Palace in an old disused warehouse. The transformation was, even to me who had visited many sets of grandeur and opulence, amazing. The cast included Jane Asher, Sophie Winkelman, Roy Marsden, Nathalie Lunghi and other TV faces. Unfortunately this story of fiction about a Richard who at short notice - and therefore unprepared - becomes the Prince of Wales was not well enough received to turn it into a long running soap opera, something we all had hoped for. On the other hand with all these artists to accommodate it was, while it lasted, a profitable venture.

In the non-fiction yet dramatised tale of Elizabeth I Helen Mirren was cast in the title role. Ironically, her next project back in the UK was to play the current Queen, thus ending up portraying both Elizabeth I and II on consecutive productions. Next to her, playing the Earl of Leicester, was our old friend, Jeremy Irons, both supported by Hugh Dancy, Toby Jones and the now famous but then little known Oscar winning Eddie Redmayne.

The show was studio based which meant costume and make-up facilities could be accommodated in the existing buildings, though I had to provide western style make-up and hair-wash chairs. What it lacked was dressing rooms that would be acceptable to the main players. It was of some concern to the local production company that they were seen to be capable of looking after major stars. That's where I came in.

In addition to the facility vehicles that I had stationed there following our previous projects two American motor homes, each towing a luxury trailer, were ordered and shipped over from the UK. It sounded as if it was going to be a hazardous journey but in fact it only meant traversing northern Germany on a continuous motorway to Kiel from where a roll-on roll-off ferry service delivered us to Kleipeda, the Lithuanian port. Another 200-mile long motorway journey and we would arrive in Vilnius where most members of the crew spoke English and who went out of their way to welcome us.

The vehicles, with their sheer size and luxurious interiors, created a bit of a stir among the locals but the artists took it all in their stride and settled into their allocated homes from home as if it they expected nothing less; never mind the fact that we were now some 2000 miles away from home in a country that only a few years earlier had been part of the Soviet Union.

There was no need to move the vehicles during filming so we left one driver behind to look after them while I returned from time to time as a public relations exercise and to introduce and market my services to other forthcoming projects.

During one of these visits I met with Milda Leipute of Nordic Productions, whose easy manner belies her determination to get the job done. She has since become a friend and was setting up a number of shows to be filmed locally; one for an Italian TV company and another for an outfit from Finland. She thus became another one of my valued clients. Other production companies that rented my vehicles to be used locally came from as far as Spain, Germany and the USA. I also returned for a number of projects that were realised in Latvia where we were able to renew old friendships.

Encouraged by the early successes, I made further and more formal arrangements to set up an operation in Vilnius. I was hoping to work on a number of international productions destined to arrive there in the near future. They included amongst others Anna Karenina with Vinnie Jones, Transsiberian with Woody Harrelson, Emily Mortimer and Ben Kingsley and Highlander with my son Jason's friend, Christian Solimeno, top of the bill. In fact, I still to this day retain a presence in the Baltics with a dozen vehicles permanently homed there.

Company Pictures, the UK production company whose project this was, went on to bigger and better things such as Wild at Heart and Inspector George Gently. Unfortunately, none of these brought them back to Lithuania.

Elizabeth I completed shooting without a hitch except for an incident after the wrap party. My driver, soon to be my ex-driver, held a substantial float to enable him to pay for fuel, parts and provisions required to maintain the trailers and to keep their occupants in good spirits. He was to settle up the account the day after the completion of principal photography. On the morning after the wrap party held that previous evening, he turned up in the office claiming that he had been mugged on his way home and that his wallet, containing all the receipts and unspent money, had been stolen. Apparently he reported it to a passing policeman but no record of it could be found.

Some production staff believed him whilst others, like me, had our doubts. It also transpired that on another production he had rented out one of our vehicles pretending it was his own and charging it to his own account. As I mentioned earlier he became our ex-driver.

On the back of these period dramas the BBC recently commissioned a remake of War and Peace. It was an ambitious project that the local production company managed to realise. With facility vehicles from our good selves, I would like to think that we contributed our bit to the ultimate success of the show.

# 45 Goal I and II (not III) 2006
## Shot in the Foot

A crew that would normally distance themselves from me managed this project from the top down. I first encountered the hands-on producer, Mark Huffam, when, as the co-owner of a location facility and transport company in Northern Ireland, he supplied a number of mobile toilets to Braveheart where I was acting transport co-ordinator. Unfortunately, a dispute about his driver's timesheets and his invoices led to a fallout between his co-director and our financial controller for which I - its always my fault - had to take the blame. I don't know whether he bore a grudge but once he moved onto the mainland and rose to the position of line producer, I did not get a chance to tender for any project he was put in charge of. The rest of the twelve (yes, twelve) producers were an unknown quantity but, as the preferred contractor of Icon Films, Mel Gibson's company who pulled out at the eleventh hour, I was not amongst friends.

My trucks were already loaded and my facility vehicles had passed the scrutiny of the relevant departments which meant it was too late to make alternative transport arrangements before principal photography got under way. I found myself surrounded by 'enemies' who were looking forward to an opportunity to declare how much better it would have been if someone else had been entrusted to carry out this job. I was 'on a hiding to nothing'. Still, my drivers and I set up the base in Newcastle where the UK scenes of the first of the three films was being shot. No complaints so far!

The film was endorsed by FIFA who gave the producers permission to use real life teams and players. Although I support Brentford (in the second tier of the league), I did look forward to meeting the then great players of Fulham and Newcastle who, on writing this, have since been relegated and are annual visitors to Griffin Park, my team's home ground.

The first of the Goal's trilogy, The Dream Begins, traces the life of a young Mexican in Los Angeles who works as a cook and helps his father in his gardening business. He plays football with friends from a car wash outfit when an ex Newcastle United player notices him and convinces him that, with his talent, he would be able to attend a trial with his former club as long as he can make his own way to England. Unfortunately, his doubting father misappropriates his savings to buy a truck for their business and he has to turn to his grandmother for help. She has faith in his ability and decides to pay for his ticket by selling some of her jewellery. In Newcastle he initially experiences several setbacks but, with the help of a fellow star player, he eventually makes the first team and is offered a playing contract after scoring the winning goal in their match with Fulham. To no-one's surprise he attracts the attention of other clubs and ends up signing up for the iconic Real Madrid. His life in the Spanish capital is the subject of the second of this trilogy.

To make sure we provided as good a service as possible I made it my business to visit the location once a week to show my face and offer additional help if it were needed. I was staying in the unit hotel hoping that, even though I was paying for my room, I could benefit from the discount negotiated by the production company. Not so. Because I had only booked in for one night at a time I had to pay the full rate which, surprisingly, matched London prices. I was made to believe that the North East wanted to attract new business; however, at these rates, I had my doubts about how they would be able to realise their plans. Disappointingly, service with a smile was not their strong point either. At work and as bystanders watching our cameras turn, stopping the crowd from chatting or, worse, shouting obscenities was almost impossible.

On a personal level camaraderie was the word. How could the same people turn from miserable at work to charming and full of banter on their way home? On second thoughts this applies to most of us, just that up there it seemed more obvious! If, however, the conversation hit a dead spot indicating a dislike of Sunderland or Middlesborough football clubs could quickly revive it. A common enemy helps to unite, especially where football in the North East is concerned.

Back at work, I received no complaints or hints of unhappiness with my equipment or drivers but still no acknowledgement, let alone praise, for the service we were giving. Shame!!

It was, therefore, even more surprising that, when Goal II, Living the Dream, went ahead and was to be shot in and around Madrid, I managed to win the contract and repeat my involvement with the project which was managed by the same crew that we worked with in smile-less Newcastle. However, this time we did not win any medals. One of my drivers who looked after Anna Friel's motor home wanted to please her by suggesting that a different trailer would be more suitable for her and her young child. Unbeknown to him, the producers had already rejected her request by telling her that no such trailer was available. Red faces all round and the driver, as usual, took the blame and had to return home to be replaced by a more discrete one. Justice, let alone fairness, is not a word often used on set.

Next came the theft of a set of Real Madrid shirts. The production rented a large secure warehouse, which we shared with the local transport company, for all the facility vehicles to be parked in overnight. One evening, when the wardrobe truck arrived, the rest of the trucks were parked in such a way as to prevent it from entering the depot. The driver, fed up and tired after a 16-hour shift, parked the truck outside the gate, locked it and got a lift back to his hotel. The following morning one of the windows in the side of the box had been smashed and, upon investigation, it was realised that the football shirts were missing. The police came and showed no interest, after all no one was hurt and, because the broken window was too small to allow anyone to enter the body of the truck, they decided that breaking it was just a way of misleading the investigators to conclude that it was indeed a break-in.

No, it was definitely an inside job! It must have been our driver who left the truck in the open and unlocked for someone to access it through the door and pretend a break-in had occurred. Of course, the fact that a local driver - who would appreciate the value of the famous white shirts and thus force our man to park outside - had blocked the entrance to the warehouse was never considered. Another casualty and another replacement driver on his way.

The third and most serious incident involved the driver who, once we wrapped, loaded up some of the crew's personal items such as laptops and cameras to be delivered, together with the film props, to Shepperton Studios; this would enable the crew to travel light without having to pay for excess luggage. The truck arrived back at our yard in Leavesden on the same evening that a large explosion and fire engulfed the fuel depot a few miles away in Hemel Hempstead. A number of the roads around us were blocked and traffic chaos ensued. To avoid getting stuck in the morning and thus arriving late at Shepperton the driver took the truck home to Twickenham from where he could get to the studio in twenty minutes. What he forgot, or so he said, was to lock the van properly and, when he opened it up to unload it, all the personal possessions of the crew had disappeared. This time I rightly took the blame for my driver's unforgivable action. When the production had to return to Madrid for some reshoots I was too embarrassed to offer my services again; not that I was going to be offered the chance. Nevertheless I left a message that I would do it free of charge. No response and the enmity that prevailed before my original involvement resurfaced.

Apart from these setbacks I very much enjoyed visiting the set on several occasions. I had the chance of taking some of the action vehicles, supposedly owned by the Real Madrid players and which included Ferraris, Lamborghinis and the like, for a spin. I also did the touristy things, visiting the Prado Museum, the impressive Plaza Mayor and taking a walk down the Gran Via on a window-shopping expedition. At one point I was able to impress Sheila by taking her along to the Footballing Mecca that is the Bernabeu and watch David Beckham, Zinadine Zidane and their teammates making a cameo appearance in the film.

Sadly, it is the mark of this industry (or maybe all industries) that all the good things and the sacrifices we made are forgotten and only the things that went wrong are remembered. Needless to say I was not invited to tender for the third film in the series, Taking on the World, and it was no consolation that the production failed to attract critical acclaim.

# 46 Defiance 2008

## Pre and Post Bond

For some reason Lithuania, with Vilnius as its capital, has, since independence, remained a backwater of the film industry with occasional low budget TV productions taking advantage of the cost of local crews and materials, especially timber for set construction. It came as a surprise that a major feature film project was to be realised there. It was not primarily cost driven, though that had some influence, but more the fact that the type of forestry and fauna in the vicinity gave the film an air of authenticity.

The Russians, during their governance, had built a studio with a couple of sound stages which survived into the present in a much dilapidated state but with workable office space, workshops and, most importantly, a canteen. Its vehicle park, apart from the trucks I operated, was due for the scrap yard.

Additional production vehicles had to be sourced from abroad. However, as luck would have it, another show came into town at the same time. Although I welcomed another client it also meant that I did not have enough good quality vehicles to go around and I had to carefully allocate them without appearing to show favour one way or another. The Palace was an ITV project to be produced by our old friends, Company Pictures. It featured a fictitious British Royal family; King Richard IV played by Rupert Evans succeeds to the thrown after the death of his father King James III. It also starred among others Jane Asher and Zoe Telford. It was going to be the first series of many, which hopefully would be turned into an endless soap. In the event it did not attract a large enough audience and the dream of permanent employment faded. The many 'faces', as jobbing actors, were more concerned with their craft than star treatment and would be happy to accept a place in one of my three position trailers.

The costume truck, because of all the royal ball gowns and formal wear involved, had to be a top of the range one. I only had one of them in the country which I had already offered up to Defiance. In the event, Defiance would not commit to it and I felt free to allocate it to The Palace in the knowledge that, in time, I would have to face the wrath of the competing production. This fictitious Royal story was to be shot on a static location with elaborate sets built in a disused factory. I employed local drivers to look after the equipment, only occasionally dropping by with words of encouragement and some wisdom (even if I say so).

Defiance is a period piece set during the occupation of Belarus by Nazi Germany. It was directed by Edward Zwick of The Last Samurai fame and is based on Nechama Tec's book of the same title. It is an account of the Bielski Partisans, a group led by the three Bielski brothers who gather together dozens of Jews trying to escape persecution and set up a community that manages to hide in the nearby forest. In spite of several casualties and sibling rivalry they manage to survive the war with Tovia, played by Daniel Craig, ending up an unsung hero as a cab driver in New York. The other players include Liv Schreiber, Jamie Bell, and George MacKay.

I had worked with Daniel Craig on Archangel before he was famous. This time, however, he was a universally recognised star. The difference from my point of view was the size of his trailer. The 'Favourite Nations' clause in their contracts demanded equal treatment for Jamie Bell and the director, Edward Zwick. So three top of the range motor homes had to be sourced for the three 'names' whilst all the other players had to be satisfied with one of the 9-cubby holes in the three 3-position trailers that we supplied for the base. Mind you, each cubby-hole included a bathroom en suite with a full size sofa, fridge and desk with both central heating and air conditioning so they did not exactly have to slum it.

For some unknown reason the management was not fast in coming forward with their requirements and, as a result, the costume department had to make do with an inferior facility than that to which they thought they were entitled and we were blamed for all its shortcomings. When I offered to ship over a better one from the UK I was told that it would not be necessary, as the costume people would make do after all.

Not so. As a slap in the face, they contacted one of my competitors and ordered a much more expensive yet no better wardrobe truck than the one I had originally offered but which, due to their indecisiveness, I had allocated to The Palace. They did not bother to consult me, pretending that all was well. I did not like that, especially as I repeatedly expressed my concern about the delay in placing the original order. What upset me most of all was that the transport co-ordinator, who a decade or so earlier I had introduced into the business in the first place and employed for many years as a driver, found it in his heart to keep me in the dark. I took it personally and was not far from just pulling off all my equipment there and then. Only the intervention of our local line producer and old friend, Gary Tuck, stopped me from carrying out my threat. It was hard swallowing my pride.

The action took place in and around a remote forest location with the unit base in a large clearing and the motor homes positioned side by side to the left, with the trailers facing them from across a passageway to the right. It demonstrated the fact that the production adhered to the favourite nations clause with Daniel Craig's motor home next to the others obviously no better or worse than he was entitled to. However, rumblings among his entourage hinted that it was not quite good enough "On the Bond films he had a much bigger and more luxurious trailer". "On Archangel, just a couple of years ago, he had been grateful for a much more modest facility" I muttered under my breath.

His chance came though when the bathroom in his vehicle sprang a leak and he could not be persuaded that it was only a minor fault that could be fixed in about an hour. Someone started whining to the producers who, for the sake of peace, agreed to provide him with a superior camper. Unfortunately, all this happened in my absence so another trailer was ordered from my unmentionable rivals and had to be shipped in all the way from the UK which would take 7 days to reach the unit base. Demand satisfied and plumbing fixed, Mr Craig's entourage seemed happy and continued to occupy their now temporary abode. He did abandon it, though, as soon as the replacement trailer arrived. We ended up with an empty motor home for which we were unable to continue charging. This time, for some unknown reason, I took it on the chin. Fortunately for the production company, Jamie Bell and Edward Zwick in the other motor homes did not kick up a fuss about why they should not be upgraded and life on this show got back on track leaving a sour taste in my mouth.

# 47 Wallander I, II  2008

## Sweat Today, No Honey Tomorrow

Kurt Wallander is the Swedish detective in Henning Mankell's crime novels. Never heard of him but my mother-in-law was a fan. From my perspective it meant that I would get the chance to visit Sweden again. I had toured the country back in my biker days when a friend of mine and I investigated what that Free Love, attributed to the Scandinavians, was all about. We had a great time even though the sex was not as easily available as we had expected. Still we each found a tall blonde to keep us company throughout the summer of 59. Happy days!

The BBC, which was looking to retain the audience that used to watch Inspector Morse, Prime Suspect and Cracker, commissioned this series of three ninety-minute adaptations. The six million pound budget, which overran by one and a half million for the first series, was contributed to by German TV and WGBH of Boston. Thus the producers, with my mentor Simon Moseley at the helm, were given a chance to create a major show without cutting too many corners. The cost of importing my vehicles and drivers seemed, therefore, to be well accounted for. The Swedish co-producer, Yellow Bird TV, owned the rights to all the writer's works. They curiously at the same time produced a Swedish version of the same stories which they, even more curiously, managed to sell and air on BBC 2 with English subtitles. (I must admit that I enjoyed watching this version better than the English one).

Kenneth Branagh was cast as Kurt Wallander, the existentialist detective who, at the same time, forever questioned the meaning of life. In the process, he suffered so well that he won awards for his performance. The cast also included the later to be famous Tom Hiddleston and David Warner whom I drove on one of my very first jobs back in the early seventies. Most of the actors came from the UK, likewise the make-up artists, costume designer and even the caterers. They all expected to be provided with facility vehicles of a standard not available locally. Just as well. An American motor home for Kenneth and American two and three position trailers for the rest, supplemented by a make-up trailer, wardrobe truck and honey wagon.

Apparently the author insisted that the film had to be shot at the very location in which he set his stories. Ystad is a tiny coastal port with a ferry service to Poland and a summer resort mainly for camping enthusiasts with hardly a decent hotel room in sight. This did not seem to bother my men who collected the hotel money and spent the nights in one of the trailers, ostensibly as night watchmen, for which again they collected a fee. With tobacco and alcohol cheap in Poland and very expensive in Sweden my drivers, one of whom spoke Polish, befriended the crew on the ferry and supplemented their income by trading these tax-free goods.

The unit base, with a couple of interior sets, occupied a disused army barracks that was optimistically described as a film studio. On the plus side there was plenty of parking space and good access to water and sewers, essential for the disposal of the waste water from the trailers and the honey wagon (no gully sucker was made available). Swedish working hours are relatively short and are strictly controlled. Drivers had time to move the production vehicles to and from location before and after the shooting day without clocking up excessive overtime which, in any case, was generously rewarded. Being partly UK and partly Lithuania based, my drivers were not bound by these restrictions. Two drivers could cope with it and only once did I have to help out, coincidently during one of my visits.

Travelling to and from Ystad I usually flew into Copenhagen from where I would hire a car, cross the sea to Sweden over one suspension bridge into a tunnel, followed by another suspension bridge. It's a very impressive structure with even more impressive charges. What was less impressive was the fact that after wrap on our way back to UK the bridge was closed to high-sided vehicles and we had to divert north to Helsingborg from where we had to catch a ferry across the choppy waters into Denmark. It added a full day to our allocated time and, with no sympathy from the producers, we had a hard time getting paid for it. Incidentally this was just the way we travelled all those years ago and I clearly remember the many Swedes treating it as the original Booze Cruise, drinking to excess and spewing up to even greater excess because back home alcohol was difficult and very expensive to get hold of.

Once I managed to fly into Malmo saving half an hour on the journey but, when I got to Ystad, the nearest hotel was some 15k away. It was a converted manor house run by a man straight out of the beginning of Christendom who took one look at me and declared that ' There was no Room at the Inn.'. However, he must have remembered that his mortgage payment was overdue and begrudgingly agreed to let me stay in the ' Stables' which he dismissively described as the annex. He took my money and handed over the keys to my room and the front door which he was going to lock at 9 o'clock.

When I got back just after 11.00 pm I noticed an old vintage open top Renault in the driveway. It was pouring down with penetrating rain. The occupants were a man and a woman shielded by heavy waterproofs that did not protect their faces - they made a sorry sight; I was curious. They explained that they were attending a rally for pre First World War cars somewhere up the road but could not get into their usual hotel because a film crew had booked all the rooms. They had been diverted to this place but could not convince the hotelier to let them in. Did not surprise me.

Well, I had the key to the annex! I let them in and they made themselves comfortable in the corridor next to the radiator. Lots of thanks and a promise to leave before the ogre got wind of my charitable deed. So it passed and I left without bothering to stay for breakfast.

On the second series the following year a new production manager/line producer took charge. Unfortunately she had, as far as I was concerned, an attitude problem. She assumed that we were incapable of arriving on time and, to pre-empt a delay, she insisted that we turn up two days earlier than agreed. It made life difficult because it now gave us only a weekend to wrap another show and travel to Sweden as opposed to four days as we had originally planned. There was no convincing her that such a precaution was unnecessary and almost an insult to our ability to fulfil our obligation. To top it all, she refused to pay for these additional two days nor did she reward the drivers for giving up their weekend to satisfy her insecurity. I later found out she had personal issues (allegedly boyfriend, drugs or both) and, being all heart, I gave up pursuing my claim.

The other setback I suffered was that I was looking forward to meeting all those tall blondes from yesteryear; no such luck. A few were still there but young enough to be my daughters. More shockingly, though, a lot of them were short, unblonde and, most disappointedly, overweight. What a difference a generation makes, or is it that my memory was playing tricks on me?

Back home in the London production office I had to listen to a sad story about a budget overrun and watch a young assistant with crocodile tears ask me to grant a discount in order to help with the overspend. There was another series planned and, of course, when it went ahead I would be the one to service it. I am not a hard man, especially as I could look forward to one of the episodes being shot in Riga which is home to a number of my vehicles and drivers.

Sweat today, but guess what? Yes, I was not given a chance to work on it.

It reminded me of another instance when we shot a pilot for the TV series of Crime Stoppers when the production manager assured me that, if I supplied my vehicles at cost, I would be getting the full rate if and when the series was commissioned. Well, it did go ahead but, for questionable reasons, I did not get the phone call. Sometimes tomorrow's honey never materialises.

# Epilogue

"Those were the days, my friends, we thought they'd never end" Mary Hopkins sang back in the mid sixties. Unfortunately, however, they did, like everything, come to an end. Where the film industry was concerned, a lot of Hollywood left California and came first to the UK and later to Europe. With it, it brought a demand for skilled technicians and better equipment. Initially the UK became their first port of call partly because of our common language, of sorts, and the willingness of suppliers like myself to upgrade their equipment to match and, in many cases, surpass what was available back at home. In addition our government was successfully lobbied to support filmmakers financially by introducing tax breaks that would allow producers to reclaim a large proportion of their expenditure. UK crews with UK based equipment not only worked on home soil but travelled all over Europe and North Africa working on international projects. In time, however, many European countries began to match and exceed the offer of the financial incentives available here and, unsurprisingly, Hollywood responded by spreading its tentacles into the continent. As a result more and more indigenous labour acquired the technical and cinematographic skills while local suppliers, especially in the location facilities section, would replace my services thus saving the producers the cost of shipping vehicles all the way from England. In addition CGI (computer generated imagery) and green screens allowed the background to be superimposed after the event. Film editors could thus project exotic landscapes on to the completed pictures without having to travel there and drag a whole unit on to far away locations.

At the same time large stages were built to house action sequences and elaborate sets which would attract the biggest corporations away from their traditional stages in tinsel town. These brand new state of the art facilities allowed a new breed of producers and directors to realise and do justice to the ambitious projects they had brought with them across from the States. Pinewood Studios are now unrecognisable with new stages entirely built to house the Star Wars prequels and sequels. In fact, its days as an open and friendly film factory are well and truly over.

What happened to the times when I could casually drive into the grounds through the old gate house with a smile and a wave from the familiar man in uniform? Today I would be asked to queue in a security hut where I would be interrogated about my business before being issued with papers that allowed me to pass through the equivalent of Check Point Charlie.

Warner Brothers went one stage further and took over the old airfield at Leavesden and built a brand new studio complex where they shot the Harry Potter series and its successor, The Fantastic Beast. They also brought over most of their other projects, many of which involved popular cartoon characters such as Superman, Spiderman, Aquaman etc. who are morphed from cartoon characters into live action silver screen heroes. Incidentally the same site is home to the Harry Potter exhibition that has become one of the most popular tourist attractions in the country, not to mention a significant contributor to the studio's income.

As a result those days of adventure and high spirits in foreign lands together with flexible payment arrangements, that would never end, did peter out. Fun turned into work and few of us old hands were able to accept or cope with the new order.

Looking back I often recall the story of a young man lying on a white sandy beach somewhere in the West Indies. He has a string tied one end to his big toe and the other end with bait and a hook attached leading into the sea. Without a care in the world he chews on a bit of grass and from time to time looks down to see if the line he is attached to is tightening up, a sign that he has caught a fish. Suddenly a shadow is cast over him when a large figure of a man stops by his side blotting out the sunlight. He is wearing an American tourist's outfit of colourful shorts with a Hawaiian shirt over his bulging stomach. His bulk is topped with a wide rimmed Stetson and he is chomping on a cigar that has seen better days; "Do you ever catch anything or do you just lie here without a care in the world and pass the time away?" "Well" said our angler "As soon as I catch a fish I take it home, gut it, and eat it for my supper. I then return the next day and do the same again"- "No! No!" bellowed the man who resembled a man with a Texan oil fortune and an accent to match "Get yourself a proper fishing rod and you will then catch at least three fish every day. You eat one and sell the other two to the beach bar over there. You will then have enough money to buy more rods and catch even more fish, which you then sell not only to the beach bar but also the restaurants in town"- "What then?" "Simple; you buy a boat and land a basket full of fish which you sell to the highest bidder in the market. You will soon have enough cash to purchase a trawler and bring in a large catch, which you could sell to outlets all over the country. You will make a fortune which you will be able to invest in a whole fleet of trawlers." "I see" nodded our beachcomber incredulously: "Sounds good, but what then?" "My friend you could then go and lie on the beach and go fishing without a care in the world!"

Although the story provides some food for thought it does not take account of the human conditions of ageing, procreation and the most recent and intrusive of all, the obligation to complete a written record of one's activities. The latter has given over control of our lives to corporate structures. Thus Willies Wheels, which could happily trade in a small bowl, found itself drowning in an ocean of paperwork controlled by an army of accountants. It shared the fate of many a corner shop when Tesco and/or Sainsbury opened supermarkets in their neighbourhood, unable to develop new administrative skills and attract sufficient funds to match their purchasing powers. As someone whose business grew organically over many years with a 'Hands On' approach to its operation, I could not create the paper trail that would have given me at least a chance to keep up with these powerful intruders.

Fortunately I managed to set up my offspring during the good times and am able to spend the autumn of my life in good health, this time, as an Oldie, taking instructions from the children of my erstwhile mentors. After all, I always made an effort to treat them well as they were climbing the executive ladder in the hope that they would remember my good deeds as they pass me on my way down. I did begin to worry, though, when on a recent production I worked on, I knew not just the father but also the grandfather of the assistant to the transport manager.

Every year the Academy of Motion Arts and Sciences dishes out an award (Oscar) to the leading lights in the industry. The winners are actors, producers, directors, and miscellaneous technicians. However, I have always felt that the transport department should have received recognition. I have, therefore, since my return to the bottom rank of the industry, introduced a Willies Wheels Award for the leading lights in film logistics. The first winners in 2015 were Jon Chu (Director) for a passenger in a leading role, Heather McKay for passenger in a supporting role (Director's P.A.), David Rosenbaum for Transport Co-ordinator in a leading role and Mark Dilliway for Transport Manager in a supporting role. 2016 saw the award for best passenger go to Patrick Tatopoulos (Production Designer), Transport co-ordinator in a leading role to Bryan Baverstock and Transport Manager in a supporting role to David O'Connor.

Recipients of the award for 2017 are Phil Alchin, as the winner of Transport Manager in a leading role, Katerina Ruskova, winner of Transport Manager in a supporting role and Marek Kalawski for Second Unit Transport Management. The award for passenger in a leading role went to Jasmine Mitchell, the schoolgirl who will, no doubt, rise from her present role as a stand-in to international stardom.

William (Willie) Fonfe was born in 1943 in Jerusalem.

As an eleven year old he moved to Munich and later Frankfurt where his father, a lawyer, represented victims of the Holocaust who sought reparation from the German government.

After attending High School he travelled extensively on his beloved motorbike through Europe and ended up in the UK where he attended, for a couple of years, the Hertford College of Further Education. He graduated with four O levels and two A levels and made his way to London where he and an old friend moved into a small flat in Hampstead. It was 1961. The Swinging Sixties, as they were later remembered, were upon us, and he was fortunate enough to be there at the right place at the right time.

The account of what follows is the subject of this, his first book.